THE COLLECTED WRITINGS OF
ASSIA WEVILL

Self-portrait by Assia Wevill, 1967–68. Courtesy of the Stuart A. Rose Manuscript, Archives, and Rare Book Library, Emory University. © Estate of Assia Wevill.

THE COLLECTED WRITINGS OF ASSIA WEVILL

EDITED BY
JULIE GOODSPEED-CHADWICK
AND PETER K. STEINBERG

Louisiana State University Press
Baton Rouge

Published with the assistance of the John and Virginia Noland Fund

Published by Louisiana State University Press
lsupress.org

Manufactured in the United States of America
First printing

Designer: Barbara Neely Bourgoyne
Typeface: Adobe Minion Pro
Printer and binder: Sheridan Books

Jacket image: Assia Wevill with papers at work in Canada, 1950. Courtesy of the Stuart A. Rose Manuscript, Archives, and Rare Book Library, Emory University

Library of Congress Cataloging-in-Publication Data
Names: Wevill, Assia, 1927–1969. | Amichai, Yehuda. Poems. Selections. English. | Goodspeed-Chadwick, Julie, editor. | Steinberg, Peter K., editor.
Title: The collected writings of Assia Wevill / edited by Julie Goodspeed-Chadwick and Peter K. Steinberg.
Description: Baton Rouge : Louisiana State University Press, [2021] | Includes index.
Identifiers: LCCN 2021012240 (print) | LCCN 2021012241 (ebook) | ISBN 978-0-8071-7135-6 (cloth) | ISBN 978-0-8071-7648-1 (pdf) | ISBN 978-0-8071-7649-8 (epub)
Subjects: LCSH: Wevill, Assia, 1927–1969—Correspondence. | Wevill, Assia, 1927–1969—Notebooks, sketchbooks, etc. | Amichai, Yehuda—Translations into English. | English poetry—20th century. | Hebrew poetry—Translations into English. | LCGFT: Literature.
Classification: LCC PR6073.E78 C65 2021 (print) | LCC PR6073.E78 (ebook) | DDC 818/.5409 [B]—dc23
LC record available at https://lccn.loc.gov/2021012240
LC ebook record available at https://lccn.loc.gov/2021012241

In memory of Celia Chaikin (1929–2019),

for Keith, Josephine, Jude, and Ruby Chadwick,

and in loving memory of Joy Gould Boyum, Bobby Cushmac,
Carol Fee, Ruth Plocinski, and Leo Steinberg

CONTENTS

FOREWORD
ON THE TRAIL OF ASSIA

Janet Malcolm has famously compared the biographer to "a professional burglar, breaking into a house, rifling through certain drawers that he has good reason to think contain the jewelry and money, and triumphantly bearing his loot away."

Well, when we started our journey on the trail of Assia Wevill thirty years ago, we didn't know where the drawers were. Not even where the houses stood. Who were the people on whose doors we may knock?

We were leafing through a book by Yehuda Amichai, the Israeli poet laureate, when we chanced upon a poem, entitled "The Death of Assia G":

I want to publicize
your death.
I sort your letters
from the others.
Let them be chosen for life.
not very long,
doubtfully good.

It was the summer of 1988. We were touched by the poem and intrigued. There was a long silence when Amichai heard our question. His voice was full of pain when he said that she was an ex-Israeli, his translator into English, and the beloved of his best friend, Ted Hughes. Hughes deplored his friends, not to mention his tragedies, in their memoirs and interviews. So Amichai was very laconic and of course didn't show us any letters. When he visited Hughes and Assia at Court Green in August 1967, Hughes told him about Assia's distress, "but I had no idea it was that deep," Amichai said. It was the first time we heard of Assia.

This set us on our quest.

We looked for her in books and newspapers but found next to nothing. In her essay "Notes towards a Biography" (1970), Lois Ames, Plath's first appointed (and aborted) biographer, did not mention Assia at all. A year later, Al Alvarez, who was a close witness to Ted's affair with Assia, published his *The Savage God* but left out Assia and the adultery.

The first one to expose the tragedy was Robin Morgan in her 1972 poem "The Arraignment," in which she accused Hughes of killing not just one wife but two:

> Her name was Assia Guttman Wevil [*sic*].
> He never married her formally—which is no crime.
> She translated poems from the Hebrew
> and was afraid of losing her beauty.
> . . . .
> A Jewish mother in the most heroic sense,
> she took her daughter, Shura, with her.

In 1975, when Aurelia Plath published her daughter's heavily edited *Letters Home,* Assia was not named but referred to as "Ted's girlfriend." A year later, Judith Kroll published *Chapters in a Mythology* and used Assia's maiden name, Gutmann, but no further biographical information appeared. In *Sylvia Plath: Method and Madness,* Edward Butscher gave an abundance of details—not always accurate—disguising Assia as "Olga."

So in the beginning, there was darkness. No letter, no single piece of paper that carried Assia's name. We began by locating childhood friends of hers in Tel Aviv; some had kept in touch throughout the years but unfortunately didn't save her letters. However, we secured our first photo of her. Our visit to the English-speaking Tabeetha High, Jaffa, gave us much insight about Assia's upbringing, but the school's archive was lacking. A memoir in Hebrew by a literary friend, Ida Zoritte, the wife of Aharon Megged, Israel's cultural attaché in London, shed light on Assia's final months. In October 1988, we published our first profile of Assia in the prominent Israeli newspaper *Yedioth Achronot.*

In the years that followed, fragments of Assia were dotted in newer Plath biographies by Linda Wagner-Martin, Anne Stevenson, Ronald Hayman, and Paul Alexander. But still, no firsthand documents surfaced.

Publicly, Hughes continued to write Assia out of his life story, but she deeply occupied his poetry. The cycle of twenty poems in a forbiddingly expensive limited edition titled *Capriccio* revealed bits and pieces of Assia's life and death: "After forty I'll end it"; "baby daughter"; "German au pair"; "six full calendar years." Hughes reprinted eight of the poems in *New Selected Poems, 1957–1994.* He was relieved that no reviewer or journalist had deciphered the autobiographical clues. "People are so dumb they don't know I have given the secret away," he told us.

It was in 1996. A dual-language edition of Ted Hughes's *The Thought-Fox* was published in Israel, and the following year, he was due to come to Jerusalem for the International Poets Festival. He hardly ever gave interviews, but this time he did, maybe because the journalist came from Assia's homeland. He probably wished to send up a trial balloon since, in those very days, he was going through his private papers, preparing them for shipment to Emory University, and was completing *Birthday Letters.* For the first time, he spoke about Assia at length and said that he had written many poems about her but was not sure that he "wrote the ones [he] should have written." The interview was published in *Yedioth Achronot,* and after Hughes's death in October 1998, we used the transcript for a front-page story in the *UK Daily Telegraph.*

In April 1999, we marked thirty years after Assia's death with an article, "Haunted by the Ghosts of Love," in the *Guardian.* By then, we had established contact with Celia Chaikin, Assia's sister, in Canada. For the first time, we saw letters written by Assia or about her.

From then on, the quest gained momentum.

Eighty-six crates with Ted Hughes's archives were shipped to Emory University and made available to the public in 2000. Hughes shared his life with Assia for seven years, about the same length of time that he was with Sylvia, but Assia was missing from his archive. He admitted that he exercised self-concealment when he sorted his papers. It was frustrating.

In the summer of 2003, Carol Hughes sold over six thousand volumes of her husband's private library to Emory. When we leafed through the books, Assia suddenly surfaced. Eighty of the volumes carried biographical fragments from the relationship between her and Hughes. Many of the books came from Assia's own library, even from her former marriages. Hughes had taken them as well as materials that he found in her death flat.

The choice of books reflected Assia's interests, and the inscriptions held many clues. On October 20, 1965, she gave Ted the *Four Screenplays of Ingmar Bergman* and inscribed it: "to mark the departure of Opal / and with love and love and love." Opal is October's birthstone, a symbol of trust and confidence.

We counted five books that Ted and Assia exchanged in October. There was no other instance in the entire collection that books were given repeatedly in the same month, year after year—except for May, which was Assia's birthday month, and August, which was Ted's. The October gift exchange indicates some kind of an intimate anniversary. Were they marking Ted's leaving Court Green and Sylvia Plath in October 1962?

Like forensic literary experts, we leafed through each book in search of annotations, dog-ears, and any other personal signs. In March 1963, six weeks after Plath's suicide, Assia terminated her pregnancy by Hughes. Even if they wished to keep their love child, Plath's suicide made it morally intolerable. Assia was recovering in Sylvia's bed, reading *The Nabobs* by Percival Spear, a study of the social life of the English eighteenth-century India.

Throughout the sleuth work, we prayed to find clues on discarded pieces of paper, which were shoved in and forgotten. We were lucky. On a card that Assia had put inside the book, she inscribed some words that caught her fancy: "The throats of our Wrists Brave Lillies." It was a quotation from "Stings," Plath's poem, which dealt with the conflict between her domestic and her poetic—her queenly—selves, aspiring to get away from the beehive that had become her prison. Underneath the quotation from Plath, Assia described her own feelings: "So this is what's like. Time stretches on and on and on . . . it's like being four again by myself . . . Tired. Not to bed, but tired, caged, slightly, upstairs."

And the pieces in the jigsaw puzzle continued to fall like manna from above.

We made long lists of friends and acquaintances of the Doomed Quartet, who were scattered all over the globe. We sent letters and emails, and nearly all seventy of them agreed to speak. For the first time. Time healed the pain, and all three former husbands of Assia agreed to cooperate. It was easy enough to locate her second and third husbands, since both Professor Richard Lipsey and Professor David Wevill acquired fame and were affiliated with universities. Her first husband, John Steele, was much harder to trace: we only knew that he had served in Palestine and then moved to London. "Firstly—congratulations on finding me—research worthy of the Mossad. And then my best wishes on the task you have undertaken: I have long thought that Assia's tragic story deserves an account in which she is not just a peripheral figure in the Hughes/Plath story," he wrote to us in July 2002 from Victoria, Canada.

We literally knocked on countless doors and always felt as if they had been waiting for decades for our visit. Those we found not only shared their memories of Assia but showed us mementos that she gave them or that they had received after her death. We held our breath when several interviewees disappeared into a back room and returned with piles of papers. We still remember rushing to the nearby photocopying machine in stationery shops to reproduce the precious materials. We urged them to deposit the originals in an archive.

In their photo albums, we saw Assia from cradle to her very last days. An eight-millimeter home movie, shot by her close friend Martin Baker, and a BBC radio program that Assia recorded with Ted Hughes as she read her translations of Amichai made her almost tangible.

We visited the many locations where the story took place: the family home in Tel Aviv; her places of residence in Vancouver, London, Devon, and Ireland; her places of work; her favorite restaurants and pubs. It was crucial to see Assia's last flat and the kitchen where she killed herself. We obtained the address from the death certificate. There was no answer when we rang the bell, and we slid a note under the door. It described our interest and, as not to alarm the current occupant, omitted the fact that our protagonist had killed herself in his kitchen. The following day, a man called and invited us in. Luckily for us, he had moved in soon after Assia's death, and he could reconstruct how the flat was then and what the neighbors saw and heard.

With her letters, journals, poems, drawings, commercial ads, and scripts that she attempted writing, we realized how much more she could have achieved. At last, we felt that we could give Assia her voice and published the biography *Lover of Unreason* in October 2006.

By then, the shutter was lifted, and Hughes's letters became a commodity. His friends felt free to write about him and included their correspondence in the archives they sold.

Thirty years ago, no one had heard Assia's name. Many of her letters and writings were destroyed intentionally, some got lost, but now, as she has become an entity of her own, we hope that in the coming years, more of her works may surface. For all those who are interested in the Doomed Quartet, *The Collected*

Writings of Assia Wevill will save a great deal of legwork and long days deciphering her handwriting scattered in various archives. But much more than that, it will enable readers to draw their own picture of the complex, vivacious personality of Assia.

—Eilat Negev and Yehuda Koren

ACKNOWLEDGMENTS

While the scope of this book makes it impossible for us to acknowledge each person to whom we are indebted, we will endeavor to name those whose assistance and efforts contributed in demonstrable ways to the book before you. We are most grateful to our family, friends, and colleagues, who supported us in countless ways while we worked on this far-ranging and multilayered volume.

Our deepest thanks belong to the Estate of Assia Wevill, specifically the late Celia Chaikin, Assia Wevill's sister, and Ira Chaikin, Assia Wevill's nephew. Likewise, we warmly thank the Estate of Yehuda Amichai, namely Hana Sokolov-Amichai, Assia Wevill's friend, for the support necessary to publish these important texts that span genres. Thank you for your confidence in us to bring forth this much-needed book.

From our perspective and experience, our publisher, Louisiana State University Press, is one of the finest of the fine in the world of university presses and academic publishers. We thank our terrific editor, James W. Long, for his leadership and expertise. The people at Louisiana State University Press embody excellence. We wish to acknowledge and warmly thank Sam Anselmo, Catherine Kadair, LB Kovac, Sunny Rosen, and James Wilson. Thank you to Elizabeth Gratch, our talented copyeditor, and Barbara Neely Bourgoyne for producing such an elegant design.

During the curating, transcribing, researching, and annotating of this volume, we had the great fortune to become acquainted with and befriend people who were close to Assia, and we are grateful for their help as well as for the kindnesses they have shown us. We wish to warmly acknowledge David Wevill, whom we hold in high esteem and whom we thank for his insight, discernment, patience, and help. Likewise, the book and our work putting it together were significantly aided by Martin Baker, whom we consider a very fine friend and to whom we are indebted for his valuable contributions. We warmly thank Patricia Mendelson, who provided letters and offered mementos and memories that would have been lost to time without her thoughtfulness and generosity of spirit.

Extra special thanks and all our very best regards go to Courtney Chartier and Kathy Shoemaker of the Stuart A. Rose Manuscript, Archives, and Rare Book Library (MARBL) at Emory University. Truly, they and the people associated with the Rose MARBL are spectacular. This book would not exist without the riches at Emory and the specialists who work there. We could not ask for better colleagues across the miles.

Archives and academic scholarship are the coins of the realm for a scholarly edition such as *The Collected Writings of Assia Wevill,* and we are grateful to the specialists, archivists, librarians, and researchers whose work enabled this book. Specifically, we wish to highlight Paul Civitelli and Yale University; Amber Kohl and the Special Collections and University Archives at the University of Maryland; Sarah McElroy Mitchell and the Lilly Library at Indiana University; Helen Melody and the Contemporary Literary and Creative Archives, Contemporary British Collections, British Library; and Mariah Wahl and the Harry Ransom Center, University of Texas at Austin.

Thank you to Emily Dill and Jeffrey Wimble of the University Library of Columbus and to Gemmicka Piper of the University Library at Indiana University–Purdue University Indianapolis (IUPUI). Thank you to Juanita Stepp and everyone associated with interlibrary loan services.

As for institutional support, we are proud to have been supported by a diversity fellowship funded by the IUPUI Arts and Humanities Institute (IAHI): thank you to the IAHI and Jason Kelly. Thank you, also, to the IUPUI Office of the Vice Chancellor for Research, specifically Steven B. Chin, Alicia L. Gahimer, and Etta M. Ward. Past support in the way of professional development grants from Indiana University–Purdue University Columbus (IUPUC) has laid the foundation for this work: thank you, Reinhold Hill, Lori Montalbano, and George Towers.

Our colleagues earn our thanks and praise; we are honored to know you. Thank you especially to David Trinidad, whose contributions are important to this book, and we thank him for his true friendship and for his own work in poetry. We thank sincerely and earnestly Gail Crowther for supplying us with photographs and an important memoir as well as for her strong friendship and support. Thank you to our colleagues and friends Yehuda Koren and Eilat Negev: we thank them for their assistance with Hebrew translations, connections to people in Assia's world, insight into the contexts of Assia's life, and their contributions to this book, with respect to letters and photographs.

Among the many people whom we have sought assistance for various aspects of the book, we wish to acknowledge and thank Cerrie Butler, Matthew Carnagua, Naomi Cohenour, Cris Craig, David Gems, Deborah Harris of The Deborah Harris Agency, Robert Jocelyn and Ann Henning Jocelyn, John Paul Kanwit, Vicki Kruse, Gary Leising, Lauren Levy, Frank Niesen, Abby Norman, Rai Peterson, George Phillips, Jenny Plath, Jennifer J. Smith, Raegan Smith, Patti White, and Susan Plath Winston. Furthermore, we are indebted to the early readers and reviewers of this manuscript; we value their critical acumen and feedback.

On a personal note, Julie wishes to thank her mentors, friends, and family, whom she treasures and whose support makes this work possible. She cannot imagine more perfect people. Also, she acknowledges the importance of friendship and scholarship in the terrific community of Plath scholars, whose kindnesses, generosity, and accomplishments pave the way for exciting and important work. Finally, she thanks Peter K. Steinberg: his brilliance, passion, work ethic, and example set the standard for us all.

Peter would like to thank Courtney, Arthur, Susan, Jennifer, David, Jon, Jack, Andrew, Janis, and Steve for their love and support, even if they didn't know they were giving it. He is particularly grateful to Julie Goodspeed-Chadwick for her dedication, professionalism, and vision for *The Collected Writings of Assia Wevill*. Being asked to participate in and contribute to a volume such as this is a privilege.

ABBREVIATIONS AND NOTES

NAMES

AW	Assia Wevill
CC	Celia Chaikin
DW	David Wevill
RL	Richard "Dick" Lipsey
SP	Sylvia Plath
SW	Shura Wevill
TH	Ted Hughes

DOCUMENT TYPES

AL	Autograph letter (unsigned)
ALS	Autograph letter signed
TL	Typed letter (unsigned)
TLS	Typed letter signed

ARCHIVES

Emory	Stuart A. Rose Manuscript, Archives, and Rare Book Library, Emory University
Koren and Negev	Yehuda Koren and Eilat Negev
Texas	Harry Ransom Center, University of Texas at Austin
Stanford	Manuscripts Division of the Department of Special Collections, Stanford University
Yale	General Collection, Beinecke Rare Book and Manuscript Library, Yale University

NOTES

Italicized text in the body of letters and journals consists of English translations of Hebrew by Yehuda Koren and Eilat Negev.

Page numbers to *Lover of Unreason: Assia Wevill, Sylvia Plath's Rival and Ted Hughes' Doomed Love*, by Yehuda Koren and Eilat Negev (London: Robson, 2006; and New York: Carroll & Graf, 2007), are to the American Carroll & Graf edition.

THE COLLECTED WRITINGS OF ASSIA WEVILL

INTRODUCTION

The year 2019 marked the fiftieth anniversary of the death of Assia Wevill (1927–69), perhaps the most notorious "other woman" in literary and cultural studies. She continues to capture our attention, as publications, documentaries, and public performances attest. Known primarily for her relationship with Ted Hughes (1930–98) and for her fraught relationship with Sylvia Plath (1932–63), Assia remains a relatively understudied figure because of the dearth of primary materials available related to her.[1] This volume presents, for the first time, a scholarly edition of important writings by Assia Wevill.

The texts published in this volume are housed in archives and in private hands in various places: from London, England, to New Haven, Connecticut, to Atlanta, Georgia, to Austin, Texas, to Stanford, California, to Jerusalem, Israel. And there are likely extant texts to be found. As it is, critical work centered on Assia is burgeoning and promising, though not yet robust. Knowing that a scholarly edition of Assia's writings is overdue, we, the editors, decided to commit to producing such an edition. What we brought to the project: enthusiasm and passion for literature and efforts in recovering lost or unknown texts and narratives; experience contributing to and accentuating (auto)biographical and literary studies; and expertise in collecting, transcribing, researching, annotating, and curating these writings. We remain eternally grateful for the support of the Estate of Assia Wevill and Louisiana State University Press. And our generous colleagues and friends Eilat Negev and Yehuda Koren provided necessary assistance. This book is a testament to the importance of relationships in many ways.

Our goal in collecting, transcribing, researching, and annotating ninety-six letters from 1943 to 1969, approximately twenty-eight journal entries spanning 1963–69, fifty-one poems, and four miscellaneous texts was to capture Assia's

1. Because of the many last names Assia Gutmann-Steele-Lipsey-Wevill assumed during her lifetime, recent scholarship refers to her by her first name, and we will follow this practice.

writing as closely as possible to the originals in order to foreground her literary contributions, unique personality, and undeniable role, influence, and impact on literature, history, and culture. Her idiosyncrasies and mistakes suggest her individuality, variability, and vulnerability, we ultimately decided, and these further delineate her as a person whose life we can learn from and situate within specific times and places. To that end, we have chosen to replicate the spelling and punctuation as she chose to write or type words, phrases, and sentences. It is our editorial philosophy to present Assia in her own words and voice as closely as possible to preserve authorial choices. Crossed-out words and phrases (when we are able to read them) appear as strikethrough text in the footnotes. Italicized passages were translated from Hebrew into English by Assia's biographers, Yehuda Koren and Eilat Negev. Additionally, readers will find that we opted to use present tense as a literary convention in our footnotes to maintain the continuous present of the letters and journal entries whenever possible stylistically. We also elected to gloss and annotate the letters and journals to provide readers with ready information that enables reading comprehension and provides contextualization of the details and allusions Assia supplies in these documents whenever possible. It is our hope that such aids will bolster readers' experience and enjoyment of this scholarly edition of Assia's writing.

The objectives of this scholarly edition include presenting new primary materials that will fuel scholarship on Assia and, by extension, Plath, Hughes, and Yehuda Amichai (1924–2000); establishing Assia's significance in literary studies; and making available materials that recuperate or restore Assia's life and writings as much as possible, while developing our understanding of Assia as a significant woman in literary history, literary biography, and cultural and women's studies who partnered Ted Hughes and achieved professional successes by her own pen. Part I is dedicated to letters written by Assia; part II is devoted to her journal writing; part III showcases her poems and translations; and part IV presents two of Assia's notes, an uncompleted and unsigned last will, and her literary introductions to the BBC program introducing her Hebrew-to-English translations of Amichai's poems. (Assia wrote and read the introductions to the poems, and Ted Hughes read the poems themselves over BBC airwaves.) It may be that other important or interesting texts by Assia surface in the future; should we have the good fortune to access such writing, an updated edition may result.

Historically, Assia has not fared well in literary scholarship, when she appears at all. We may find Luce Irigaray prescient to some degree when we evaluate Assia's life within the context of Assia's letters, journals, poems, other texts, and biography. Irigaray claims, "Woman, in this sexual [patriarchal, psychoanalytic] imaginary, is only a more or less obliging prop for the enactment of man's fantasies. That she may find pleasure there in that role, by proxy, is possible, even certain. But such a pleasure is above all a masochistic prostitution of her body to a desire that is not her own, and it leaves her in a familiar state of dependency upon man" (*This Sex,* 25). In other words, one interpretation of the world in which Assia found herself entails that we take into account patriarchal norms: women are to be valued for their physical bodies and how they can be utilized in a patriarchal system. Female bodies are the playing field, battlefield, or canvas upon which normative male desires are projected, pursued, or enacted; the female body is an accessory, then, of what Irigaray defines as male fantasies. Women very well may discern pleasure in being sought after and treated as desirable, but the end result, in Irigaray's psychoanalytic, feminist schema, is that women will be diminished and displaced—and the latter word was selected by Assia as one she used to describe herself—with respect to their own bodies. In such a configuration, women become dependent on men for, as we may surmise, their self-worth and identity in what Irigaray also identifies as "a dominant scopic economy" (26). We could ask ourselves what kind of expectations we have and how we bring them to bear on Assia and, by extension, the texts that follow. How does what we know of Assia through Sylvia Plath or Ted Hughes, for example, shape the image or identity of the historical person, literary character, and cultural entity we will soon (re)encounter? Being aware of these filters or biases may allow us to receive and approach Assia's writing and the author herself across genres in new and different ways, all of which would not be possible to the same extent without these surviving writings. Indeed, we expect that readers will encounter perspectives and experiences of the world—that of Assia's lifetime and relevant in various ways now—that show us what it means to be a subject with agency more broadly as well as what it looks like to be enmeshed in the historical, social, and cultural circumscription of gender more specifically.

Not until the mid-twentieth century would people tend to invoke what we now think of as markers of social identities—sex, race, class, nationality, and religion—to describe their own or someone else's identity (Appiah, *Lies That Bind,* 3). These markers, or categories, are "culturally prescribed," Alvin Gouldner and Kwame Anthony Appiah insist (5). Thus, Assia's social identity is constructed through culturally prescribed categories: she emerges in others' accounts of her, as we will see shortly, as a beautiful but destructive woman who is somehow always an example of alterity and not at all to be associated with the English, albeit she spoke and wrote fluently in English and even translated Hebrew poems into English. Furthermore, she also married and partnered English and Canadian men and lived and worked in England, among other places. In various accounts, she comes across as a sophisticated, exotic femme fatale instead of a multinational, multiethnic, accomplished, cosmopolitan woman who defies categorization and assumes more both-and possibilities than either-or categorizations in terms of markers of identity. We anticipate that readers will see how Assia's own voice, as represented in her writing, supports, undercuts, modifies, and changes or enhances received and perceived notions about who she might have been and how she is perceived today. In this vein, it is important for us to remember this caution by Appiah: "Once identities exist, people tend to form a picture of a typical member of the group. Stereotypes develop. They may have more or less foundation in reality, but they are almost always critically wrong about something" (12). And yet the importance of identity is underscored by Appiah: "Not only does your identity give *you* a reason to do things, it can give others reasons to do things to you." He elaborates: "Dominant identities can mean that people will treat you as a source of authority; subordinate identities can mean you and your interests will be trampled upon or ignored" (10–11). Indeed, many subordinate identities intersect to render Assia particularly vulnerable to mistreatment, ostracism, and silencing.

Truly, it is incredible that Assia's writing across genres exists—with respect to the quality and quantity of the documents we have—given the complicated history attached to Assia's life and writing: her life writing, so to speak. In a letter dated October 3, 1963, to Assia, Hughes requests, "Keep a journal and send it [to me]" (*Letters of Ted Hughes*, 223). Assia's own letters to Hughes "ring sincere," he tells her in a February 9, 1964, letter (229); she strikes him as honest and authentic. By 1965, though, Hughes begins to worry about Assia keeping a record of their lives and their relationship. He implores her in a February 1965 letter: "Past experience is bad enough to cope with, but it clears itself—it doesn't really oppose our present lives, whereas those letters & that diary of yours do. They're in our way. They've already caused enough trouble. So please burn all my letters" (236). Assia neither stopped keeping a journal, nor did she burn all her beloved's letters. Because of these texts, we have documentation that provides a more complete record of Assia's life as well as more complete biographical records of those close to her. In addition to these aspects, we also have a record of her time, of her world as she saw and experienced it, and in the texts collected in this edition, Assia, as a talented writer, proves she was often an astute chronicler of people, places, and events.

Perhaps the surest sentiment we can express about Assia is that she comes across as a complicated person, perceived differently by different people at different times, as are we all. While that tends to be the case, a great deal of commentary has been generated about her physical appearance. Gerald Hughes, Ted Hughes's brother, describes Assia as "a strangely beautiful woman," who "had an exotic quality and was artistic" (*Ted & I*, 168). Poet Richard Murphy, a friend of Ted Hughes, confesses, "The Babylonian beauty of Assia's raven hair, dark eyes and voluptuous bosom astounded me" (*Kick*, 229). These responses, focusing on Assia's body and its attractiveness, are typical responses from the men who knew her. Women also take especial note of Assia's physical features. For example, Plath, in an October 9, 1962, letter to her mother, calls Assia a "triumphant model with her exotic looks" (850).

But Assia was more than her corporeal beauty, although that appears to be one of her defining characteristics. We document here the conventional treatment of Assia to underscore reception, but we wish to emphasize the philosophical strain in our approach to Assia: Assia's work emphasizes and enhances her subjectivity. Clearly, she is a subject, not an object. Her close friend Patricia Mendelson recalls Assia's "tremendous personality and enthusiasm" and remembers her as a much-loved mother. In a letter dated April 13, 1969, three weeks after Assia and Shura, the daughter of Assia and Ted Hughes, died at the ages of forty-one and four, respectively, Mendelson writes to Celia Chaikin, Assia's sister, about both Assia and Shura, providing an intimate glimpse into their lives:

> Unless [Assia] was going through an intolerable patch [she] would always be gay and fun to be with on the surface and was good at hiding from us all just how desperate she was. She and I had become very close during the last years and she was the only one with whom I could laugh about certain things; we would talk German to-gether and somehow had something in our relationship which I don't have with my English friends. She had changed so much since Shura was born, become softer, and much more understanding of women, which she

> had not been before—more vulnerable too. You are wrong about Shura, Celia, thank God Assia took her with her, she (Shura) loved her Mummy so much and already suffered so much by the instability of Ted's relationship—she would be heartbroken each time he went away again. Assia's loss would have dealt her a blow she could <u>never</u> have recovered from.

In an interview she gave in 2013, Olwyn Hughes, Ted Hughes's sister, indicates that the instability and insecurity of Assia's and Shura's lives with Ted Hughes would not have improved. According to Olwyn Hughes, Ted Hughes "didn't even know that Sylvia would find out about [the affair with] Assia. He'd done everything he could to be very discreet. It was just one of those things. . . . [. . .] But he didn't leave [Plath] for Assia. That's just not true." From the perspective of someone we might label as an insider, we see that, in this instance, Assia is not positioned in the Plath-Hughes mythology as the main catalyst in the breakdown and breakup of the Plath-Hughes marriage. Running counter to dominant biographical narratives swirling around Plath, Hughes, and Assia, Olwyn Hughes's narrative mitigates faultfinding with respect to her brother and his lover and, later, partner. In poems published in *Capriccio* (1990), such as "The Error" and "The Other" (retitled "Rules of the Game" in *Collected Poems* [2003]), Ted Hughes considers Assia as a victim in the aftermath of Plath's suicide. In his unpublished poem "So there he sits in the web he has spun," he castigates himself for mistakes he could not know would claim three lives. In a different account, Lucas Myers relates what he remembers: that Assia said she would never have had an affair with Hughes if Plath had been pleasant to her (*Crow Steered,* 129), and by 1969, Myers is convinced that Assia and Shura would be living with Hughes in Scotland within a year (135). Having lived with Assia and David Wevill for a time in Belsize Park, in Sigmund Freud's former residence, Myers became close to Assia. He describes her as "good company" and "born to conduct a literary and artistic salon." He adds, "She dressed with taste but a good deal of panache, had striking looks, spoke with great articulation and a kind of bejeweled accent, and was fundamentally a very vulnerable person and capable of authentic human affection" (127–28).

In many examples—from the records, memoirs, and reminiscences we encountered—Assia's contemporaries found her "likeable," to use Richard Murphy's word from a 2007 interview (Murphy and O'Connell), and lovable, as evidenced in two of Ted Hughes's unpublished poems about her, "Sunlight" (dated October 1962) and "Only Your Ivory Smooth Body" (undated). In "Sunlight," the speaker yearns for his lover and gestures to the manner in which, though physically absent, she is ever-present in his thoughts and, therefore, close to him. Visual imagery captures the loved one: she is linked with fish, nature, a wedding, gardens of flowers, and an enormous absence that keeps the speaker awake and thinking of the lover all night. "Only Your Ivory Smooth Body" makes use of biblical allusions, comparing the beloved's body to Eden, his own personal Eden. The speaker finds the woman's body refreshingly pure, like snow water, and their kisses are likened to young flowers. The poem ends as it begins, with reference to the woman's ivory body. These are desire-laden love poems. Conversely, after Assia and Shura died, Hughes also wrote poems, in *Capriccio,* in which he represented Assia as both a dangerous threat to his selfhood and a monster, while he wrestled with the traumatic losses of his partner and daughter. (Assia died by suicide, and Shura died by maternal filicide.)

In the letters he sent to different addressees after her death, Hughes occasionally brought up Assia. In the April 14, 1969, letter to Chaikin, Hughes remembers Assia as "my true wife and the best friend I ever had" and Shura "as the most wonderful little girl, full of fire. And really beautiful" (*Letters of Ted Hughes,* 290). More than twenty-eight years later, in his November 19, 1997, letter to Jutta and Wolfgang Kaussen, who were translating Hughes's poems into German, Hughes discusses Assia in connection with the *Capriccio* poem "Shibboleth":

> The "you" was an exotic and by fashionable standards very beautiful foreigner whose mother tongue was German but who now spoke (left Germany in 1935, though her mother was Prussian) an elocutioner's English rather more lofty than the élite English who sat around her (German behind English can sound super-echt English). True to type, all were disturbed by her. They were out of their depth with her, of course, at some point their attentions turned nasty. She had no defences, being a born refugee: a jew born in Hitler's Germany (Father a Russian Jew); later, a German in Israel (Mother as I said Prussian); later, in Western Canada, a continental freak (married to an English ex-Army officer); later, cosmopolitan beauty and wife of a wandering Canadian student in the far East, eventually settling in England—but never forgetting for a moment that she was on the run and belonged nowhere. But a big personality. Passionate about Tolstoy.

Hughes continues:

> The "game"—her—it now becomes clear, has been winged (hit on the wing), has fallen, and has been seized, and is now held, by one of the dogs. Held in that fashion—broken-winged (pinioned) and held trussed (pinioned), she is both held to be killed (as the game bird) but also held arm-pinioned, for cruel interrogation, as a human alien. So she floatingly exists in my lines simultaneously as the wounded about to be killed bird held in the mouth of a dog, as all the hunters stare down, and as a foreign fugitive suddenly dragged upright, arms screwed up her back [. . . .] It has now dawned on the whole table that they have here not only a disturbingly exotic woman who is faking her English manners (like a spy) but who is also actually a savage Tartar probably begotten by some big black geni out of the Arabian Nights. Hence the coup-de-grace—the Englishman's ultimate social skull-crusher: "Lick of the tar-brush?"—a phrase from colonial days meaning "tainted with native (Indian or African) blood." (697–98)

In his letter to Chaikin, Hughes signals his love for Assia, and in this letter to his translators, he gives a snapshot of her biography to us, a biographical sketch that features her as an exotic, fashionable, literary, beautiful, cosmopolitan, global outsider with "a big personality" whose very presence disturbs proper English folk. Be that as it may, she is delineated as defenseless and vulnerable; she is, in the course of the sketch, persecuted, Hughes suggests. She is thereby wounded, caught, and likely about to die, and we are told in that moment that she is an imposter Englishwoman; really, her essence is that of a multiracial, multiethnic savage. This take is one of the more dominant, enduring views regarding Assia. However, this edition takes its cues from literary recovery efforts, and while we wish to introduce readers to Assia in these prefatory pages, we hope that readers will encounter her in the pages that follow and develop their own interpretations of a significant life.

Other members of Assia's circle offer sometimes different and sometimes convergent perspectives to that of Hughes. Her friend Nathaniel Tarn posits that Assia's behavior is a result of terrible insecurity in his journal notes for August 1962; he surmises that she is a compulsive gossip because gossiping keeps her aware of and/or involved in current affairs and events. On October 1, 1962, he chalks up the love triangle and drama associated with Ted Hughes, Assia, and David Wevill as the equivalent of a Greek play. In his October 10, 1962, entry, Tarn records that Assia wants to keep her job and maintain her independence; specifically, she does not want to become dependent on Hughes. Tarn learns, perhaps from Assia, that Plath is naming Assia in divorce proceedings and, consequently, hiring detectives. By December 7, 1962, Tarn explains that everyone knows about the Hughes and Assia affair because Plath told everyone about it at the English PEN party, a writers' association get-together that took place on October 29, 1962. He relates that Peter Porter, who appears to be the source of what transpired at the PEN party, conjectured that Assia's behavior overall stems from wanting to keep her dignity intact publicly. After Plath died, Tarn writes, on February 16, 1963, that all the women blame Assia for Plath's demise. Almost a month later, on March 12, 1963, Tarn details his lunch date with Assia; she does not eat and looks unwell and rattled. While he has previously dismissed her as calculating, Tarn labels Assia as supremely naive toward the end of his journal entries; by this point, he has captured her confidences to him and his observations of her from 1962–63. On June 23, 1963, Tarn describes Assia as incredibly isolated and feeling like an outsider. She does not feel she is coping adequately, and to add to this development, she is mesmerized by Plath—so much so that she thinks she may write a biography about her ("Nathaniel Tarn Papers").

Assia's coworkers Julia Matcham and Ann Semple characterize Assia in their own respective writing. Matcham served as art director at Colman, Prentis and Varley and worked with Assia, who was a copywriter there, in the early 1960s. According to Matcham, Assia "was a pirate on the sea of life, and life could not possibly ignore this rather beautiful and rather animal woman. She was charming, but she did not exploit her power. Like a satisfied lioness, she waited" (qtd. in Koren and Negev, *Lover of Unreason,* 78). In a letter from February 2, 1987, that Matcham penned for Linda Wagner-Martin as part of Wagner-Martin's biographical research on Plath, Matcham delivers a long discussion of Assia that is not particularly favorable ("1990–1991, Wagner-Martin MSS"). Matcham thinks of Assia as ruthless and, at best, entertaining, someone who generated extravagant and unorthodox ideas. Matcham notes Assia's sexual charisma, claiming that Assia matches Hughes in this regard. Dubbing Assia a subtle prima donna, Matcham declares that Assia intentionally seduced Hughes during the May 1962 weekend the Wevills stayed with Plath and Hughes in Devon. After Plath's suicide, she goes on to say that Assia (initially) did not feel remorse because Assia believed Plath's physician had prescribed the wrong pills, which Assia concluded was the primary factor in Plath's demise. Matcham informs Wagner-Martin that Assia's group head, Angela Landels, thinks Assia's behavior could be summarized as having been primarily motivated by envy. At the end of Matcham's letter, she conjectures that Assia's suicide stemmed from one of three possibilities: revenge; the need to shift attention to herself; or a bad gamble with what Matcham calls playacting, an act that ultimately would have failed to result in any satisfaction for Assia, after a lifetime of performing that way.

By contrast, Semple, who worked at Ogilvy & Mather with Assia in the late 1960s, holds a much more favorable opinion of her colleague. In a letter to Assia postmarked July 15, 1968, Semple, who had left the advertising agency before Assia did, writes, "You were the only REAL LIVE writer left in that hell-hole" (Semple, qtd. in Koren and Negev, *Lover of Unreason,* 183). Using terms of endearment, such as *darling* and *dear heart,* Semple urges Assia to seek a top job and not settle for a position at a mediocre agency, despite what she suspects must be Assia's panic and financial angst (Semple), to which Assia would have been prone, given that she was a single mother who did not receive child support and who served as the head of her household. Semple also refers to Assia as the only true woman at the agency, and she calls Assia an "earth-mother" twice in her letter postmarked June 6, 1968, all notions that run counter to the manner in which Assia has traditionally been represented. And Semple comments that Assia is a writer who is both brilliant and inspired; she would make a suitable creative leader in advertising, encourages Assia's friend and advertising colleague.

For his part, David Wevill wrote several poems commemorating Assia, two of which are "Assia" (1987) and "Departures" (2001). These poems provide a sympathetic but also a beautiful and despairing vision of who Assia was from her third husband's point of view. In addition, they paint a portrait of her and the quality of her life toward the end of it. "Assia" begins with the speaker describing Assia in the doorway of a shop about to close, an unraveling white ribbon affixed to her hair (3–5). Her eyes conceal what she has lost, such as a lost property (6–7). Much like the fading light of the poem, Assia's life is also fading (8, 14). She belongs to a "dark generation" and a "wandering kind" that manages to escape persecution (9–10). Left alone, finding the "stage hers," she "weeps, silently" and becomes "less and less visible," until she is the "whole of darkness waiting to go" (11, 13, 14). In "Departures," Assia is cast as Anna Karenina. The speaker reflects that the Anna Karenina figure's difficult, transitory past is one that she has escaped ("They hung / stations from her eyelids / with real trains—" [1–3]), but the future promises doom nevertheless: "The lonesome train of her heavy century / long gone. Explosions still to come" (10–11). At the end of the poem, Assia is alluded to as a Daphne character, the extraordinarily beautiful daughter of a river god in Greek mythology. Daphne, requesting an intervention from her father, is turned into a laurel tree, specifically to prevent Apollo from pursuing her with, presumably, the intention to rape her. These two poems, "Assia" and "Departures," ask us to entertain the idea that Assia deserves our sympathy and maybe pity, too, for the circumstances she faced in her life.

Frieda Hughes, daughter of Ted Hughes and Sylvia Plath, remembers a blended family arrangement with Assia and Shura in Ireland and Devon, England, in her autobiographical poetry collection *Forty-Five: Poems* (2006). She writes in "Sixth Year 1965," "In Ireland, my father was searching for a new / And different life to take us to" and that the "family of three / Was sometimes five" (22–26).In the next poem, "Seventh Year 1966," the speaker depicts the father and son as bonded and Assia and Shura in similar fashion, with the speaker serving as observer of—and not participant in—the activities of the scene. While Ted Hughes and Nicholas Hughes are preparing bait for fishing, the Assia and Shura characters are crafting paper angels with feathers for wings. From the phrasing of these two poems, we are given to understand that Assia and Shura are their own family unit and a tacked-on addition to the Hughes family, sometimes integrated and sometimes not. These portrayals align with what Assia herself confided: that she was "a displaced person"—and also that "she had created the woman she seemed to be," as her friend and advertising colleague William Trevor recorded in his memoir (*Excursions,* 119).

In that memoir, Trevor weaves a complex portrait of Assia. While "she could not properly make her imagination work for her" in 1962, when she met Plath and Hughes, he figures, "One day she might have the right" to be included in "the charmed poetic circle" of Hughes, Plath, and David Wevill (*Excursions,* 117). He maintains that Assia "exaggerated" in stories she told him "only in the interests of what she saw as a greater veracity" (118). And yet to Trevor, it is striking that Assia simply wanted to be "loved for herself alone," not for her physical appearance (117). All the same, Trevor reports that, to Assia, it was important to be considered attractive (116). And she succeeded. Here is how Trevor describes Assia: she was "tall and beautiful, her features reminiscent of Sophia Loren in a tranquil moment. When she spoke it was huskily, her tone aristocratic," and she reminds him of an F. Scott Fitzgerald character in her charm, attractiveness, and unobtrusiveness, with "innocence brushed over with sophistication" (115). About a month before she died, Assia and Trevor conversed about her life in great detail. Assia confided in him that she wanted a new life: a marriage and a new start with Shura, away from Primrose Hill and the literary world. She was done with poets, she said. At their parting, Trevor observed a fleeting disturbance in Assia's composure: "Defeat, suddenly there, faintly distorted her features, dragging at the corners of her mouth. 'Actually, I'm afraid,' she murmured, before she smiled again and went away" (121). That was the last time Trevor spoke to her.

In closing, we predict that Assia's life and its stories will continue to be bound up in the life stories of Sylvia Plath and Ted Hughes. May Assia's writings across genres further bolster those stories and her own from countless perspectives and approaches. It is our hope that these letters, journal entries, poems, and miscellaneous texts will serve the purpose of bringing into focus and enhancing a complex, important woman and significant artist who has her own stories to tell.

WORKS CITED

Appiah, Kwame Anthony. *The Lies That Bind: Rethinking Identity.* Liveright/Norton, 2018.

Hughes, Frieda. "Seventh Year 1966." *Forty-Five: Poems.* HarperCollins, 2006, 9–10.

———. "Sixth Year 1965." *Forty-Five: Poems.* HarperCollins, 2006, 7–8.

Hughes, Gerald. *Ted & I: A Brother's Memoir.* Thomas Dunne / St. Martin's, 2012.

Hughes, Olwyn, and Sam Jordison. "Interview: Olwyn Hughes, Sylvia Plath's Literary Executor." *Guardian.* Guardian News and Media, January 18, 2013. Web. June 29, 2019.

Hughes, Ted. *Capriccio: Poems.* Gehenna, 1990.

———. *Collected Poems.* Farrar, Straus and Giroux, 2003.

———. *Letters of Ted Hughes.* Selected and edited by Christopher Reid. Farrar, Straus and Giroux, 2007.

———. "Only Your Ivory Smooth Body." MSS 644. Subseries 2.3 Uncollected Poems. Box 83, Folder 46. Ted Hughes Papers, Stuart A. Rose Manuscript, Archives, and Rare Book Library, Emory University, Atlanta. March 22, 2018.

———. "So there he sits in the web he has spun." MSS 644. Subseries 2 Writings by Ted Hughes, ca. 1949–90. Box 57, Folder 11. Ted Hughes Papers, Stuart A. Rose Manuscript, Archives, and Rare Book Library, Emory University, Atlanta. March 14, 2018.

———. "Sunlight." MSS 644. Subseries 2.3 Uncollected Poems. Box 84, Folder 29. Ted Hughes Papers, Stuart A. Rose Manuscript, Archives, and Rare Book Library, Emory University, Atlanta. March 22, 2018.

Irigaray, Luce. *This Sex Which Is Not One.* Cornell University Press, 1985.

Koren, Yehuda, and Eilat Negev. *Lover of Unreason: Assia Wevill, Sylvia Plath's Rival and Ted Hughes' Doomed Love.* Carroll & Graf, 2007.

Myers, Lucas. *Crow Steered, Bergs Appeared: A Memoir of Ted Hughes and Sylvia Plath.* Proctor's Hall, 2001.

Plath, Sylvia. *The Letters of Sylvia Plath,* vol. 2: *1956–1963.* Edited by Peter K. Steinberg and Karen V. Kukil. HarperCollins, 2018.

Semple, Ann. "Letter from Ann Semple to Assia Wevill, June 6, 1968." MSS 1058, Box 2, Folder 1. Ted Hughes, Letters to Assia Wevill, Stuart A. Rose Manuscript, Archives, and Rare Book Library, Emory University, Atlanta. April 28, 2018.

———. "Letter from Ann Semple to Assia Wevill, July 15, 1968." MSS 1058. Box 2, Folder 1. Ted Hughes, Letters to Assia Wevill, Stuart A. Rose Manuscript, Archives, and Rare Book Library, Emory University, Atlanta. April 28, 2018.

Tarn, Nathaniel. Nathaniel Tarn Papers, M1132, Department of Special Collections, Stanford University Libraries, Stanford, CA. August 17, 2018.

Trevor, William. *Excursions in the Real World: Memoirs.* Penguin, 1995.

I. LETTERS

TO KEITH GEMS[1]

ALS, Koren and Negev[2]

Thursday, November 18, 1943

9 Balfour St.
Tel Aviv
Palestine
18.11.43

Dear Keith,

I wonder if you still remember me when you finish reading this letter, I hope you do; I suppose John Steele[3] told you about me (he[4] gave me some hints about that). The cause for this sudden and I suppose quite unexpected letter is that I haven't heard from John for a long time about 2 months, I am very much worried, and wondered if you had any news from him lately, as I learned from John you are corresponding regularly, so you are my only source of information. Do you think you could help me? I shall be very gratefull if you do;

I have imagined the worst, so nothing would surprise me, but it is still harder and most unpleasant to stay in doubt, and not be sure of anything.

Do you like Suez better now? and how are you in general? I have never known very much about you, so there isn't anything in particular I can write about or ask you, John hasn't told me much about you, although I was always very curious, his stay was brief and passed very quickly; we had a very good time, and as a result lean raw now (a little). Have you[5] ever seen the Yarkon river? it is

1. British architect Keith Gems (1922–2016) is a British airman at the time of this letter. AW met him when he was stationed in Israel in 1943. He was close friends with AW's first husband, also an airman in the military, and became a lifelong friend of AW's second husband.

2. The letters to Keith Gems (as well as the 1946 letter to John Steele) that begin this volume were provided by Yehuda Koren and Eilat Negev, who obtained their copies from Keith Gems in December 2003. In some places, the quality of the initial copies is dark and/or some of AW's text is cut off. We have identified these instances in the text (<illegible—Eds.>) and in notes. In 2018 and 2019, the editors contacted a Gems family member who was unable to locate the originals.

3. John Steele (ca. 1923–2007) would become AW's first husband; they married in 1946 and divorced in 1952. He is an English soldier stationed in Israel whom AW is dating at the time of this letter.

4. "me ~~a little~~ (he" appears in the original.

5. "~~Did you~~ Have you" appears in the original.

a beautiful place at least this is what Tel Avivians think, In some parts it looks very much like an English country side, and really worth seeing I have joined a course which prepares me for the London Matric,[6] which I hope to take in June, it demands a lot of work, and all my evenings, and as Maths are my weak point, I have chosen the lower paper and ∴[7] take 6 subjects. I have an idea of joining the W.A. W. f's after the matric, but I am sure I shall change my mind at least twenty times,[8] it has many bad points in it, but quite a change from the sort of life I have led for such a long time, and then one meets so many different people.

I am afraid I shall have to stop here, wishing you the very best

Sincerely yours
Assia Gutmann.

TO KEITH GEMS

ALS, Koren and Negev

Sunday, January 30, 1944

9 Balfour St.
Tel-Aviv
Palestine.
30th January 1944.

Dear Keith,

I won't start with a list of explanations and excuses for not writing before, because I know you won't believe any of them. Two are true—I was working a frightful[9] lot for Matric at the end of December, and I was ill twice.

In the meantime three of the 24 weeks[10] of waiting for the results "elapsed," I hope I have done well, I am very doubtful about maths, though. The languages and literature were all cakes, I was lucky in the history questions because they gave me precisely the periods I learned most. I have discovered too, that my only hope of passing the thing was by stuffing in the periods in questions a week before the exams. It worked some how!

And how are you Keath? by the way what's the weather like down at your

6. AW references a matriculation examination.

7. AW uses the symbol for *therefore*.

8. "at least ~~for a~~ twenty times," appears in the original.

9. "frightfull" appears in the original.

10. "24 ~~months~~ weeks" appears in the original.

place? It has been pouring down here for the last month with a break of one glorious, bright week, just enough breathing[11] for the press to regain and roll off long pathetic stories about the floods, and the ghastly time a fellow had burning in his tent, which was struck by lightening. All this went on for seven consecutive days.

Do you know Hanna,[12] Cecilia's[13] friend? She has a spaniel, and it came to pass that Cecilia accompanied her friend to a dogs' nursing house. [Lucy—the spaniel had pneumonia][14] They met a very chering lady who asked Hanna whether she would like another spaniel as she wants to give hers away, Hanna said that Cecilia wants one, and it was brought home. The loveliest cocker-spaniel you could think of, with a lovely sheen on a wonderful black coat. It was called Kushey [have you noticed that most dogs' names end up in "ey"?] and was most intelligent. John wasn't particularly enthusiastic, both Cecilia and I were mad with him for that.

Strangely enough, Kushey wouldn't eat anything but chocolate and biscuits. He grew thinner and thinner, and we began to worry. He came to us on a Sunday, on Friday just as we[15] were about to give up, the bell[16] rang at 3 o'clock and a clean shaven man with a remarkable yellow tie entered coyly. He said he wasn't a patient and that his name was Mayer. It was all extremely interesting, and I just bought a "Picture Post,"[17] pealed off an orange and was about to have a "gorgeous" afternoon nap. He came in[18] connection with the dog. I woke up my father[19] [who was also having the ritual friday afternoon nap].

He explained that he[20] was the manager of "the" Gat-Rimmon[21] and that his wife had a nervous break-down (e.g. a lunatic) that's why she gave the spaniel

11. "just enough ~~time for~~ breathing" appears in the original.

12. Hanna Weinberg-Shallit, a friend of AW and CW, whom AW met at the Ark, a Service Club Entertainment center in Tel Aviv.

13. Celia Gutmann Chaikin (CC [1929–2019]) is the sister of AW.

14. AW largely uses parentheses in her texts; however, there are five instances in which she employs square brackets.

15. "on ~~Monday~~ Friday just as ~~I was abo~~ we" appears in the original.

16. "the ~~door~~ bell" appears in the original.

17. *Picture Post* is a photojournalism magazine published in the United Kingdom that operated from 1938 to 1957.

18. "He came ~~abo~~ in" appears in the original.

19. Dr. Lonya Gutmann (1896–1969), AW and CC's father. He is referred to throughout the text as "Vatick" or more frequently as "Vati," which is German for "dad" or "daddy."

20. "that ~~his~~ he" appears in the original.

21. Gat Rimon is a moshav (a cooperative community of farmers) in central Israel, founded in 1926.

away. He stayed and had tea with us and promised us a puppy in three months time. Ain't that somethin'?

My hand writing is telling on me isn't it! my only excuse—that I am in bed. Both Cecilia and me have an ear inflammation, not really as grand and important as it might sound. We had a bad time at first, but at the moment we are having a grand time. My mother[22] says I ought to finish reading the "History of England" by Andrée Mauras.[23] Instead I read the adventures of Tom Sawyer; and the life of Huckleberry Finn.[24] Great fun, great fun. It really is you know. makes one[25] regret having been born a girl.

The first two after Matric I had a wonderful time, I have been asked to parties every evening and I stayed out untill ones and half past ones. But there was a great obstacle—you see I developed some kind of a friendship with a girl my parent dissaprove of. She is terribly witty and intelligent, very soigme,[26] but some how every body says she makes[27] an impression as if her morals aren't particularly high. She is definitely in the Tel-Aviv smart set, but my parents don't like me to take part in it. I will though. It's fun, and the people I meet are more broadminded,[28] and are intellectuals. Still I am going to get my freedom through evolution.

Please, please pardon the terrible stains and crossingouts.[29]

Yours sincerely,
Assia.

P.S. Congratulations Corporal!
Keith P. Gems Gems
Gems

22. Elizabetha Gutmann (1889–1965), AW and CC's mother. She is referred to throughout the text as "Mutti" and "Muttinka." These are nicknames derived from *Mutter,* which is German for "mother"; AW and CC's mother is German.

23. French author André Maurois wrote *A History of England* (London: Jonathan Cape, 1937). Immediately after this mention, AW wrote some text but heavily crossed it out, adding a note: "Can you read this brother?"

24. Samuel Langhorne Clemens (pen name: Mark Twain [1835–1910]) wrote the canonical American novels *The Adventures of Tom Sawyer* (1876) and *The Adventures of Huckleberry Finn* (1885).

25. "makes ~~you~~ one" appears in the original.

26. AW means *soignée,* which is French for "dressed very elegantly; well groomed."

27. "everybody says ~~her mora~~ she makes" appears in the original.

28. There is approximately a line of text crossed out here.

29. There is a line of text crossed out here.

TO KEITH GEMS

ALS, Koren and Negev

Monday–Tuesday, June 5–6, 1944

9 Balfour St.
Tel-Aviv
Palestine
5th June 1944

Dear Keith,

At long last I am on holydas, and able to answer your May letter. As a matter of fact, your letter was written exsactly a month ago (in the meantime I am 17!) The answer (which) was postponed from week to week—then John came, and then again there was a continuous disturbance which lasted for 7 extremely pleasant days.

You have never told me whether you liked the expresso or not, I am nearly hurt. But here—well, this is a mere matter of personality—if one appeals to the bar-maid, she gives you a double portion of ice cream, shows you a row of golden teeth which mean a commercial gain; the result a wonderful oozing Expresso, too much for the small glass, here the extra quantity spreads itself on the dirty marble counter, and when you or I lift the glass it leaves a nice brown stain on a newly starched dress. I am an old customer (being antialcoholic) been an older acquaintance of the proprietor's son—I have some oozing expressos—many more brown stains.

6th of June

An unexpected visitor interrupted this letter, which I planned to end last night. I was tired to death, and nearly fell asleep while he was telling me the amazing history of his father's career as a judge.

Yes, Mr. Gems, I thoroughly agree with you that there are lots of subjects which would have served most interesting topics for lively conversation after a refreshing drink[30] (3 glasses of water only tasty when drunken with tea spoons,) such as: a.) why Americans chew chewing gum? b) Why Coca Cola is not very popular in Switzerland, even less popular in Palestine? c) Why Maths. Mistresses are such favourites in most girls' schools.

Cecilia has suddenly decided that the ideal life for her would be in the country—that is living among blessed hills of Palestine. Her parents have decided to send

30. "drink ~~of~~ (3" appears in the original.

her to an agricultural boarding school where she will learn to appreciate rural surroundings (!!!) and love the smell of cows and horses. So young Cecilia will probably be a happy farmer's wife someday—and study with great interest the prices of dotted cattles in N. Zealand, compare them with local prices the way our friend Thaches did (further information from John He[31] proposed to me while washing my hand with lifebouy[32] [what a wonderful plot for an advertisement]!) instead of knowing exsactly whether Bette Davies likes boiled or fried eggs[33] for her breakfast. As a matter of fact I don't like the idea in the least, but then again Cecilia dreads the idea of ever having to sit in a tidy office. I am a little snobbish about it as well, though farming nowadays is made simplified, it is still hard physical labour quite unsuitable for women.

I have become quite a dangerous <illegible—Eds.>[34] at least this is what my father he thinks, he said so quite openly the other day at Lunchtime, he said that I am losing all my aesthetic feelings, and he even suggested that this is a prelude to a vulgarized way of thinking; well, well, well. As I am not particularly fond of dancing, and don't let myself go, the way some girls do when learning <illegible—Eds.> I think it is quite harmless, isn't it? I think the actual reason is, that all this <illegible—Eds.>[35] stops him from hearing 11 times a day the same news in three different languages.

I hope you will write to me again Keith, I enjoyed your letter immensely.

Yours sincerely,
Assia Gutmann

TO KEITH GEMS

ALS with envelope, Koren and Negev

Wednesday–Saturday, August 2–19, 1944

9, Balfour St.
Tel-Aviv

31. "John ~~H~~ He" appears in the original.

32. Lifebuoy is a brand of soap launched in 1894.

33. "boiled ~~of~~ or fried eggs" appears in the original.

34. A hyphenated word is illegible. The first part of the word may be *swing, seeing, saving,* or *sewing,* and the second part of the word may be *fan.*

35. This word looks like it is the same one as the first part of the hyphenated word that is illegible in this paragraph.

Palestine
2nd August 1944.

Dear Keith,

After practically giving up all hope of ever hearing from you again, your letter arrived at last. By the way, there wasn't one spelling mistake, I was a little amazed, you know.

Will you believe it, I drank a whole bottle of Coca-Cola; it was awful. So as to not offend the Canadian who gave me the Cola, I tried to put on a sweet smile, and uttered something silly about it. This story might seem a bit suspicious, so I think I might as well go into further details. The Canadians liked a building in Ben-Yehuda road, put a tremendous sign on one[36] of its balconies and called it "Canada-house." A week later the Services Club got an invitation for a dance there. I was among the eight girls who went there. It started on with calm Coca Colas and Johnnie Zeros on a tremendous radiogrami,[37] then their "girl friends" appeared, you know the suspicious looking girls who roam about "Hyarkon" Street;[38] I was terrified and decided to leave at once. at that time, the Canadians got near the bar, and showed us what Canadian spirit was like. I sneaked quietly to the Cloak room, took my bag, and ran out; that was the first time that I have seen what jitterbugging was like. I began to wonder whether these are first signs (of their kind) of deterioration of man kind.

Cecilia isn't going to that boarding school after all; by the way the whole reason for those great deep feelings which dragged her to rural surroundings, was that out of 800 points in her exams she passed with 403. But now, after the great row at home of which she was so frightened didn't occur at all, she preffered to stay in Tel-Aviv and read her monthly "True romances."

Now my mother is going to Jerusalem during the summer;[39] Cecelia has asked her best friend Hanna, have you met her? (the girl with the wild spaniel?) to stay with us. That means, the wildest jitter bugging parties at home when my father will be out, the wearing of all my dresses and shoes (ignoring protests). I shall tell you about the results later. By the way both of them are

36. "sign ~~of~~ on one" appears in the original.

37. AW may mean a radiogram, which was a piece of furniture with a built-in radio and record player. "Johnny Got a Zero" (also known as "Johnny Zero") was a popular 1943 song.

38. HaYarkon Street is a major street in Tel Aviv that runs parallel to the coastline.

39. "Jerusalem ~~for~~ during the summer" appears in the original.

ardent[40] Scoonatra[41] fans. I am cured of that now, after listening with disgust to the most amazing exclamation of American girls through recordings of "hit parades."[42] Do you like him? Another sign of Cecilia's growing up is that she seems to be very fond of smoking but please don't ever tell that my mother! she smokes two cigorettes* weekly in the bathroom! I admire her spirit though.

I'm afraid I was rather horrified at the amazing names you gave to those kittens of yours.

*this is a spelling mistake!

19th August

My mother has gone to Jerusalem on holidays, and I think this is the first time in my life that I feel as if I was half mistress of my liberty.

Tonight I have seen Lena Horne in "Stormy Weather";[43] have you seen it? I was rather disgusted, you know, with all those black, flat figures disappearing in clouds of smoke and jitter bug. Though I couldn't help admiring Lena Horn's beautiful face and "husky" voice, if not for her typical negro finger nails and hands, one can often forget that she is coloured, but of course the colour of her skin is probably grey, but that is an attraction of its own, isn't it?

John hasn't been posted to Palestine after all, as he[44] told me he probably would be, he seems to be very keen on that Maths. affair, though it is so much involved with maths. (he told me that wasn't a very strong point of his). And how about you mister? haven't you grown sick with paddling yet? In case you do, you ought to read John Masefield's "I must go down to the seas again,"[45] if that won't have any in effect—learn it by heart. That reminds me of school, which is opening on September 1st. That means 4 months of ruthless studying;—although I have done some during these Holidays. My weakest point are Maths. I often think it is a hopeless struggle, but then I somehow manage

40. "~~aradent~~" appears in the original.

41. AW probably means Frank Sinatra (1915–98), acclaimed American singer and film actor; he was considered a cultural phenomenon by 1943.

42. AW may mean the American radio program *Your Hit Parade,* frequently called *Hit Parade,* which featured Sinatra and ran from 1935 to 1953.

43. *Stormy Weather* is a 1943 musical film starring Lena Horne.

44. "~~he~~ as he" appears in the original.

45. The poem "Sea-Fever" (1902) is by John Masefield (1878–1967), who was the British poet laureate from 1930 to 1967. "Sea-Fever" begins with the line "I must [go] down to the seas again, to the lonely sea and the sky."

to solve the simplest problem, and I get new courage. Cecilia grumbles about switching off the light, and if I won't stop right now, her slipper is surely going to hit my arm any minute.

Yours sincerely
Assia.

TO KEITH GEMS

ALS, Koren and Negev

Wednesday, October 4, 1944

9 Balfour St.
Tel-Aviv
Palestine.
4th October 1944

Hey Paddler,

Well, you asked for it. Thanks a lot for your letter, as usual I enjoyed it immensely; and by the way, I think you are a very good letter writer.

For fifteen days now have I been thinking of what to write you about. I must tell you first that I am ill, I have hay fever, at least I had it, and at the moment I am having a relatively good time. Like Ali-Baba's wife I am eating apples (If you remember, Ali-Baba is a fellow who lived in Baghdad, and who owned 40 barrels of oil, in which some 39 robbers had the illfortune of dwelling).[46]

Except being ill during my holidays—I learn. Although John might not affirm it, but he always interrupts me, and you can tell him that. By the way, I am the only girl in a class of 12, having a, well, I can't find the right adjective, I suppose it's good. (In this case it would be adjective, attributive, descriptive, describing the name "time.") I have grown into a dreadful habit,[47] I parse every sign on the street. I have seen an amazing one the other day it read like: "Butcher, kills himself every morning": I am awaiting comments. I shall let you know a secret, a real one. A friend of mine, an Irish officer, and a dumb New-Zealand private (who was in the meat trade . . .) had a very low dive into "a beautiful and exotic garden" as was in the Paper. And it was a real low dive. (for

46. "Ali Baba and the Forty Thieves" is a story collected in *The Thousand and One Nights*, or *The Arabian Nights;* the stories are of uncertain date and authorship.

47. "dreadful ~~word~~ habit" appears in the original.

the first time.) Later, we discovered that the "Lorenz"[48] was a sort of place where everybody is sure he won't meet any of his acquaintances, amazingly enough they all meet there. Neither of my partners could dance, so that we had to be contended with a freezing lemonade (on a cool night) and[49] free staring at our neighbours who definitely did not altogether act like ladies and gentlemen. The New-Zealander told us about the meat trade and how he thought of being the manager of his department one day. I enjoyed myself immensly, because all this occurred without my parents knowing,[50] and I trust YOU Mr. Gems.

By the way, I am not in the least content with the amount of freedom which is granted to me. My parents insist on knowing about every visit to the library or to the pharmacy in order to buy apacket of Shampoo. But this point seems to be quite hopeless, as they remember exactly, how young ladies behaved 40 years ago. The war doesn't seem to have changed their ideas.

Rumours say that you are going to visit our holy and green land in November, we shall be both happy and honoured if you will bestow a visit upon our humble abode,[51] LEOPOLD Keith Gems! (By the way did you know that my ear-less Giraffe is called Leopold?)

Thank you very much for the two books you sent me, I passed them over to John, but he gave them to me. I am very happy with the nonsense poems of one of them. Belloc, have you read the "modern Traveller"?[52] his stories are horrible, his historical essays are boring, but his essays are really pleasant little things. You said you could send me a book with R.A.F. slang, I'd love to have it, if you could spare it. Unfortunately, I have very little buisness with the real men of the R.A.F. as both my family and I decided to stop frequenting the Club until January. It is rather hard, but it is all for mother's sake.

By the way, how many pipes do you possess? And haven't you changed over to smoking yet? Please tell whether it is true, that pipes go out from time to time, and how does one light a pipe. Don't ask why;

48. AW probably references the Lorenz Café, which was a popular meeting space, formerly located at 57 Eilat Street, Tel Aviv.

49. "night) ~~with~~ and" appears in the original.

50. "without ~~the knowledge of~~" appears in the original.

51. "abode, ~~Mr. Gems~~." appears in the original.

52. Hilaire Belloc (1870–1953) is a French-born writer who became a naturalized British citizen in 1902. *The Modern Traveller* (London: Edward Arnold, 1898) is a book of verse.

How is your yacht? have you added anything else to your private fleet? What colour is she?

Please answer me before November[53]—

yours very sincerely,
Assia.

TO KEITH GEMS

ALS, Koren and Negev

Friday, November 10, 1944

9 Balfour St.
Tel-Aviv
10th Nov. 1944

Dear Keith,

Thanks for an extremely enjoyable letter, and for the book on "services slang." I'm afraid I can't be very polite regarding that—I think[54] it's awful. The wittiest and "dirtiest" words are really missing, and especially those I really want to know about, and don't dare ask anybody. The following is a rather innocent sounding sort of thing, which an irish man who was no so innocent said, and wouldn't tell me what it is—Oxometer?

So you are coming? I hope you aren't going to skip my humble abode, and miss the chance of being introduced to a real Mickey Rooney—Judy Garland sort of "Ice Cream Bar,"[55] with wonderful "Sundays," "Mondays," "Tuesday" and "Wednesdays," "Brooklyn Specials," "Banana Split," and that and Bananas. By the way the owner of the place, an extremely fat sort of woman who has eyes like Bette Davies, and talks like Ida Lupino in "High Sierra"[56] was mentioned in the 'Readers' Digest.'[57] John saw her—wasn't impressed.

53. "before ~~October~~ November" appears in the original.

54. "that ~~matter~~—I think" appears in the original.

55. A scene in *Love Finds Andy Hardy* (1938) features Mickey Rooney and Judy Garland having ice cream sodas.

56. *High Sierra* (1941) is a thriller starring Humphrey Bogart and Ida Lupino.

57. Founded in 1922 in the United States, *Reader's Digest* began publishing in the United Kingdom in 1938.

After four years[58] my old class decided to meet again, and arrange a party. So I am going. One of the girls is married. ∴ we didn't invite her. Have you seen any good films lately? I have, "Manhattan Tales."[59] Very good; I went for two reasons. The first because my father bought me a ticket. But there is a long story behind that too. On a Saturday night, about 7 days ago, my father my mother and myself decided to go to the Cinema. So Cecilia, very efficiently bought the most expensive and worst tickets possible (with a humble smile on her tiny lips which expressed a wish to go out). She presented them. Her wish was granted, and we went to the cinema. It was a beautiful moonlit night, and my father told me a joke. When we reached the Cinema—we were late. But funnily enough the audience was still standing outside. After ten minutes a short, bald headed little man stepped out, and said that his operator quit him—but still, he can't give the money back. So people broke the windows, and ate the chocolate in the buffet, and out on the seats which were made of wood.

That is the 1st reason for my going to see Manhattan Tales. Secondly—because my favorite actor took part—GEORGE SAUNDERS.[60] Strangely enough, he always gets the 2nd rate rolés, I think he is a marvellous actor, and very good looking.

How is your cat? how is your other cat? And by the way, do you like the stories in "Esquire"?[61] If so, I shall lend you one when you go to Syria, but here is a but—I would like it back.[62] You know, you can't scribble off a sentence very well, I read what you tried to cover last time, and this is the way to do it.[63]

Yours sincerely
Assia

P.S. I don't like your signature.

58. "After four ~~yours~~ years" appears in the original.

59. *Tales of Manhattan* (1942) stars Charles Boyer, Rita Hayworth, Ginger Rogers, and Henry Fonda, among others.

60. AW means Russian-born, to English parents, George Sanders (1906–72).

61. *Esquire* is an American magazine founded in 1933.

62. AW heavily crossed out a short sentence.

63. AW has drawn an arrow from the end of this sentence to some text she scribbled out at the end of the previous sentence.

TO KEITH GEMS

TLS, Koren and Negev

Sunday, April 8, 1945

9 Balfour Str.
Tel- Aviv
April 8th 1945.

Dear Keith,

I hope you don't mind me typing this, but my hand writing has grown to be so bad lately, that I thought it would be absolute cruelty to send you some more of it. As a matter of fact there is another reason for doing so, and that is, that at the moment I am actually on duty, and as there is practically nothing else to do, and as the boss said reading in an office is not good form, I thought i might as well try my best to keep my correspondence up to date.

I suppose I ought to tell you more about my job. Well, it started like this: exactly a week ago, one of my platonic boy freinds told me that one of his platonic girlfriends was leaving her job, would I like to take it over? would I . .? wou I. I thought it was a wonderful chance because, not very much is required, and the salary was relatively speaking fairly high so accepted, accompanied by sqeals of joy and strong protests from my parents'side. They thought that I ought to have fin my secretarial course, and then take a half time job.

I am not frightfully good youknow, but fortunately my boss has patience and a sense of humour. One of the great dis advantages is that I have got to be here at eight o'clock inthe morning, which is not a particularly refreshing thought after late nights. Last night I went to bed at two O'clock after a very jolly party, as I came back I thought I have had my job.[64]

And how are you keeping? I suppose you are busy studying at the moment; no comments. . . . I have also heard that you will be seeing dazzling Tel-Aviv again soon. That reminds me that I shall have to show you round the American Ice cream Bar, which has been renovated and turned even more prettier. Except that they serve two slices of peaches insteat of one, and honestly the ice-cream is much better. Personally I have around four banana splits a week, a traditional one on friday afternoon after listening to a rotten broadcast in "the most popular services club in the middle east" quoting a[65] poster, but this of course is tripe,

64. "I thought ~~I had~~ I have had my job" appears in the original.

65. Two lines of text are struck through by AW.

and I have long ceased to understand why people go there at all.[66] Between you and me this Club is meant more for officers than for anybody else, I think.

Something rather unpleasant happened to John, some sort of a Met baloon exploded inhis face, as a result of which his face is completely burned, and he looks rather like that fellow in "Phantom of the Opera,"[67] a more Northern type though.

By the way, I had a peep into the Bedside Esquire,[68] and it is practically nothing but an anthology of modern American Literature. Very good though. That reminds me Keith, Do you remember something about some Esquire I promised to lend you before you went to Syria? did you take or not? Just let me know if you did please.

That's all really.

yours sincerely
Assia.[69]

TO KEITH GEMS

TLS, Koren and Negev

Tuesday, June 19, 1945

9, Balfour St.,
Tel Aviv.
June 19th 1945.

Dear Keith,

Thanks a lot for your letter and as you have probably realised by now I am working again. This time I am a secretary to the Maccabi World Union[70] Tel-

66. "why people ~~flock there~~ go there at all" appears in the original.

67. *Phantom of the Opera* is a novel (serialized 1909–10; published as a book in 1910) by the French writer Gaston Leroux (1868–1927). It has been adapted as a film many times; AW may be alluding to the 1943 American version, directed by Arthur Lubin and starring the English actor Claude Rains (1889–1967) as the Phantom. In this adaptation, acid is thrown in the face of the man who becomes the Phantom, scarring him and prompting him to wear a mask.

68. *The Bedside Esquire* (New York: Tudor Publishing Co., 1940) was edited by Arnold Gingrich.

69. Beneath AW's signature are the words, in her hand, *Monichal, conscience,* and *monocle.* Another word was crossed out.

70. The Maccabi World Union is the longest-running and largest Jewish sports organization in the world.

Aviv branch, which is a golly good job. You know, none of any dull business routine, and everything rotates around sports and games. Except cutting out excerpts from papers all about the Jewish Brigade[71] and their heroic activities, then sticking them on a special file (the excerpts) there is scarcely anything else to do. I spend nost of my time reading magazines and keeping my correspondence up to date.

And how are the boats? I suppose that by now you are pealing all over (pealing is a spelling mistake) and the Mediterranean climate must have worked wonders on your spirits energy, etc.

We have a puppy, a rude little white and black spaniel, who makes a lot of noise and does not show any signs of outstanding dog intelligence, Cecilia insists he has plenty. As both of us work, mother has all the trouble with feeding for himd and trying to bring him up. We play, make pretty and hackneyed remarks.

Do you remember me telling you about the great May Festival in the Ark and all about the show they were palanning to put on, well according to the papers it was a terrific success, the show was super duper, and polite everbody were surprised at the great deal of talent displayed. By the way the critic was praising Hannah Weinberg in a big way and devoted her five words which was comparatively quite a lot, By the way I don't see much of her lately, but this is mere coincidence as she is busy being ill and reading dirty French short stories. She sends regards.

The pictures Sherrif took did notcome out, because while he was developing them, Palestine was in the midst of a great khamsin session[72] and the film

71. According to the United States Holocaust Memorial Museum, "The Jewish Brigade Group of the British army, which fought under the Zionist flag, was formally established in September 1944. It included more than 5,000 Jewish volunteers from Palestine organized into three infantry battalions and several supporting units. Under the command of Brigadier Ernest Benjamin, the Jewish Brigade fought against the Germans in Italy from March 1945 until the end of the war in May 1945." Further explanation and background is provided by the museum: "Beginning in 1920, Great Britain ruled Palestine under a mandate created by the League of Nations. The British were to facilitate the establishment of a modern Jewish homeland. Due to Arab opposition to the proposed Jewish homeland in Palestine, the British initially refused to establish a separate fighting unit of Jewish volunteers from Palestine. However, wartime manpower requirements and the strategic need to defend the Middle East induced the British to permit the formation of 15 Palestinian Jewish battalions. These units were incorporated into the British army in September 1940."

72. The *Oxford English Dictionary* defines *khamsin* as an "oppressive hot wind from the south or south-east, which in Egypt blows at intervals for about 50 days in March, April, and May, and fills the air with sand from the desert."

simply melted away. He says that the prints are alright but he can't enlarge them as black spots will appear all over the place.

May I remind you that what I have typed so far is equal to a whole sheet of handwritten effort.

By the way, I have decided to take up something quite different for my future carreer. I would like to take pure art in university combined with interior decoration, so that I shall end up with painting lampshades and china. I am optimistic enough to think that I have talent. John decided to go to University after all and take up psychology. He thinks of being one of those industrial psychologists in our brave new communist world. Good idea that.

I am gald to hear that that long expected friend of yours arrived at last, I even remember his name -Malcolm- that right? Hanka is the girl with the not too beautiful legs, right? did he really look as dazzling as Hannah and I decided he did on that photo?

Well that's all. (the"all"is finished with going up into minor key)

sincerely,
Assia.

TO KEITH GEMS

ALS, Koren and Negev

Monday, October 1, 1945

9 Balfour St
Tel-Aviv, Palestine
October 1st 1945.

Dear Keith,

I think it would seem rather silly if I started with a long list of apologies; I read all about your heroic activities in saving all the Greeks from perishing as the lowest of the low of all papers put it ("THE MID EAST MAIL"), and then Cecilia told me you were a Sgt. and I felt like scribbling Sgt. Gems, and that's why I'm writing because I like, [I don't know how to finish the sentence so I'm leaving it at that].

I am working for some Contractors who are extending Lydda airport,[73] and

73. Lydda Airport became what is now Ben Gurion Airport.

I work (sigh) in a little hut in the middle of a semi-desert. I work here because I get exactly[74] 3 times the dough I got in my former job, except this I ought to add that I am cursed with jobs where I do nothing, so that there is plenty of time for developing some of my latest philosophical thesis.

I failed[75] in maths, passed in everything else (logical[76] isn't it?] The London University is so good as to let her wartired students sit for one subject only if they failed in it, so that I shall take maths. in January. The authorities don't let any unmarried women students into U.K. at the moment, that will be valid for another three years, so that I don't think I shall be able to go to University, but I will go to an Arts school and take drawing and lithography. This is real hell, and I swore when I heard it, with no effect whatsoever. You needn't let John know about it, because he will immediately jump into conclusions, and that will be awkward.

I am sick and tired, sick and tired, sick and tired of the ark, and the Services Club and all everything that went with it. I have some friends whom I met before I worked in Lydda and who are fortunately stationed there except this, the boy-friend-situation is rather acute. You might know one of them, he flew with the Air Sea Rescue up at Haifa,[77] a fellow called Lefebure, a 1st Lient. They took me flying twice and I went over to Trans Jordan[78] and back. A lot of fun, especially when climbing, but I felt awfully sick when I came back. We have a constantly full refrigerator around here, and as my[79] bosses are away most of the time, they linger around, and my bosses think that it must be very hot in Lydda because the consumption of drinks is terrific.

Cecilia is going to take part in next years tennis tournaments; you know Hanna, her friend don't you? she did this time, and won in a mixed game, she is going strong in basketball too, and is in the Palestinian representative team now. In point of fact she only sleeps and eats at home, the rest of her time is spent in eating ice-cream with Egyptian tennis-champions, and Syrian Basket-ball players, grim looking fellahs with semi-bald heads.

74. "~~exsa~~ exactly" appears in the original.

75. "~~All my~~ I failed" appears in the original.

76. "(~~makesense~~ logical" appears in the original.

77. Haifa is a city in Israel.

78. The Amirate of Trans-Jordan is a British protectorate, established in 1921, that became what is now Jordan.

79. "~~most~~ and as my" appears in the original.

Except all this we are expecting trouble in Palestine; but[80] I lost some very good friends by talking politics, and discussing Politics, Imperialism.

So Solong,
Assia.

TO KEITH GEMS

TLS, Koren and Negev

Tuesday, November 6, 1945

R.A.F. Station Lydda.
November 6th, 1945,

Dear Keith,

I am not leading a fast and immoral life. And I am not interested in psychology to the extend of reading literature about it, and I am interested in the prizes you won in sailing races, and I liked your letter. Are you really coming on the 26th of this month? that will be swell (forgive this). I hope Palestine will still be in bounds for troops by that time, and that reminds me , how were the riots in Egypt,[81] was it really hot? to me the whole thing seems more like a social revolution than anything else. Of course according to the local papers the riots were purely antisemitic, but I think some of the good and miserable Felahs[82] rather coveted some of the window displays in the more elegant Cairo shops. What do you think?

There was a terrific amount of tension in Palestine during last week, some shots were heard, stones were flung at cars on lonely roads, and people felt queer. I don't think there is much chance for the solution of the Palestine problem in favour of the Jews(a sentence)[83] I hope you don't mind my chatting about all this, but that is the only[84] thing people do talk about these days, except the weather.

John is certain that he will be in England by the end of December he probably won't be, and then he will go into fits of temper which will last during the whole of January, and at the end of it, he will go home.

80. "in Palestine, ~~which is most awkward~~ but" appears in the original.
81. AW refers to the Balfour Day riots on November 2 and 3, 1945.
82. In Arab countries, a "felah" is a peasant or agricultural laborer.
83. Visible in our copy is "(a senten."
84. Visible in our copy is "onl."

Where exactly does your sister study, I sent applications[85] to about four Art Schools in London , but I don't expect an answer until sometime next year. They might be more decent though.

Do you think you could fly over here, I could arrange transport back by air (Ah Ah) . I really could.

Do you remember that friend of mine dear Hanna Weinberg[86] whom you met on the first day of leave last time? she is an announcer[87] in the P.B.s. now, by the way strictly Children' hours.

This is all . Pardon the typing.[88]
Please[89]
Assia.

TO KEITH GEMS

TLS, Koren and Negev

Tuesday, January 15, 1946

9,Balfour Strreet,
Tel Aviv.
January 15th, 1946

My dear Keith,

Last week I wrote you a very long letter; two pages of closely typed non-sense, and somehow they got lost, I mean the pages, the only possible solution is that Beffi (our Spaniel)has mistaken them for his supper. He is really cute, you know, but I suppose you know all about him already. I am rather annoyed about that letter, it took me a whole morning to write, that is four hours, in between telephone calls and pretty compliments from my boss. I left that Airport job, in favour (they finished building the camp, if you are interested, all the messes are leaking, and the paint is coming off, but that really is besides the point), in favour of a job as secretary to a well to do lawyer, who has his slick and well

85. Visible in our copy is "applicat."

86. Visible in our copy was "Weinbe."

87. Visible in our copy was "announc."

88. AW refers to the appearance of her typed words. The *h* key jumped, leading to that letter appearing not inline with the rest of the text but above it, almost like superscript.

89. *Please* is handwritten.

furnished offices in the Barclys Bank[90] building, I am sure you remember it, don't you?I only work in the mornings from 9 to 1, and overuse the elevator. Except this, I do a lot of drawing, still lifes, portraits of impossibly plain girls, in whom we are supposed to find beauty, Yemenite charwomen, and squalid and bearded old men. I study at the studio of a well known Palestinian artist, who has the quaintest ideas about art, rather difficult to cope with at first, but then he is supposed to mould us(please don't misunderstand me!) twice a week I get messed up with charcoal, and comments from my fellow students, everyone of whom thinks he is an undiscovered genious, rather tedious at times.

Tell me all about your journey home,and about the lines you shot (or did you?) I was going to ask you whether you were sea-sick, but suddenly remembered that I should like an answer to this letter.[91] You must have arrived at the time ovf those storms, the press was so full of at the time;[92] were they really as "shordid and shinishter" as most correspondents claimed? or merely sensationalism, ah that's a word I am very fond of lately. Please forgive this attempt at literary outbreak, but, I have no excuse . . .

Have you seen John at all?It's ages since I have last heard from[93] him, and I have been wondering, the Bromley belles, you know. . . . . How is your sister, and her artistic inclinations? and the most beautiful[94] suburb in London(quoting thee) Ealing?[95] and what is your release number, and what do you expect to do for a living? is begging illegal in England?

Hanna Weinberg is going to Australia in March, she is accompanying her mother as secretary, Her mother is deeply interested in the social problems of this world, and is a memeber of the executive of the WIZO (Women's International Zionist Organisation),[96] hence this journey to Australia, the necessity of which (considering limited shipping space) is subject to individual[97] judgement. She is probably going to marry an Australian Lt.Colonel, a jew who is also a

90. Founded in 1690, Barclays is headquartered in London and is a multinational bank.

91. Visible in our copy is "lett," and we have supplied the rest of the word based on context.

92. "so full of at ~~that~~ the time"; appears in the original.

93. Visible in our copy is "fro."

94. Visible in our copy is "beautif."

95. Ealing is a borough of London, between central London and the western periphery of it.

96. The Women's International Zionist Organization (WIZO) was founded in London in 1920 and was active in Israel at the time of this letter; it is an organization dedicated to the needs and welfare of Israeli society, with a special focus on women and children.

97. AW handwrites *individual* after crossing out a misspelling of it.

distant relative of hers, She says that she has already planned her partners for future double crossing. Great woman, Hanna. I hope you don't resent this, but these are the bare facts, and knwing Hanna slightly, you can come to your own conclusions.

About Cecilia; at the moment she is in love with a dumb but beautiful captain of a football team in Tel Aviv. She uses lipstick, looks prettier without it, smokes, and no longer in the bathroom, and on the whole is quite a useful citizien of this world. We still don't get on at all, and quarelling is pretty frequent, but I think this is no longer funny, but rather sordid. How are the goil friends[98] and how is your social life on the whole?

So long, & love[99]
Assia

P.S.
I didn't under line my signature because according to you this indicates a weak character—now jump to your own conclusions . . .

Assia.

TO JOHN STEELE

ALS with envelope, Koren and Negev

Monday, January 21, 1946

January 21st, 1946

Dear John,

For God's sake tell me why you never write? Even if you wanted to stop, why didn't you let me know? I am addressing this to Keith, so that I shall be assured, that you will finally receive it.

By September transport facilities to England will not be as impossible as they are now, and I hope to sail at the end of August. Financially, things are not as difficult as I expected and I shall be able to get on fairly well if I live in the College's hostel. The greatest difficulty is my acceptance at a college. I should have loved to study art, but I think an 18 month's course at a Commercial Col-

98. AW strikes through a phrase here.

99. "& love" is added by AW by hand. The *o* in *love* is the shape of a heart.

lege will be more practical. What I need is a letter stating plainly that on such and such a date there will be a vacancy for Miss Assia Gutmann in such and such a class. An entry Visa will follow immediately. John, could you please arrange this for me? I might as well add that I don't think I shall be very welcomed as a Palestinian, so that if I merely entered into correspondence with some of these colleges, I shall be ignored as I have been so far by 3 colleges. Could you apply to *1) The Polytechnic, Regent St, 307–311. 2) Clark's college—address unknown. Or any other presentable commerce school with moderate fees.

*)I wrote to the Polytechnic, explained the situation very badly, and expect a flat refusal.

Of course it is superfluous to add how much a year's stay in England means to me. At this moment, friendless, miserable, and lonely, this is the only thing I am looking forward to and please John, don't feel as if you owe me something. If your feelings have changed—I shall always try and understand. I shall only be most grateful if you could possibly help me to be accepted to one of colleges I have mentioned. I wrote four letters before sending this one, it is so difficult to write to you nowadays. I never know how my letters are accepted.

If I will come to England in September I shall never call on you or ring you up, unless you want me to—please, you needn't fear any Barbara Stanwyk[100] sincopations.

Assia.

P.S.
I am so tired that this letter really is some mess. I am too tired to think hence the impossible arrangement of sentences and choice of words. Am I forgiven?

<Written on the verso of the envelope—Eds.>

Keith dear,

Will you please hand this over to John perhaps I suspect something rather about the fate of my letter. If it isn't true, I shall go crimson with the shame for 8 weeks.

Assia.

100. Barbara Stanwyck (1907–90) is an American actress.

TO KEITH GEMS

ALS, Koren and Negev

Monday, January 28, 1946

9 Balfour St.
Tel-Aviv
Palestine
January 28th 1946.

My dear Keith,

Something rather unfortunate happened to me yesterday, and as a result I decided to leave for England as early as possible. Hanna's sister went to some polytechnic college in London, where she took up commerce. I want to do the same, even if it is only for the sake of an excuse. I wonder if you'd find out for me all about accomodation, the minimal amount of expenditure per month, whether there is any chance of getting[101] a part time job, and what have you. I am frightfully miserable, and if I see you again I shall tell you all about it.

I haven't heard from John, and I don't expect to either, I have given up long ago. I wonder whether my letters reach him at all, as he hasn't written since arriving in England. I have applied for an entry visa this morning, will you tell John that he can be an awful lot of help, even if he doesn't feel like it. All about "honouring his promises" is sheer rot, and I am not going to impose myself on him. After all people's emotions are there to be changed, every now and again, and I can't blame him for not feeling the same. There are all sorts of complications in connection with my going over; I have[102] a few strings to pull, which might be of some help. I am afraid I shall have to rely completely on English Zionist sort of organizations, like W.I.Z.O and the Maccabi. They are bound to help me, being a member in their Palestinian branches.

I might as well add that I shan't be too well off as far as the financial side of the thing is concerned, I hope[103] I shall get enough lessons though to be able to keep up.

Will you answer me as soon as you can, please Keith?

Love
Assia.

101. "~~for~~ of getting" appears in the original.
102. "over; ~~and I~~ I have" appears in the original.
103. "concerned, ~~so that they~~ I hope" appears in the original.

TO KEITH GEMS

AL,[104] Koren and Negev

Thursday, April 25, 1946

9, Balfour St.
Tel-Aviv
Palestine
April 25th, 1946

My dear Keith,

This long lapse is not entirely my fault. The Post Office has been striking for the last three weeks, so that there was really hardly any point in writing.

Actually I wrote before. It was an air letter, and wouldn't get posted (WaWa—grammer!!) after three weeks of lying around in my bag, I was too ashamed to post it. So here is to you. . . . Keith.

How are you getting on, and how is Keith's blue eyed lady? or have I read too much between the lines? Are you still in Scotland? and is the blond hair real Scootch?

We are having a lot of fun in Palestine. We shoot and fast, and don't celebrate Easter. Post office, and on the whole all Government Offices, are staffed by the wives of Senior Government officials, who feel awfully patriotic. Twice a week my country men and women raid "Police Fortresses," and empty the armouries. We feel like frightful heroes, and think the world is a wretched place. Except this, we are awfully well fed we are overstuffed with food, nylons, American cosmetics, and white combs, and we stab Airborne troops, while enjoying an orgy in Tel-Aviv. Please don't take a dim view Keith dear, it's all very exciting.

John, who promised faithfully to bestow his winning smile on some of the many principals of art schools in London, did less than nothing so far. It looks quite prospectless of some of these schools will accept me. What was the name of that school in Easling, you sister goes to? do you mind sending me the address again, pliss? and above all, does she like it?

Most of my friends here, left for England; the rest are about to go. At the moment, I am[105] spending Saturday nights in the Officers' Club in Tel-Aviv (the only place left in Town, where I can be seen with any non-Palestinian friends

104. Only pages 1 and 2 of the letter appear to be extant.
105. "moment, ~~that~~ I am" appears in the original.

of mine) with Airborne people. Some of them even ex-<illegible—Eds.>. You know, tall, and what have you (Are you jumping to conclusions?).

Saturdays are wonderful. Do you remember those jeeps full of Coca-Colas[106] and G.I.'s on the Bat-Yam Beach?[107] These minus G.I.'s minus Coca-Colas, but repeat performance here. The weather is ideal, hot and dry. The beach is practically empty, and the sand has become much cleaner, <letter unfinished or remainder lost—Eds.>

TO KEITH GEMS

ALS,[108] Koren and Negev

Tuesday, May 21, 1946

9 Balfour St.
Tel-Aviv
Palestine
May 21st 1946

My dear Keith,

I haven't heard from thee for ages now, and for the life of me can't remember whether I answered your last letter or not. I hope I have. There is so much time on my hands nowadays that letter writing has become <illegible—Eds.> and this town has been out of bounds for the last 4 weeks, and I don't feel like pretending that I couldn't care less. Yes I could, and more than less. My Airborne friends (I think I told you about them in my last letter) are hopelessly unpopular here, and being seen with them is sheer suicide, hence—boredom, and boredom and boredom. Hanna Weinberg went on a holiday to Haifa, so that I am completely alone and fairly miserable.

People here think it is high time for me to change my ways. How dare I, in these days of great a National rebirth associate with non jewish people and thus "expose" myself to an ever-increasing danger of complete assimilation. This is the voice of the more reasonable, the well meaning "odd acquaintances" I have, fellows who think an inspiring <illegible—Eds.>-talk over a Pims N° 1[109]

106. "full ~~with~~ of Coca-Colas" appears in the original.
107. The city of Bat Yam is located on Israel's Mediterranean coast, just south of Tel Aviv.
108. The letter has very dark staining, which has obscured some text.
109. Pimm's is a gin-based liqueur flavored with herbal botanicals, spices, and caramelized orange.

at the Gat Rimon will have the right effect and so on. I think it is rather superfluous to talk about the hotter heads. They run around handing me little notes on the street which "work" me, and so on. It is all so disgusting, and such also like fascisim (fascism), that I want to cry. You will be surprised to find Tel-Aviv so utterly changed, the pleasant, sunny, fairly hospitable little town has completely vanished. I can hardly describe Tel-Aviv now, without being unkind and insolent. Of course people are justified to a certain extend—but this is not the way. But one shouldn't say this, not aloud, for the second step is something alternative to the black list of "collaborators" in France.

I have heard from my German Cousin in Germany. We haven't heard from her for 6 years, I only have 4 relatives in the whole world. 2 pretty girl cousins who worked in the Japanese Embassy in Berlin, and 2 boys who were prisoners of war. Elizabeth (the one we heard from) now works for the *A. M. G. She spent some years in England, so she should get on quite well.
*(Allied Military Government)

She was twice arrested by the <illegible—Eds.> for un Patriotic feelings (Must be in the family).

How is thyself getting on? Are you still in Scotland, and seeing something of John (I last heard of him, having a holiday in Lancashire with a battle green shirt and white lizard tie, I am afraid it doesn't coincide awfully with my taste.). I was at last accepted at the Polytechnic (or I think I was) and hope to be in England by September. If you remember—we asked you to be the best man . . .

If there is anything I can get for you Keith—such as nylons for £2 a pair, let me know. The shops are packed with all the luxuries in the world here. Is there still a shortage of cosmetics in England—if there is please let me know if there's anything you want. And by the way—would you remind John if you see him, to ask the people at the Ealing School of Art whether there are any vacancies for the next term—please?

Please write again—

Love
Assia.

TO KEITH GEMS

ALS, Koren and Negev

Tuesday, June 18, 1946

9 Balfour St.,
Tel Aviv
Palestine
June 18th, 1946

My dear Keith,

Thank you so much for another letter. Actually I lost account of the letters answered, answered twice, or didn't answer at all, but I don't think I answered the lost one yet.

At long last I was accepted at the Polytechnic with all the pomp and circumstance befitting the occasion. Now comes the visa, which I shall probably get within the next two months, and then, Heck, the shipping. . . . There is supposed to be a promised improvement by September, how that will affect me, I don't know, but now that the greatest difficulty is overcome I have some very good chances, I might even get a priority . . .

How is John? our relationship, if you can call correspondence a relationship, has been very quaint lately. He doesn't write as frequently as he used to, and there is always some ravishing female waiting for a telephone call or for a dinner date. Not that I can blame him. Hell, I wish I could, but a year is a long time to wait for any one, and with John's explorations into the mysticism of femininity—well, I am slightly sore, and very slightly jealous, and nothing can be done about it. Maybe I shouldn't have written all this, it is unjustified because you can't be objective, and you are in a rather awkward situation all round.

Has he changed a lot? As I remember him, he used to be awfully clean cut, with principals, very puritan, and an overgrown school boy. I didn't realize it at the time, but I can afford to look at him differently now. We used to get on very well together, slowly I tried to adjust myself to his sense of humour, and towards the end of his stay in Palestine, we scarcely ever quarrelled at all. We had a lot in common, and I don't think we ever bored each other. Of course I met lots of people in the meantime, and I suppose I changed as well, so that the thought of seeing John again, terrifies me slightly. I hope he hasn't idolised me, and I do so hope that I shan't disappoint him.

I am working rather hard these days, but there is quite a lot of <illegible—Eds.> nearly going as well. The political situation over here has passed the stage of tiresomeness—it is morbid, and arouses mixed feelings. I suppose I should be a hero and stay here, but, there are lots of buts. No, I am not going to ask you what you think about it, I don't suppose you give a damn, anyway. You shouldn't. We, around here, like to think that we are in the headlines all the time, but seriously, how do people react in England?

I am glad to know you are going to University, what are you going to take? Will you go before September? If you remember, you promised to take me sight seeing, Uncle Keith. By the way, thanks awfully for being so good and willing to vouch for me.

Love,
Assia.

TO KEITH GEMS

ALS,[110] Koren and Negev

Tuesday, February 8, 1949

Cherry Bank Hotel
818 McClure St.
Victoria B.C.
Feb. 8th 1949

My dear Keith—

John promptly delivered your platonic love—I return same heartily.

He was wildly[111] excited about the Pamful letter and kept talking (he still does, rocking on a schintzy chair, reading LIFE)[112] about the dim prospect of seeing you in this flower-potted Ye Olde English Towne accompanied by Pam and the 4 kids (well spaced)[113]——

110. Letter written on Canadian Pacific Hotels letterhead. AW crossed out "Empress Hotel, Victoria. B.C."

111. AW wrote "W" above the *w* in *wildly,* as it was not clearly formed.

112. *Life* is a general interest American magazine, founded in 1883.

113. Iris Pamela "Pam" Gems (1925–2011) is Keith Gems's wife, and they have four children. Pam Gems went on to become an accomplished and prolific English playwright; she was nominated for Tony Awards in 1997 and 1999.

I don't think I have written to you since the I.O.W.[114] and I am sure I haven't apologized for behaving so badly—I am terribly sorry for embarrassing you so dreadfully, but I couldn't help myself—the idea of leaving Europe with all its delightful decadence was—well, I will say no more.

I have done various things here, graduating slowly from chambermaiding, hat checking, and modelling furs, to secretarying for a local radio producer and a mad actress, with whom I became very pally, and from whom I got hardly any salary at all.

John works very late most evenings, and I am left to the New Statesman[115] u[116] Nation, Soap operas and "Folk Dancing" (wobby—middle aged females "feeling young" with elephant thighs); oh yes, the roller-skating instructress (all part of PRO-REC)[117] is called Daisy Goodspeed . . .

My papa has arrived, with the appropriate African Souvenirs, hippo-skin canes, little negro statues and all—gave us some square meals, was very happy and departed for Vancouver the next day. My mother will follow in a month.

If you want any butter (Black) cigarettes, gold watches, American cars, apply to

Balfour De Havilland[118]
352 Welbeck Mansions,
Hampstead NW3

P.S. Whisper on the phone!

Assia

What's Pam's size in stockings?

114. AW uses an abbreviation for the Isle of Wight. The Isle of Wight lies off the southern coast of England in the English Channel.

115. Founded in 1913, *New Statesman* is a British progressive periodical, known for its coverage of politics and culture. In the twentieth century, it was associated with literature and with authors such as George Bernard Shaw and H. G. Wells.

116. *Und* is German for "and"; when AW uses *u* in her writing, it functions as an abbreviation for *und.*

117. Pro-Rec is the Recreational and Physical Education Branch of the Department of Education. In 1952, there were 300 members in Victoria. Activities included weights, dancing, boxing, and badminton, among others.

118. Probably AW means photographer Edward Hay Balfour de Havilland (1920–).

TO CELIA CHAIKIN

ALS, Emory

Undated, circa September 1952[119]

Hello dearest Zilli,

I got your letter, but I can't write Hebrew, oh my, I've almost forgotten spelling entirely, I'm sure you don't write "forget" this way.[120]

To Hell with it,

Thanks for writing anyway—you're a good kid, sometimes; and because of the distance I was all aglow with forgiveness and pleasure to receive your letter. Thank you very much, really . . .

On Monday UBC starts[121]; on Monday is your birthday—the first fills me with terror, the second—well, I'll kind of miss you; even though we are no longer children, and the pleasure of presents and the morning excitement of birthdays is so quickly dissipated on the bus to work.[122] Damn it, why couldn't we remain children for another 10 years, or better, for ever—we seemed to have enjoyed every thing so much more then, new thrills, new things which "never happened before" every day. And now—we run to the movies like a drug, no more "*tag*" with its thousands of excitements—

I see nothing but another extremely bleak year ahead. With "early nights" and dreary Saturday nights. But for you, there are a Great many more open worlds—I envy you in Montreal.

The Sumer was lovely, I loved the North, and the Cannery wasn't too bad—it had boats, and water in Summer afternoons, and an immediate life, with the future as unreal and unimportant as death.[123] I should like to live in that country. I guess I'll be able to, when I teach.[124]

119. Letter is dated from internal evidence.

120. Throughout the book, all English translations of Hebrew are italicized; translations are by Yehuda Koren and Eilat Negev.

121. AW studies at the University of British Columbia in Vancouver, British Columbia, Canada.

122. CC's birthday is September 22. She is turning twenty-three; AW is twenty-five years old.

123. AW worked in a fish cannery in Namu, British Columbia, during the summer of 1952. See Koren and Negev's biography of AW, *Lover of Unreason: Assia Wevill, Sylvia Plath's Rival and Ted Hughes' Doomed Love* (London: Robson, 2006; and Cambridge, MA: Carroll & Graf, 2007), 46–47, for a discussion of this job. Page numbers to *Lover of Unreason* are from the Da Capo, American edition.

124. AW writes about her experiences working as a teacher in her May 22, 1953, letter to CC. See pp. 54–55.

Thanks for your kind offer re the coat, but I can't afford it. I shall have to wear my old tweed one again, which is fine. I can see no males I want to dazzle on the Campus.

Nixon I saw, and found that he had absolutely no appeal for me, not now. I don't care if I never see him again, actually I rather hope I won't—because we had nothing to say to each other the last time. I feel free to fall in love with someone else, at long last, now that I know N. means nothing anymore. It's a great relief, in a way.

Many happy returns. I hope your birthday is gay and that someone takes you out to a Ritzy Restaurant.

Love—
Assia

TO CELIA CHAIKIN

ALS, Emory

Wednesday, October 1, 1952

Oct. 1st 1952

Dearest Cilly[125]—

I guess you've heard by now. He's wonderful, really wonderful—kind, considerate, polished, well mannered, very clever and has money besides. Above all, I love him.[126] So . . .

The point of the letter—I'm going to visit you for two days. If you can put me up, well and Good, if you can't, I'll stay at the Y.W.C.A. Could you reserve a room for me for two nights the 17th u 18th of October?[127]

Hold the coat business until then, o.k? very kind of you to have offered to send me one. Have you bought a coat for yourself yet? if you haven't, wait till I come, and we'll chose one together, o.k.?

125. AW uses an affectionate name for CC. At the time of this letter, AW is living in Vancouver, British Columbia, and CC is living in Montreal, Quebec. AW frequently uses other pet names for her sister, such as Cillinka.

126. AW is referring to Richard "Dick" Lipsey (RL), who was her fiancé at the time of this letter and who would become her second husband. RL came from an affluent family and was pursuing a master's degree in economics at Toronto University at this time.

127. "the ~~16th u 17th~~ 17th u 18th of October?" appears in the original. This proposed trip may have turned out to be the one discussed in Koren and Negev, *Lover of Unreason*, 50.

It's 1 a.m. I'm sleepy—and no further news.

By the way, be sure to lock your closet doors and have a key made before I come—[128]

Mother threatens to rent our room, which I think is a very bad idea—I feel they should move to a smaller apartment, you write to them and tell them.

If you're doing nothing for Christmas, perhaps we can plan something together, i.e. come and stay with us in Toronto.[129] How's that?

Write soon.
My sleepiest love
A *Assia*

TO CELIA CHAIKIN

TLS with envelope, Emory

Tuesday, November 11, 1952

59 Admiral Rd.,
Toronto, Ont.
Nov. 11th, 1952

Cillinka Dearest,

Just a short note to let you know that

1. I'm still alive
2. I have moved (see address above)[130]
3. I have received the poster—it's beautiful.

Thank you so much for the odd notes you have sent me in the past. May I remark that you letter writing has improved beyond all comparisons. You write, fine, delightful and amusing letters, and I'm very proud of you.

128. AW is invested in fashion and how she dresses; she would often borrow her sister's clothes without asking permission to do so. She also had a history of buying clothes for herself and charging the expenses to CC's account.

129. AW and RL marry on October 21, 1952, in Toronto, and AW relocates to Toronto with her husband.

130. AW and RL experienced challenges in securing and maintaining desirable lodging. They were evicted from one residence because AW hung up on callers on the shared telephone line if the calls were for the landlord and not for her. In another domicile, AW and RL's neglect of domestic chores bothered the landlady, and RL consequently assumed responsibility for the domestic work.

The damned apartment was never heated properly, and the man took our portable heater away—it was agony getting up in the mornings, and the weekends became fiercely cold. Then we decided that we're spending unnecessarily vast amounts of time and money on street cars. We decided to move somewhere near the University. We have found one large room with a private bath, which will do, until we find some more faults with it. Also, I have found a job—a beastly one, filing clerk in the Toronto General Hospital which sounds, and probably is dreadful.[131]

I had a letter from Doris. She said you and D. were going to have lunch together sometime. But she is such a scatterbrain, and forgettor of plans and times, that I think it would be quite allright for you to nudge her (via telephone) after a reasonable lapse of time has passed. I had a letter from Mutti and a parcel containing various goodies for the house. She seems awfully loney, but perhaps she isn't really, and just feels loney when she's writing us. How are your finances? if they are very poor, perhaps Dick can lend you some, until times improve for you. I would hate to think of you going without things you need.

Still like Montreal?[132]

I'M beginning to miss Vancouver, badly. Especially my friends there. I don't seem to meet anyone here I really feel much in common with. Perhaps one only makes friends at school and University. What a ghastly thought. Write again on T. C. A. time . . .[133]

Yerr everr leving sisterr
Assia

When will we see each other again. I can hardly write in Hebrew anymore.

131. "and probably is, ~~beastly~~ dreadful" appears in the original; "dreadful." is handwritten. Previously enrolled as a student for three years at the University of British Columbia, AW had not completed a program of study for a degree; instead, she acquired various jobs, including typist, chambermaid at the Harrison Hot-Springs Resort and Spa Hotel, and worker at a Namu fish cannery from 1950 to 1952.

132. "Still like ~~Toronto~~ Montreal?" appears in the original.

133. CC worked for the Trans-Canada Air Lines (TCA), which was based in Montreal. It was a Canadian airline that operated from 1937 to 1965. It was renamed Air Canada in 1965.

TO CELIA CHAIKIN

TLS with envelope,[134] Emory

Monday, January 19, 1953

Dearest Cillinka,

Od pitka ktana leefnay she ani holechet habaita, beetzem, mipnay she ain lie shum davar acher laassot.[135]

Did you get my cheque?

I shall send the gloves on again tomorrow. Next payday I'll send you some towels too, as a bonus. Oh God, your coat—it really baffles me. And I had two very nasty letters from mother. Tell me when your friend gets to the airport, that would be simplest, I haven't got a box large enough to put your coat in, and when can I get to a post office when I work from 8.30 to 5?

Still, my love and apologies.
Assia

TO CELIA CHAIKIN

ALS with envelope,[136] Emory

Monday, March 30, 1953

116 Bedford Road
Toronto.
Monday Morning

—Shalom Cillinka

forgive me for not writing earlier—we have moved—the office is intolerable, and I just sink into bed when I come home at night.

However.

134. The date is supplied from the postmark. The letter is written on McClelland & Stewart Ltd., 25 Hollinger Road, Toronto 13, letterhead.

135. This sentence is transliterated Hebrew, and it can be translated in English as "*[Just a] small additional note before I go home, essentially because I have nothing else to do.*"

136. The date is supplied from the postmark. On the verso of the envelope, written in Hebrew, is the line "If a man will phone, tell him I'll meet him at 11 at tennis. Z." Koren and Negev do not believe it is AW's handwriting, but probably that of CC, likely writing to her mother. The *Z* references CC's Hebrew name, Zilli or Zillinka.

Are you going to New York for Easter? if not, may I come and see you in Montreal over next week end? Dick is working hard, the exams are on next week, so he can't possibly come, and I'm at a loose end.[137]

However, if you have already made plans, don't let me interfere by any means.

If you're going away, please let me know as soon as possible—o.k.?

I feel horribly sleepy this morning—I'm writing in the office. I'll tell you about the ladies here when I see you. They're killing me.

my love
Assia

TO CELIA CHAIKIN

TLS with envelope, Emory

Wednesday, April 22, 1953

April 22nd

Dearest, sweetest Cillinka,

I received your post-New York letter with some anxiety, I don't think I have known you as depressed as your letter suggested.[138] But perhaps it was just a morning mood, or perhaps you got carried away with writing—I know how even the smallest beginnings of dissatisfactions become enlarged and alarming when one faces them with a clean sheet of paper—however, I have heard no more from you since then, and I presume it's all over, and you are pleasantly concerned with clothes and this evening's entertainment again.

Then I was alittle concerned with what ever you said about your boyfriend, is it Abie?[139] (forgive me for forgetting his name, but I don't have your letter here). Don't, don't marry him—unless you can resign yourself to the thought

137. AW's biographers document AW's social life, which interested her more than pursuing her academic studies. Having a full and vibrant social life was important to AW. See Koren and Negev, *Lover of Unreason,* 45–47 and 51. RL was completing exams for his master's degree; he would embark on his doctoral studies in September. He became a decorated economist; among other awards, he became an officer of the Order of Canada in 1991.

138. "I don't think I have known ~~as~~ you" appears in the original.

139. Rather than "Abie," AW likely meant "Arnie," the man who became CC's husband. Celia met Arnold Abraham Chaikin (1925–2015) during the winter of 1951–52 while skiing at St. Sauveur in the Laurentians, north of Montreal.

of no more 'romanticule' relationships with anyone but him for an indefinite period of time. I shall never forget the session with John Steele, and I now think I have learned, I repeat, learned rather than seen or understood both sides of the story. There is nothing more abysmally depressing and monotonous than the constant companionship (which is a magazine euphomy) of a man who is tolerable before marriage, but who lose 80% of his mal-nourished charms afterwards. However, you are a wise and strangely mature girl, and I hesitate even to comment on what you wrote. In your case, I would say emphatically—<u>you,</u> know best.

I didn't know whether you realised it, but I think you knew how funny it sounded when you wrote: "I bought a pink dress with a hole in the back, by Peck and Peck."[140]

<u>PEOPLE</u>

I met Corinne's sister in the super-market. She looked impossibly beautiful, but too thin. She seems to do nothing, she sleeps, and eats dreadful things like parsnips and porridge. She's looking for neither job nor husband, is reserved and shy, and painfully affected, but in a pleasant inoffensive way. We had her up for Sunday supper last week, and she terrified Dick, because she was so beautiful.

How ridiculous that you should have seen that girl Jean in New York. As far as I remember she was a real prostitute, wasn't she? Is she still pretty, or is she thick and faded? she was incredibly stupid if I remember right. I'm dying to hear what you talked about.

PLANS

We are leaving, I think Saturday week, i.e. May 2nd at the earliest. Off to Ottawa to see John, and then to Montreal. I hope you realise that by going to see you we shan't be able, as we hoped we would drive through the South and New Orleans, but God knows when I shall see you again, and we've seen each other only once, during all the time that I've been here. However, as soon as I'm absolutely positive about coming, I shall let you know. Or rather, I know, we're coming, I mean absolutely sure about the date. I would like to meet your boyfriend.

140. Founded in 1888, Peck & Peck is a New York retailer of women's clothing located on Fifth Avenue. In the latter part of the twentieth century, Peck & Peck was sold in piecemeal fashion to various groups. As of 2008, Stein Mart has owned the Peck & Peck trademark.

THINGS IN GENERAL.

Naturally delightful, because I'm leaving this Hades of the Chief Accountant and the thirty wicked virgins. I come to the office outrageously late, and I write these letters. I hopw to God this is my last job in an office.

I'm looking particularly shoddy and drab these days. I'm still wearing my black watch skirt and the three changes of sweaters, because I8ve packed the rest away. Oh, but I'm ready for a rejuvenation, and summer clothes and short hair again. I am seriously thinking of dying it blonde, what do you think? certainly I'm having it cut . . . I'm so afraid of shocking mother, though.

I have bought 3 summer dresses, or rather 2 dresses and one lovely cotton suit. All blue, and all slim. Butthey are packed away meekly, becuse the weather is so lousy. But I really look bloody awful, as only I can look—and you know how awful that is. Mostly, this is due to having to get up in the mornings, I really am interested in only one thing in the morning—sleep. Clothes are there to cover one's nightgown, no more. Beauty comes with laziness and indulgent sleep. But you will disagree because you are neither lazy nor sleep-mad.[141]

Richard is working hard and cruelly. I rarely see him. I'm going to see "I'm a Camera"[142] tomorrow, with Jane McKinnon, an American girl in Toronto whom D. & I like tremendously.

Be good and pretty, and we shall see you before the end of Spring.

A

Assia

141. AW possesses a history of valuing her sleep. She irritated her in-laws, the Lipseys, by oversleeping when she and her husband were living with his family in spring 1953. More than a decade later, Ted Hughes stipulated in his draft of a list of house rules that AW should adhere to while they were living together: forgo sleeping past 8:00 a.m.; avoid lounging in her nightgown in the morning; and refrain from taking naps (TH, "Draft Constitution: For Suggestions and Corrections," MSS 1058, folder 66, Ted Hughes, Letters to Assia Wevill, Stuart A. Rose Manuscript, Archives, and Rare Book Library, Emory University, Atlanta, GA).

142. John Van Druten's play *I Am a Camera* was performed at the Royal Alexandra Theatre, King Street, Toronto, for one week, beginning April 20, 1953.

TO CELIA CHAIKIN

ALS, Emory

Friday, May 22, 1953

72 Palace Ct.,
Bayswater,
London, W.2.
May 22nd 1953

Dearest Cillinkale—

For your letter—thank you. I am relieved to hear that the pictures have arrived, but I fear Arnie doesn't like them, which is sad, but cháque a son gout, which is the wrong spelling but nevertheless French for "each to his own taste."[143]

Look, this is the first letter I have written for two months, I just don't write letters any more (but I will again) which is no excuse, but all the same, fact. There are so many things going on here all the time, that I simply don't get around to it.

I am delighted to hear of your impending motherhood—congratulations! I am sure you will make a devoted and excellent mother, as long as you treat your progeny more gently than we did each other some years ago. No, seriously, I am very happy at the news! I am only sorry to hear about the physical discomforts. Why spend $200 on maternity clothes, when you can make them yourself very easily—try it, or ask mother to make you some—You will find that after your confinement you will be so depressed that $200 to spend on clothes will be marvellous.[144]

I am still teaching. This is the best thing that has happened to me since October 1952[145]—I love it, and apparently the children like me. The last school I

143. In French, "each to his own taste" or "to each his own" translates to "à chacun son goût."

144. When AW and CC lived in Israel in the 1930s and 1940s, their mother made their clothes and was successful enough in doing so that people took AW and CC to be members of a well-to-do family.

145. AW references her wedding day. In October 1952, she married her second husband and took on the name Pamela A. E. Lipsey, which was the name (P. Lipsey) AW listed with the return address on the envelope accompanying this letter. AW's given name was Assia Esther Gutmann; she assumed the first name of Pamela to Anglicize her name in order to minimize teasing over her Russian name. Back in 1949, AW began using the name Pamela, or Pam, as her own; for instance, AW enrolled as a student under the name Pamela A. E. Steele, using the surname of her first husband, at the University of British Columbia. Not until 1953 did her second husband learn that her given name was Assia Esther and not Pamela or Pam. See Koren and Negev, *Lover of Unreason,* 45, 52.

was at, presented me with large bunch of flowers on my last day. I nearly cried. They call me "Miss Lipsey"—it's always "Miss"—"oh, come on, Miss, please Miss" in sharp little Cockney accents. I teach in the toughest districts in London. In China Town, in the Dock districts, among fascists and communists, and the children of families who all sleep in one bed. But they are good, children, responding quickly to fair-play and kindness.

No Summer clothes for me—no Summer. It is as cold here as it was in February, and it seems folly to buy any clothes.

Yet another visitor has arrived this minute—so short of postponing this letter again—I shall finish it now.

By the way, what I would like for a birthday present would be a nylon slip or stockings, size 11 they are very expensive here. Or—a pair of saddle shoes, if you can get them cheaply.[146]

So good bye. Write soon, and my love
to Arnie.
Assia

TO CELIA CHAIKIN

ALS, Emory

Monday, July 13, 1953

2825 Cambie St.
Vancouver B.C.
Julie 13th 1953[147]

Ma chêre Seur—
—*Hello Cillinka*
Mein liebes Cillichen—
Ma liddle sister—

To begin with—my best wishes, congratulations, says Emily Post are only offered to prospective bridegrooms, so my very best and sincere Good wishes.[148] No opinions (for which I have not been asked) neither Questions (those have

146. AW's birthday is May 15; she had just turned twenty-six.

147. AW means July 13, 1953.

148. Emily Post (1872–1960) is an American writer, known for her advice about etiquette. AW discusses the etiquette expectation, stemming from the Victorian era, that one offered "best wishes" to the prospective bride and "congratulations" to the prospective groom. The idea behind the

long been answered)—but do be happy, and kind and good, and don't lose your temper.

I was really very excited to hear about the forthcoming marriage—I am very sorry I won't be there.[149] We seem to marry in isolation, you and I.[150] But we're doing pretty well. 3 in one family is pretty Good . . .[151]

I am here in this humanity-forsaken, God confounded town again, with all its dull Ghosts to haunt me in vaulted beer parlours and academic lawns.[152] It is an empty, pretty, bitter city of middle class prosperity. Everyone is happy, good-looking, tanned and fairly well off—Oh they bore me, bore me to distraction . . .

I have been at the University for a week now; a week of depression and plain misery; I feel I have been satiated with everything that the University has to offer, I have outgrown it emotionally, if not intellectually—I simply cannot go back. Today I have decided not to return. I shall stay here for a while until mid-August, anyway, and then return (appropriately) for the remainder of my life in North America—to Victoria. To die in sunshine and sail boards and Douglas firs.

Mutti u Vati look remarkably well, especially the first. She is really pretty and well-Groomed and in extremely Good humour—so is father. Of course they are delighted with your marriage, but that is only natural.

I like Arnie. He was very kind to Marga[153] and me, and he was an extremely Good host that evening, of course I only got to know him on a superficial level, but I trust your judgement, (I mean that.)

I bought the Hillel u Aviva record in Montreal, the sun bent it, and Dick

---

difference lies in suggesting that the groom is lucky to have made the match. In offering a woman congratulations instead of best wishes, the well-wisher suggests the woman did not have her choice of suitors and that it was not a given that she would secure a marriage for herself.

149. AW refers to her sister's upcoming wedding to Arnold Chaikin, which took place on October 7, 1953.

150. AW's family was unable to attend her wedding in Toronto. Her parents were in Vancouver, and her sister was in Montreal.

151. Presumably, AW is alluding to the three marriages between herself and her sister; AW is in her second marriage at the time of this letter.

152. AW is living approximately two miles from the University of British Columbia at the time of this letter.

153. Probably AW means Margaret Bosher (ca. 1933–). Margaret Bosher is listed on the same ship manifest for the RMS *Ascania* as John Francis Bosher, a student with AW at the University of British Columbia. The ship departed Montreal on September 2, 1953, and arrived in Liverpool on September 10, 1953. Both travelers list "Transit to France" as their proposed address in the "United Kingdom."

bought me another one in Toronto.[154] I have learnt most of them, but I can't make out the words in the *"A caravan in the Desert"*—can you? let me have them please, if you can.

How is Ahuva? I liked Ahuva—tell her that I liked her, and give her my regards.[155]

Oh I'm so silly this evening, I can't write you the sort of letter you deserve.

What would you like for a wedding present?

My love, and again, my blessings, for
what they are worth
Assia *Esther* Pamela *Gutmann*—
Steele—Lipsey

TO CELIA CHAIKIN

TLS/ALS with envelope,[156] Emory

Friday, December 4, 1953

10 Green St.,
London W.1.
Dec. 4. 53

Shalom Cillinkalebubilemotekle,[157]

Thank you for your beautiful Christmas card, also for the letter. Now I'll tell you why Ihaven't written earlier—because for the last three bloody months I have been looking for a decent job . . . I can get relatively well paid (for the low English standards of pay) clerical jobs, but Iknow how bloody bored I'll get in no time, and how disgusting and sordid office-boredom is, and I'm looking for something where I can use my tiny little brain if only to take it for a walk every day . . . but no, no, no. You've got to know people in order to get a job like writing copy foran advertising agency, getting a little beastly job inthe B.B.C., or in fact anything which sounds, butisn't really glamorous. So there. And now, until

154. The record is *Shepherd and Other Folk Songs of Israel, Sung by Aviva and Hillel* (Folkway Records & Service Corp., 1953).

155. Negev explains that Ahuva is an Israeli name, meaning "Beloved." She believes that Ahuva likely is a friend of AW or CC.

156. The envelope is postmarked December 11, 1953.

157. *Bubile* (or *Bubale*) means "darling," "sweetie," or "dolly," and *motek* means "sweetie" in Hebrew.

Christmas I'm working in the book department of a huge, ugly department store at $15.00 a week!

However, we work every day from 8.45 a.m. to 6 p.m., on Thursdays until 7 p.m.—beat that, there is 25¢ per hour for overtime. Oh, I'm fed up, or rather fad oop, as my colleague in the book department says.

I must wash my hair and have a bath, I absolutely stink—our bathroom hasn't been cleaned for 25 years, and one has to arm oneself morally for a whole week before one can actually brave the journey into the great outdoors which is where the bathroom is.[158] England is rotten without a generous supply of money—I hate it, and so is the rest of Europe, too. John Bosher,[159] in Paris is really sufering, he has no bathroom at all, no lavatory (honestly, it's hard for anyone in Canada to believe that) and they spend all their money on small quantities of food and tram fares. So really in comparison we live like the Duke and Duchess of Vancouver!

I8ve started to learn speedwriting. It's quite easy but needs persistence. I'm doing it by correspondence through since I've worked at Selfridges[160] I find it extremely difficult to concentrate in the evenings, I'm so terribly tired. Did I tell you that we are going skiing in Austria? look, have you still got your discarded brown ski-pants? I think you bought a pair of navy-blue ones instead didn't you? they are terribly expensive here, and if I can help it, I won't buy any, I'll ski in Jeans. Could you send me the brown ones[161] to get here by the 24th—if you can't get them here by the 24th, don't bother about them. O.K.? I got two Holbein prints for you as a Xmas present, but I had them framed, and now they are ready, and I haven't got enough money to pick them up—God damned it—they are

158. More than half of British households did not have bathrooms in 1950: 46 percent of residences contained bathrooms, and 8 percent shared one. See the article "More than Half of British Homes Don't Have a Bathroom—Archive, 1950," *Guardian,* https://www.theguardian.com/society/2018/mar/21/british-homes-without-bathroom-archive-1950.

159. AW means Canadian John Francis Bosher (1929–2020), a professor of history who was educated at the University of British Columbia, University of Paris, and University of London. AW and Bosher were romantically involved before AW became engaged to Bosher's best friend, RL.

160. Selfridges was founded in 1908 and functions as a British high-end department store today; it is the second largest store after Harrods in the United Kingdom. AW likely worked at the London flagship store at 400 Oxford Street; her home was one-fifth of a mile away and would have required a walk of only two or three minutes. These days, Selfridges is open until 10:00 p.m. on most nights.

161. From this point on, the letter is handwritten.

lovely prints, I think you will like them.[162] I'll have to wait till I get my Canadian income tax returns before I can get them for you, O.K.?

I'm awful sleepy. And Dick sends his love—

Write soon
Assia

TO CELIA CHAIKIN ALS with envelope, Emory

Friday, December 11, 1953[163]

<Drawing of a praying woman with a halo over her head; there are numerous red stars scattered across the page.—Eds.>

Sweet Cecilia!

Unsainted muse,
Oh, maid of infinite, kindly use,
Sister kind,
Daughter unblind
(To mercy)
Take, yeah, take this curtsy,
And accept this gift
Of Yule and
Double birth
And remember your kin
Of now equal girth.
A Merry Christmas . . .

162. Hans Holbein the Younger (ca. 1497/8–1543) is an accomplished German artist who worked in various media, achieving the most success with his portraits. His work is displayed at the National Portrait Gallery in London. Alternatively, AW may have been alluding to the work of Hans Holbein the Elder (ca. 1460–1524), who also produced notable work.

163. The date is supplied from the postmark on the envelope.

P.S.

No, I am not pregnant, only fat, yes, very fat.

Have you, by any chance had the misfortune of receiving 3 earring of my own making which I posted months ago, to mark your birthday?

Are you well?

I am not. I have:

(a) Rheumatism

(b) disturbances in my kidney

(c) Too little money.

I hope you are faring better. And these two, are two Victorian serving spoons, which I hope you will like.

Your loving
sister

Holy night,
still night, all is calm, all is bright . . .

TO CELIA CHAIKIN

ALS, Emory

Tuesday, September 14, 1954

28 Westbourne Gdns.
London W.2.
Sept. 14

My dear Cillinka—

Since we have returned from the continent, I have been living off one small suitcase—the rest of the stuff is packed away and is inaccessible—included in the stowed cases is my address book—all of which goes to explain, why you never received a single postcard from me. I can't, no, I couldn't possibly describe the trip again—we went to Paris and Venice, and on a fantastic fairy book wine-tour of the Rhine.[164] I was very impressed with Germany, and although, as hitch-hikers we were shown extravagant kindness on many occasions, I still believe that the Germans are Germans are Germans, and we shall see some form of Naziism in full flourish in about 3–5 years. I now possess a Nazi party

164. The Rhine River is a river that flows through Germany and is an important artery of global industrial transport.

button given to me by an old Nazi at whose house we stayed. I didn't tell this to either mother or father because I thought it would distress them, as it did me.[165] We went out of our way to Dachau—(the Concentration camp town) gruelling surprise![166] it is a dreamy innocent looking South German town with pretty Rathhouse,[167] murals, pigtails and innocuous inns—the camp now spruced up, is run by the Americans—you would never dream that anything out of the ordinary had ever taken place in this peaceful, pastoral setting with its flower bedecked market square.

Many happy returns on your birthday—I don't know how old you are now, either 24 or 25, but it doesn't matter, Hell, it really doesn't. I don't mind getting older now, and I have stopped fibbing about my age—however, I shall respect any deductions you care to make on yours.

I am now officially a company-director, and my "firm" has a bank-account. The partnership with Marga Bosher is now dissolved. She was really disinterested, inefficient and largely unreliable, although as a person, very charming. If I continue to expand, I shall hire a girl on a piece work basis. I have just sent off 72 prs. to Kenya! mind you, I have been working a 17 hour day. School in the morning, ½ hr. for lunch, and then earrings until midnight. So far I have made £100—about $350. I love this business—and would love to go on with it. I have designed you a pair of white earrings, which you will be able to wear with a lot of things. I shall send them off the moment I have a spare minute. If anyone asks the price, say they are $2.10, and can be had by mail.

We are moving into Keith's old flat in 2 weeks. It is in the French section of Soho, and is rebuilt with wall-to-wall carpets[168] on the top floor of a 300 year old slum house for $8 a week, fully furnished. Mind you my full school salary is only $16 a week!

165. AW and CC were born in Berlin, Germany, to a Jewish father and a Protestant mother. The Gutmann family lived in Berlin until 1933, escaping fascist Germany shortly after AW's sixth birthday.

166. Opened in 1933, a few months before the Gutmanns fled Nazi rule, Dachau served as a model for other concentration camps. In twelve years, 200,000 people were imprisoned, and of these, 41,500 were murdered in Dachau and subsidiary camps. AW and CC's uncle, Vanya Gutmann, was killed, along with his wife and young daughter, by Nazis during World War II. Koren and Negev report that AW could not make herself go past the gate of the Dachau concentration camp. For a discussion of AW's trip to Germany with RL, see Koren and Negev, *Lover of Unreason*, 55–56.

167. *Rathaus* is German for a city, town hall, or civic center; generally, it is the chief administrative building of a city or town.

168. "wall-to-wall ~~cupboard~~ carpets" appears in the original.

I hear you are suffering agonies with your spine—God, I am sorry to hear that Cillinka—but it should soon be over, shouldn't it? What are you going to name the child? how about Natalie, Natalia, or Natasha if it's a girl, or Alexandra?

We are living with Thirrell[169] at the moment. God she's changed. She is fat, ugly and more mannish every day, if you can believe it. I am afraid we don't get on at all well. She is mean, tight fisted, and I have not seen a generous gesture on her part yet. I think she probably finds equal faults on my part, but at least I am <u>not</u> mean. I am acquiring an obssession about her, I really <u>hate</u> her—bloody little hypocrite . . . I am sorry for this outburst, but I can't very well tell Dick about it and I have to tell someone. She is getting married in Boston in June—poor Billy. For God's sake don't <u>ever</u> mention anything to him.

This is all, write soon and again, happy birthday.

Love to Arnie.
Assia

TO CELIA CHAIKIN

TL, Emory

Wednesday, August 24, 1955

August 24th, 1955

My dear Cecilia,

I feel even guiltier descending on you from this English Sahara, unheralded, than I do for not having written for such a shamelessly long time.[170] I hope you are well, further more I hope Arnie and child are equally so.[171]

Mutti (who by the way has sent me some photographs of the house which looks enchanting, but which need raw silk curtains over the large windows, which I would dearly love to buy her, if only I could afford to) says that child is delightful, which I am sure he is. But not having seen him or played with

169. Thirell Lipsey is RL's sister, AW's sister-in-law.

170. After they were married, the Lipseys moved to London the next year so that RL could pursue his doctoral work at the London School of Economics. They divorced in spring 1960.

171. CC gave birth to her first child, Ronald Eric Chaikin, on December 21, 1954. CC's son, Ira Martin Chaikin, was born on March 12, 1958, and her daughter, Tamara Ruth Chaikin, was born on August 31, 1960.

him, I find it difficult to remember that he does in actual fact exist. I have often found myself standing in front of childrens' shop windows in London, and thought, how marvelous . . . and then I thought of Ronnie. The things here are absolutely exquisite, there are no more elegant childrens' clothing in the world than those in the childrens' department of Fortnum and Mason,[172] or some of the other American Tourist specialists—prices, unfortunately are equally "equisiste." And I wish I could buy him a beautifully tailored white doe skin coat with hat to match, or a navy blue one with gold buttons and a white linen collar, and beautfilly tiny white gloves[173] . . . but my diet this week has again consisted of sardines and unbuttered bread for lunch, tomatoes and home-fried potatoes for dinner . . . oranges, are a mere window decoration in green grocer shops. Melons, grapes, apples, pears, and peaches are so expensive that only miners and dockers can buy them. England is thickly in the midst of an inflation, not an outrageous one, but one tall enough to have increased the cost of living by 20% since we first came to England.[174] This means that people living on a fixed income (like us) can afford to buy less and less, or 20% less than we did when we first came here. Meat we only eat once a week—since we have no refrigerator we eat no butter. Our main staples, are potatoes, cabbage, tomatoes and sausages. All highly spiced with onions and pepper (real pepper ground freshly in a pepper mill). However, the very worst times are over. You may have heard about Dick's job—he is a lecturer at the London School of Economics, which is a "good thing."[175] Indeed a splendid, shiningly wonderful thing. He is working with one of the greatest economists in the world, a man by name of Robbins.[176] All this means, that if he stays at L.S.E. for another two years, Dick can, on returning to North America, call his own tune, or rather his own salary, and a professorship at the age of 29 . . . At the moment he is also teaching statistics to American Officers at their camp near London, which he will do for the remainder of the year, which brings his salary up to a point where it will

172. Fortnum & Mason is a luxury department store based in London. It was founded in 1707.

173. "tiny ~~little~~ white gloves" appears in the original.

174. "20%~~, which~~ since we first came to England" appears in the original.

175. RL acquired a tenure-track position as an assistant lecturer at the London School of Economics in 1955.

176. Robbins is Lionel Charles Robbins (1898–1984), a decorated economist at the London School of Economics who became Baron Robbins CH CB FBA.

no longer be necessary for me to work.[177] I am working again at the moment, because I am trying to save up enough money to go to Paris for two weeks on Sept. 15th. The Boshers are living there again, on a fat Canadian Government scholarship, and have offered me accommodation in their sumptuous Latin Quarter flat. Through a French Canadian we got to know rather well this past year, I have learnt quite a bit of French, I hope the measly two weeks will polish it to a degree where I can overhear morons on the tube.[178]

Next Summer we shall return to Canada for a few months. In June, in fact. This will be financed by one of those nebulous jobs, with the vague title of "consulting," which trapped Lipsey in the Vancouver City Hall, oh so many Summers ago.[179]

London, with the exception of Goodge St. has been transformed into a sort of inferior Deauville,[180] a dustier, dowdier deauville, but with a startling similarity between inhabitants.[181] The goloshed acneed typists who huddled unprotesting at bus stops with bus after ful bus muddying past them, of other[182] English Summers, have suddenly been transformed into H-lines of cheap "shocking" pink[183] (past its fashion prime)[184] masquerading happily for the international divorces of the Mediterranean. Baroque gaming Salons, compete here with pin-machines, and the same crooners implore for love from the T.V. and Record shops here as they do from loudspeakers of side-walk cafes in the

177. "for me to work~~s~~" appears in the original.

178. "where I can ~~hold~~ overhear morons on the tube" appears in the original.

179. AW and RL returned to Vancouver, Canada, the following summer; RL taught summer classes at the University of British Columbia. Koren and Negev describe that summer and Assia's activities during it in *Lover of Unreason*, 59.

180. "a sort of ~~superior~~ inferior Deauville" appears in the original.

181. AW and RL lived on Goodge Street for a time during their marriage. Goodge Street and the West End in London in the 1950s could be perceived as exciting: one might find newly emerging coffee shops or rock and roll music. AW and RL, however, lived in a very modest arrangement due to their limited means: a one-room flat without a refrigerator and with a shared bathroom, which was located three floors down from their room. Deauville is a destination beach resort city in France that historically has attracted the wealthy, from the Continent and abroad, as both a place of residence and a vacation spot.

182. "past them, ~~have suddenly~~ of other" appears in the original.

183. "of cheap ~~cotton~~ "shocking"pink" appears in the original.

184. Shocking pink is a hot-pink color associated with the experimental fashion designer Elsa Schiaparelli (1890–1973), who brought the color to prominence with the packaging of her perfume Shocking in 1937.

Riviera. The heat is groggy and relentless. Yesterday it was 90 in the shade, and the employees of a glass factory walked out on their employers—The English are inequipped to deal with the heat—they are gorgeously stupefied by the sun they are used to see in the cinema and on travel posters . . . what other culture devotes so much of its lyric poetry to heat, sun and Summer as do the English? even love, finds an inaccessible competitor in Summer ". . . Shall I compare thee to a Summer's day?"[185] Go, catch me a Persian Poet saying that . . .

Only the Germans, with either round, soup-plate-like straw hats, or student caps, with ribbons, and red perspiring faces, take this phenomenon entirely for granted—but they cannot reconcile[186]

TO CELIA CHAIKIN

TL, Emory

Sunday, October 9, 1955

39 Goodge St.,
W1.
October 9th, 1955.

My dear Cilly,

I have just returned from Paris to find your letter, which I have since lost, and consequently your new address. I hope to goodness, that unlike me, you leave forwarding addresses behind you. You probably do, I have full confidence in your efficiency and good sense. I must say that when I do break my impolite silence, you greet me with such a tirade of bad temper that I am quite frightened to write back, but tonight I feel strong and courageous, and I hope you will forgive this little outburst of really quite unjustifiable anger. You might like to know, that however bad the result of my literary effort may have been, I spent a whole evening on the story I wrote you, and you dismissed it rather cruelly . . . all of which makes me a little sad.[187]

185. This line alludes to the first line of William Shakespeare's Sonnet 18.

186. This letter is either unfinished or the remainder of it has been lost. The letter is typed on letterhead with the top section cut off. At the bottom of the stationery is printed: "Industrial Compressing Machinery, Tablet Machines, Pharmaceutical Equipment, Metallurgical Equipment, Special Profess Plant." AW probably worked at this establishment and used its paper for this letter.

187. There is no evidence that AW's stories exist any longer, but five original poems do, which are collected in this volume.

It is incredible to think of Ronny being almost a year old—this is all quite fantastic. Do please remember, that for me Ronnie has absolutely no reality, I have never seen him, he is just a name, and I don't really believe that he exists at all until I see him, and that is the reason I don't enquire about him, or make any reference to him in my very few letters. Although you probably can't imagine yourself without Ronnie, I can't imagine you with Ronnie. Do you understand, or does this sound like a mawkish and very unconvincing excuse for my neglect of him? because, you know it isn't.

I don't know whether mutti told you, but we are going to Canada for the Summer, in fact late May, but by then Ronnie will have ceased to be an infant and will be a real little boy, all of which is very exciting!

Your reports of David sound most distressing. It is a long time since I have written to him, in fact I have lost touch with him altogether, and rely on you to give me news of him, which you do, but only very sparingly. Just how does he mistreat Phyllis? and why has Phyllis become very nice? and how do the Dane and his wife fit into all this? is David in love with Eleanor? if so, how sad for all concerned.

How wonderful about your house, you never mentioned it before, I must say, you are a surprising girl, husband, infant, house, all in two years . . . I am lagging behind, oh such decades behind. I own practically nothing besides a husband, and that is not like the ownership of objects or children, it is a sort of indefinite loan, really. I own three tea cups and four plates, and various bric a brac in Victoria, which I shall probably give away when I see it again, my tastes having changed so much.[188] The thought of an ornate silver (plate) cocktail tray makes me drunk with revulsion . . . How, oh how shall I ever live in Canada again? I don't know, I doubt the event more and more. England has very definite limitations, especially as far as money is concerned, (and this is the most serious limitation any country can impose) but it is so seductive; one always feels that all the glorious stuff like splendid houses and the luxury of an old European capital is within reach eventually, which of course is quite untrue, and a terrible, pityful illusion. I am as far from a box at Covent Garden and a theatre supper

188. AW's contemporaries praised her sense of style. Her biographers note that later in her life, about 1966, she became involved with antiques: "With her artistic flair, Assia went into business with one of Ted's local friends, an antique collector. Hughes was very proud of her taste and keen eye, finding a Georgian set of drawers, a much-coveted fifteenth-century lead gargoyle taken off a church, and several paintings." (Koren and Negev, *Lover of Unreason*, 157).

at Roule's with a little Dior dress as I shall be ten years from now.[189] But when it comes to leaving all this here, illusions and all, it is so painful, that I would rather live in hopes. Perhaps, perhas not. I shall be able to tell more accurately at the end of this Summer.[190]

Do go and see Jungle Blackboard,[191] or Blackboard, and think of your sister. Not that I ever encountered quite the raw brutality which the man in the film did, but many situations in the film were so painfully familiar to me, and the schools I taught in last year were the London equivalent of the part of New York in the film, it was a real traumatic experience that film, it took me hours to get over it. Oh God, thank God I am out of teqching.[192] I am doing nothing at the moment, but I shall have to think seriously of getting a job in advertising which is what I want to do; this time there is no financial pressure, but I have come to the conclusion that I must have a job, an interesting job in order to be reasonably happy.

We are considerably better off financially now than we have ever been before. The life undergraduate is over now, (just in the nick of time, too), another year and I would have been a raving lunatic with a perpetual cold. It's rather pleasant to be on the other side of examinations, or rather to be the wife of the other side of examinations.

Thank you very much for the offer of the dress, I should love to have it—if you are sure it is of no further good to you. I remember it as being wonderfully warm.

Well—I shall see you in May—quite a thought. I am sure we have both changed I am terrified to think of the first moment.

Give my regards, nay, love, to Arnie, and the gentlest kiss to R. And stop saying to him "If you don't stop crying I shall call the bogeywoman, Assia."

189. Located in London's West End, Covent Garden is London's main theater and entertainment district. One will also find luxury goods stores and award-winning restaurants. AW likely means Rules (rather than Roule's), which is the oldest restaurant in London, located in Covent Garden. It was established in 1798 and offers traditional British food. Dior is a French haute couture brand, founded in 1946–47.

190. Koren and Negev note that socioeconomic class was important to Assia: "Unable to bond with Germany and turning her back on Israel and Canada, she threw herself on Britain. It was doomed from the start—Lipsey thinks—because only by birth could one find a place within the British class system. Assia aspired to something she could never get" (*Lover of Unreason,* 56).

191. *Blackboard Jungle* is a 1955 film directed by Richard Brooks. It was shown at the Empire, Leicester Square, London, in September and October 1955.

192. AW means *teaching.*

TO CELIA CHAIKIN

ALS, Emory

Wednesday, November 2, 1955

39 Goodge St.
W1.
Nov. 2nd 1955

My dear Cilly,

Thank you for both letter and photographs. What a bright and clean infant you have—he looks by far the cleanest infant I know personally. His eyes, of course are like the perennial raisins, and he looks as though he should flutter over some Egyptian Venus[193] in company with another brown cherub, in one of those Baroque[194] ceilings in Italy, or for that matter in any chi chi aristocratic bed-room in England . . .

I am sorry you are so bored—and pained by your back. What a dreadful combination. Can anything be done about the back? Surely one can do something, the thought of you dragged down by a vicious pain like that really distresses me—really.

I have all sorts of sinister and revolting things wrong with my female innards—which cause me pain, discomfort and irritation with myself.[195] It is indecent to have "conditions" at my age, it is premature, unjust, foolish.[196] Apparently all can be cured by having a child, but I don't want a child. I am very happy as I am at the moment. Some people accuse me of selfishness, which I find astounding. How can one be selfish towards an unconceived, unborn child? and I don't believe in duties toward "society,". . .

Of course, now that you have written and told me about your imprisonment in your house (now that you made me almost tearful with compassion) you will write back and say that having a child is all full of mystic wonder, that you don't regret it for a second, and will conclude by intimating, that indeed, I am selfish.

Oh, to Hell with it.

193. Venus is the Roman goddess associated with love, beauty, and fertility.

194. A stylistic movement in architecture, literature, art, and music of the seventeenth and eighteenth centuries in Europe, Baroque art is distinctly extravagant and particularly ornate.

195. AW may be referring to symptoms of cystitis, of which she suffered recurring bouts. Cystitis is an inflammation of the bladder and is often caused by an infection, a urinary tract infection. Bacterial bladder infections may occur in women as a result of sexual intercourse, and antibiotics are used to treat these infections.

196. AW is twenty-eight years old at the writing of this letter.

About Canada. We are returning for a mere visit which I believe will last from the end of May to the end of September. I think we have said our residential farewells to Canada. Neither Dick nor I have any interest in it any longer; it has acquired for me the aspects of a Geography lesson, and its attractions are equally pulling. I dislike it—its mineral resources, the red hunters' caps, the wedding showers, the wonder roads, the prodigial constructions, the rarified social-life.[197] I have in fact changed. One always does, and one is always full of contempt for one's previous attitudes and metamorphoses. As before, I think that what I am now will remain with me forever—which is foolish. If we return, Dick will be the proverbial big fish in a dull pond—removed from International economics, forever playing with the wilting posies he acquired at L.S.E.[198]

Perhaps I have infected him too much with my affectations if you like. He is no longer the brush-cut sallow cheeked youth "who wanted to get to know Europe"—but you will judge for yourself this Summer.

Of course I shall pay for all this one day. When I am old I shall have neither house nor child to care whether I live or die. But surely the ways of expenditure depend on one's temrament.[199] It is rather like inheriting a fortune—I am squandering it, you are wisely investing it. The difference lies in the fact that you can always be smug—now <u>and</u> later.

Thirrel: is in Venice. Vague as her brother, I have no idea when she will be back in either England or Canada. I believe she wants to return to America. I don't know why. She is a fishy girl, neither firmly fleshed nor poisson[200] (pun!)

We see a good deal of Keith Gems and his brilliant wife. They have bought an old house and are gradually converting it into something filthily elegant (and I mean this literally). I like them very much, if only they would bathe themselves, infants, animals and house more frequently.

In March we shall ski in Norway for a change.[201] Althogh I have become really attached to Austria, I know too well just exactly what we shall eat, what

197. Recalling AW in London, her friend Keith Gems asserts: "She was a woman with intellectual aspirations, immersed in books. Leaving Europe with all its delightful decadence, and settling in Canada, which meant intellectual death for her, was something Assia could not bear." Gems is quoted in Koren and Negev, *Lover of Unreason*, 41.

198. RL earned a doctorate from the London School of Economics in 1956.

199. AW may have intended *temperament* here.

200. The French *poisson* means "fish" in English.

201. According to Koren and Negev in *Lover of Unreason*, "Despite Assia's ineptitude on the slopes, she insisted on ski vacations abroad each Christmas" (55). A Norwegian newspaper published three photos of AW in her skiing costume, taken during one of her vacations.

the Three Wise Men will sing on Christmas Eve, and the feel and the smell of the new Year in Tyrol.[202]

Now I come to a point which has worried me a lot about Mutti u Vati. I have not heard from them for a month. They usually write within four days of receiving my letter, and I have already written twice. For God's sake answer immediately, have you heard from them?

Do Go and see them in the Summer if they want you to. They are, after all slightly bored, and so lonely, and Vati is obviously longing to see Ronnie. Please be kind, and forget about money. It comes and goes, and really, unless one has nothing at all, or too much, it is so unimportant. I feel so much guilt when it comes to them. I love them so much—in a way, more than anyone else in the world. Their possible death haunts me as cruelly as it did when I was a small child—: mother does not look well on the photograph. I dread seeing her and discovering any signs of real age. Do tell me what she was like when she was with you.

I am going now. I am lunching with Dick in the Senior Common Room.[203] He has a large and elegant office with arm chairs and curtains and a telephone. . . . I am so silly.

Please write soon. Thank you for the dress. If you want to send me something send me 89¢ nylons—very fine ones. They are brutally expensive here. Or a ready pie mix.

My love to Arnie—a kiss for the child.
to you with a serious love—
Assia.

London is full of Israelis. I know two of them. they are full of brains, but have just a tiny drop of tact.[204] *And they are all in love with England. Why? but.*

Do you still correspond with Debora?

202. A state in Austria, Tyrol is considered a desirable place to ski because it is situated in the Alps.

203. Still in existence, the Senior Common Room is located on the campus of the London School of Economics.

204. This is the literal translation. Koren and Negev supply an additional streamlined translation: "They are very clever but have very little tact."

TO CELIA CHAIKIN

TL[205] with Envelope, Emory

Friday–Saturday, March 9–10, 1956

March 9th, 1956.

My dearest Cillinka,

I am writing with tears of shame and repentance scalding my cheek—I apologise with all my heartfor not having the good manners, if not the gratitude, to thank you for your wonderful Christmas present, as well as for the shipment of ski equipment which arrived several weeks ago, also for your own thank-you letter. You must have divined with nothing less than intuitional genius that I needed underwear. The pants are superb (unlike British nylon on which I am slowly become an expert of sorts—see heading, these do not discolour after frequent washing, and there is nota snag in sight in spite of the fact that I have worn them for three months now)the nylons are also very good, but I don't believe they cost anything under two dollars, they are far too good for 99 cents[206] . . . you were very generous, thank you. Dick's tie is also in constant use; mother,you and I, seem to be the only women in the world who know what sort of ties men like . . . Thank you dear Cillile, and do forgive my swinishness in not thanking your earlier.

Plans for the Western Trek are slowly, and in the most appalling disorganization,taking shape.[207] Dick has accepted a Summer School lectureship at UBC, though this entire sum, (I mean the total pay)[208] will not even pay for our fares—how we shall solve this, I do not know.[209] But, something, something always turns up. Actually this trip causes me many a sleep less night—I have

205. The letter is typed on British Nylons Spinners Ltd., 25 Upper Brook Street, London, W.1, letterhead. The British Nylon Spinners is a British company, founded in 1940 and merged with Imperial Chemical Industries in 1964.

206. AW would have been most familiar with nylon as the material used for hosiery. Nylon had replaced silk as material for stockings in the first half of the twentieth century because nylon proved more durable and less likely to snag and run than silk. Stockings were considered an essential part of women's wardrobe for much of the twentieth century.

207. "slowly, ~~though~~ and in the most appalling disorganization,taking shape" appears in the original.

208. "~~will not even pay~~ (I mean the total pay)" appears in the original.

209. RL accepted a summer teaching position at the University of British Columbia in 1956. RL and AW resided with AW's parents in Vancouver during the week and spent the weekends with RL's parents on Vancouver Island.

this new job, which I took on an understanding between my ego and I that it would be permanent. It is interesting and could lead to an escape from routine and detail, of which I have had quite enough during my working life. I am in the Public Relations office, and since this[210] whole field of dubious activity is relatively new to England, there is no knowing at present where this might end. Of course the trip to Canada spoils my chances of a "career"—but I suppose this can't be helped.

Friday—10th.

I have learnt several things about nylon, which you might find useful. Don't wear your stockings inside out, don't ever use soap when washing nylons, especially white nylons (therefore use your washing machine with detergents i.e. daz, tide,[211] etc. and ruin your washing machine.) Wash them frequently and don't let them sit around dirty. Always drip-dry weaves, and wring out tricots.[212] End of lecture.

I returned home last night to find Dick at the point of tears. His term at L.S.E. doesn't finish until the end of June, or rather July 2nd, the term at UBC starts on July 4th—we can't afford to fly, i.e. we simply don't have enough money to fly, and the Director at L.S.E. is rather a school master, which means cringing appears for pity which sounds detestable. Poor Dick, has to work all the time, including evenings, week ends . . . Oh God, it's absolute Hell, for so little monetary reward, for a pittance in fact. I never see him. He can't type because if he types I can't sleep, and I must sleep, otherwise I feel as though my head were bored through by maggots the next morning. All this takes place in one room, you will bear in mind. Eating, working, ironing, sleeping, "entertaining"—thank God there is a little kitchen attached. And everything is covered in a greasy yellow film, where it comes from I don't know.The white paint has long gone yellowish, in spite of weekly washing down. But now that I am working I want to live during week ends, (if only by myself) not scrub woodwork. What snobs the English are—we used to employ an agency of itenerant servants at a price,£1 for four hours, which is a lot of money. But they refuse to come now, because of

210. "and ~~this~~ since this" appears in the original.

211. Daz is a laundry detergent introduced in England and Ireland in 1953 and manufactured by the American company Procter & Gamble. It is a lower-price option to a sibling detergent, Ariel. Launched in 1946, Tide is a laundry detergent also manufactured by Procter & Gamble.

212. Tricot stockings were made out of finely woven or knitted nylon. *Tricot* is a French word meaning "knitting" or "knitted fabric."

the disreputable neighbourhood . . . there couldn't possibly be any other reason for complaint, because I never saw them, and I always left the place tidy for them, all they had to do was clean.

I haven't written the paretns for a long time—I don't know why. I feel very guilty. Time was when I wrote to them every week, and they only answered haphazardly, and I worried like the white rabbit.[213] But I shall write after this letter. How are you Cillinka? and how is Ronnie? and Arnie? are you still bored? or are things looking up. Be charitable to your old sister, and write in reply, though the Lord knows, I don't deserve it. Thank you for the beautiful parka. We are leaving for Norway on March 17th. Will send you a pipe, perhaps.

TO CELIA CHAIKIN

TLS with envelope, Emory

Tuesday, May 29, 1956

39 Goodge St. W.1.
May 29th/ 1956

My dear Cilly

Thank you very much for both letters and the birthday card—I am sorry I have been so long in answering either. Mutti is quite right, we are flying from New York, and will therefore have to miss Toronto and Montreal. We are flying because Dick has to be in Vancouver on July 3rd (the beginning of Summer School) and the University term in London does not end until July 2nd—with some difficulty he managed to get earlier leave, but the leave is only just early enough to get him to Vancouver at zero hour.

We are sailing with the "Ile de France" of the French Lines; this ship leaves Southampton harbor on June 22nd (it doesn't really dock at Southampton, but is on the verge of the 3 mile limit) I believe it really leaves from Le Havre (in France). Quite frankly I am not absolutely certain when we arrive in New York, I think it will be on the 28th of June, but perhaps the most reliable information should spurt from the shipping offices of the French Line in Montreal.[214] What

213. This allusion is probably to the White Rabbit featured in Lewis Carroll's book *Alice's Adventures in Wonderland* (1865).

214. According to immigration documents, AW and RL sailed in the tourist class of the *Ile de France* from Southampton, England, on June 22, 1956, and arrived in New York on June 28, 1956.

delight it would be to be met in New York, the thought of arriving in New York does more than dazzle me, it frightens me just a bit, and since you usually go about matters of arrival and departure in such a relaxed and unlunatic way, I can think of no one I would rather see at New York harbor. By the way you might also like to find out at which dock the Ile de France docks, there are, I believe, about 37 different docks in New York port, covering an area of several miles. . . . Oh I do hope you can come, it will be marvelous.

Because we are flying, because we are virtually paupers, and cannot pay for excess baggage, we shall only arrive with 40 lbs. of luggage—the thought of this drives me mad. I shall have no winter or for that matter, any warm clothing with me whatsoever, and will therefore probably freeze in North Vancouver, and stifle in New York. My summer clothes (those that I own) are designed for a moody summer day, which begins with a cold mist and ends with an Anglo-Saxon Garden party shower, probably quite useless for any other clime, but what the Hell . . .

I am very excited about leaving this pleasant but despair-driving country.[215] But more when I see you. I can hardly wait for June 22nd. I have counted days for the last two months, and can't believe my luck. However, this trip will cost us the little capital we had which we wanted to invest in a down payment for a house. I suppose we shall never own a house now. But what the Hell. I must go now.

Thank you for wanting to come, and
let me know if you are really coming.
Assia

They returned to England via Montreal, Canada, on the *Empress of Britain*, arriving at Liverpool on October 1, 1956. It was on this return trip to England that AW met David Wevill (1935–), the poet who would become her third husband. AW professed her love for DW to him on September 30, before disembarking.

215. According to 1956 British immigration records, AW and RL indicated that they intended to make Canada their country of future permanent residence, estimating that they would reside in Britain for another nine months upon their October return to England. While AW would live in Ireland in 1966, she would ultimately make England her primary country of residence from 1956 until her death in 1969.

TO LONYA AND ELIZABETHA GUTMANN

Postcard,[216] Emory

Friday, January 3, 1958

3.1.1958

Hier ist ener verwundetes kind, am letzten tag 1957.
Wir fahren jetzt gerade weg.[217]

Adieu.[218]
Asia[219]

TO PATRICIA MENDELSON[220]

ALS, Stanford

Tuesday, June 30, 1959

Red Sea—June 30th 1959[221]

Dear Pat,

How very kind of you to have bothered writing to me—thank you very much, really thank you.

I must say I'm slightly shocked about the Situation Tampax—I mean, one can't very well bring a suitcase full . . . never mind. Also dismayed by absence of nail polish remover. In fact rather dismayed by the East, now that we're in the Red Sea,.

The ship is intolerable. It looks and sounds as though a train-load of "To

216. The front of the card is a photograph depicting AW with a cane. She is accompanied by a person in a polar bear costume. Snow is heaped in mounds in the background to the left of the photo; where AW stands has been cleared of snowdrifts. A park bench next to a tree also appears in the background toward the right of where AW stands. She wears boots, a midi-length coat, and a long scarf. Swiss postage stamps are affixed to the postcard.

217. Translated into English from German, the text of the postcard reads: "Here is your wounded child, on the last day 1957. / We are now driving away."

218. *Adieu* is French for "goodbye" and is commonly used in many parts of Germany.

219. AW signed "Asia" on the postcard.

220. Patricia Renate Mendelson (1933–) is a friend of AW. Mendelson traveled to Burma with her husband on the *Derbyshire,* which departed Liverpool on May 2, 1958.

221. AW is on her way to Burma (now also known as Myanmar) to reunite with DW. She separated from RL, saying goodbye to him at a London train station before making her way to the port at Liverpool, where she would embark on a ship bound for Rangoon, the capital city of Burma. AW boarded the *Derbyshire* on June 19, 1959. She writes to Patricia Mendelson, who is in Mandalay, in care of DW. AW's occupation listed on the ship's manifest is "Teacher," and her English address is given as "19 Hans Place, Knightsbridge, S.W.1."

the Sales in Kensington High Street" from Wimbledon has taken over the ugly middle-aged Derbyshire for a cruise.[222] I'm turning into a sort of paranoid Robinson Crusoe reading over and over again a 3 week-old "Observer."[223]

Look—I'm afraid I'm running rather short of money, and unless I can borrow some, I may not be about to buy the flash-bulbs for your husband.[224] I'll try and borrow some though.

Again thank you for writing,
Assia Lipsey[225]

TO LONYA AND ELIZABETHA GUTMANN TLS, Emory

Friday, July 17, 1959

Trincomalee, Ceylon,[226] July 17th 59

My dearest, my sweetest, Muttinka und Vatile,

Thank you, thank you for your letter which you sent to Colombo[227] (dated July 3rd! and I received it today.) I am so glad that your arm is better, my dearest Muttile, your handwriting was as normal as I remember, which relived me. And I'm so glad and so relieved about the equipment in Vati's office—that's wonderful, especially since we didn't expect it. But you <u>must</u> be patient about the house, Mutti, and not generalise despair from one or two enquiries.[228] It takes a long time to sell a house, which is what we all knew, and precisely why we urged you to begin selling it so early, do you remember? Oh oh muttichen—please please, you're doing it again . . . Bubale, be patient.

Oh how you would despair if you were on this ship now, like me, totally

222. Kensington High Street is a fashionable shopping district in Kensington, England. Wimbledon is a district in southwest London.

223. AW alludes to the shipwrecked and stranded main character of *Robinson Crusoe* (1719) by Daniel Defoe. The *Observer* is a British newspaper founded in 1791.

224. AW refers to American poet, writer, and translator Michael Mendelson (pen name: Nathaniel Tarn, 1928–).

225. In the *Derbyshire*'s passenger manifest, AW apparently identified herself as "Miss. Assia E Lipsey," rather than using the title "Mrs.," as some passengers did in the report, signaling her separation from RL.

226. Trincomalee is a port city, and *Ceylon* denotes the republic now known as Sri Lanka.

227. Colombo is a port city in Ceylon, now Sri Lanka.

228. AW's parents are living in Vancouver, British Columbia, Canada, at the time of this letter.

alone, nobody really to speak to, and delayed indefinitely in this strange exotic desert island harbour. The journey is getting on everyone's nerves except the captains, who seems to have the patience of Job,[229] the blood pressure of a refrigerator and the pompousness of a magistrate. There are only 12 passengers left in a space designed for 100. The majority are small, monkey-like Burmese officers who look like aged children, especially their bodies, which look like those of 11 year old boys. They spend all their time gambling or being extraordinarily arrogant and rude to the dozens of Indian stewards who have the misfortune to have to earn their living in this way, or perhaps they are fortunate, being Indians, to earn any kind of living in any kind of way. They are as patient as nuns, and they call me 'Memsahib'[230]—which is wha I remember Myrna Loy was called in a film about India[231]—this is absurd. Suddenly, absolutely suddenly, after 5 days in this harbor of terrible heat (my face is always wet with sweat—very good for the skin someone said) a great loud Monsoon wind has begun,; the sea is ruffled, it's cloudy with black murderous clouds, and the ship is swaying slightly. We've been here for 10 day now, the day of departure is delayed every day because the Singhalese[232] don't know how to unload cargo (they are unused to it in this port) and the unloading takes a long time at the best. I have described Trincomalee in the other letter which I am sending with this one.[233] I was going to copy the other letter on to this, which is why the first paragraph in this letter is exactly the same as the first paragraph in the other one—but I really can't bring myself to write the same letter twice. I'm beginning to run extremely short of money—because of the delay, and there is no way of getting any more, at least not for a woman of my temprament . . .

Then there is a Buddist priest on the ship—whose baggage consisted of 5 books, a set of yellow robes which he washes every morning, and a plant in a

229. AW alludes to Job, who is referenced in the Book of Job in the Old Testament and in James 5:10–11 in the New Testament. Job exhibits great patience and noble perseverance in facing enormous hardships.

230. *Memsahib* refers to a white married or upper-class foreign woman in India; at the time, it was a respectful form of address by nonwhites to whites. *Mem* is thought to be an Indian pronunciation of *ma'am,* and *sahib* functions as a polite title or address for a man. The word derives from Hindi and Urdu.

231. Myrna Loy (1905–93) is an actress starring in *The Rains Came* (1939), which is set in India. The film won an Academy Award for Best Effects, Special Effects, and was nominated for five more Academy Awards.

232. AW means *Sinhalese,* which refers to the ethnic group of people associated with Sri Lanka.

233. The letter may not be extant.

pot. Both his arms are heavily tatooed up to the elbow, and he only eats once in every 24 hours . . . He's thin, and doesn't speak to women unless he can sit on a higher level than they.

Ah, at last we are sailing—today, I mean we are sailing tomorrow, but today is the latest I can post this.

Today I went into Trincomalee again—the monsoons are fully on with a fantastically high wind—60 or 70 miles an hour and rain. I quite like all this—it smells strange and nothing looks safe enough to eat—but the people respond touchingly to smiles or any show of good temper and friendliness. I took some photographs today which I shall send you when I have them developed. I spent £4 on a Zeiss Ikon[234] which I bought in Aden,[235] it looks as though it should do good things for me—the first camera I have ever owned. Aside from this I feel very strange, but I'm getting used to being alone and dependent on myself—I don't like being by myself, and I hate seeing the wonders of the world by myself—I mean without people who speak my language and whom I love—like you two. Oh how I would have loved to see all this with you—except for the heat which you couldn't have stood. O I remember you aren't much interested in the East. When I next write I shall have seen David and Rangoon. It will be a good 8–9 days before you hear from me again. My sweet dearest parents, thank you for being so sympathetic in your letter. Thank you½

Assia

TO PATRICIA AND MICHAEL MENDELSON

TLS, Stanford

Undated, circa August 1959

8 University Estate,
Mandalay.

Dearest Pat and Mike,

It seems absolutely fantastic , privately fantastic, that I once imagined Mandalay as an enormous white palace sitting on top of a vast jade rock, surrounded by a

234. Founded in 1926, Zeiss Ikon is a German company that specialized in cameras. It folded in 1972.

235. Aden is a port city in Yemen on the Gulf of Aden, which connects the Red Sea and the Indian Ocean, in western Asia.

luxurious cemetry. And there was young Kipling[236] in spanking clean white ducks making love to a beribboned princess, and going to a real lavatory made of bamboo. But that's enough—both of us are in really awful gloom, depths of. We miss you very badly. We suddenly realized last night that we are to all intents and purposes totally alone now , which makes me feel slightly panicky.[237]

The Informer still calls occasionally looking jelloid and cadaverous, rather like a neurotic middle-aged Berliner Hausfrau[238]—I almost feel for him, but not quite.[239]

Maung Maung is sick, disrespectful (in the broadest sense) and madly successful at comfortable survival. Poor Maung Po, we realise is simply, archaically mad. He talks to himself. This genuinely moves me. But I'm not in the least moved by M.M. for whom[240] I have conceived a manic, distressing dislike, and have successfully infected David with it. If you know a cook in Rangoon etc. It is shame-making, idiotic to be so obssessed with trivia like this, I mean M.M. etc.—but one's silly life is hemmed in, framed by these minutiae of 2 bland tasteless curries a day, and I forgot to buy sugar and oil, and therefore, as today, we had 2 pieces of buttered bread and tea for lunch. Na, wirklich . . . also bitte.[241]

We've decided not to come back here after March, it really is unsupportable, and I now realise was only tolerable as long as you were here. Surely this is a manifestation of something or other.

Have you, by any chance, looked into the tiny matter of the pick-up head?[242] are you well? are you happier? what news?

Oh what a bitchy letter this is. I'm half ashamed for writing it, and feel like tearing it[243] up. There must be some virtue here, somewhere, unrecognised by

236. English writer Rudyard Kipling (1865–1936) wrote about Burma after spending a short time there. AW may have been familiar with his poem "Mandalay," which was published in *Barrack-Room Ballads* (1892).

237. AW, DW, and the Mendelsons enjoyed spending time together in Mandalay, Burma. A photo of AW and Michael Mendelson at a tea party in Mandalay in 1960 was reprinted in Koren and Negev, *Lover of Unreason,* in the plates section between 142–43.

238. The German *Hausfrau* translates to "housewife" in English.

239. The "Informer" may be the "ex-Palestine Police officer" whom AW mentions in her letter to her parents, dated September 7, 1959. See pp. 80–82.

240. "for ~~him~~ whom" appears in the original.

241. "Na, wirklich . . . bitte" translates from German to English as "Well, really . . . please." *Bitte* also is used when saying "you're welcome."

242. AW asks about a part for a record player.

243. "tearing ~~up~~ it" appears in the original.

all of us. T.E. Lawrence[244] would perhaps have seen it. That sentimental Queen Collis[245] spotted it in an unthwarted flash, see—so what's Collis got that I ain't? or you, yes, you ain't?

Much love
Assia[246]

<Added by Assia Wevill on a separate sheet of paper—Eds.>

Today I got an extension visa for another 3 months.
We shan't go down to Rangoon—no money, the chiefest reason.
Hate not to see you before you leave.
Has Martin Morland[247] delivered my letter?
You said you'd write—
P-l-e-a-s-e look after yourself.

love
Assia

TO LONYA AND ELIZABETHA GUTMANN

TLS, Emory

Monday, September 7, 1959

8 University Estate,
Mandalay, Union of Burma,
September 7th 1959

Dearest Muttinka und Vatile,[248]

Meine lieben guten Bubale[249]—

Thank you very much for your letter which I received 2 weeks ago. I was very disturbed by your reports of Dick, and surprised. Since leaving England I

244. British archaeologist, military officer, and writer T. E. Lawrence (1888–1935) is mentioned here.

245. This reference is probably to the novel *She Was a Queen* (1937) by Maurice Collis.

246. A postscript by DW follows: he says he agrees mostly and hopes the planning in Rangoon is not as absurdly complicated as it sounds.

247. Probably AW means Martin Robert Morland (1933–2020), who later served as the British ambassador to Burma from 1985 to 1990.

248. At the top of the letter, AW has crossed out holograph text that appears to have been the start of a different letter. The return address is handwritten.

249. The German "Meine lieben guten Bubale" translates to "My dear good Sweetie" in English.

have only had 2 letters from him, in reply to 10 of mine. A third letter arrived today—very cool, mostly reporting about his visit to you, where he said that he found you as sweet and charming as ever . . . Mutti said she thought he still loved me—well, that can't be true, I'm afraid, unless you have reasons of your own for thinking that which I don't know about. Shortly before I left England, I suddenly couldn't face the thought of leaving him, wanted to stay, and begged him to let me stay, but he said to go, that I must go . . . well. I went weeping bitterly and regretting everything, but he seemed completely unmoved. Since his letter told me about nothing but his visit to you—judging from his silence and the tone of his letter, I should think that he is more or less indifferent. I know of course, that you must think that it serves me right—well, if it does it does, and there is nothing I can do.

David and I get on extremely well—but we both are unnerved by the virtual isolation of this place. There is nobody in our age bracket, and only an ex–Palestine Police officer here and his Chinese Wife, with whom I particularly do not get on at all well (I mean with the man), and neither does David. But I paint and David writes a lot, and the days somehow contract between an early bedtime (I got to bed at 9 and sleep by 9.30, and get up again at 6) and an early cool morning.

How to begin to describe life here? it is so totally different from anywhere, anything I have ever lived before, that I should really compile a long list to give you the beginning of an idea. Now that my stomach is used to some germs I can at least move about more than I could at the beginning. Sights like lepers crawling about in the main street don't horrify me quite as much as they did during the first weeks. There is a leper hospital and colony here run by Franciscan nuns[250]—but the poor patients are thus condemned to years of total isolation and inactivity with only a chance of a cure, whereas if they are outside they are at least free though they are doomed to their terrible end sooner. There are a lot of Indians here, who seem to play the role of Jews in Europe. They are largely disliked, cleverer and more energetic than the Burmese, they are also considerably richer. (This is because of a difference in their religion—Buddhism places no value at all on earthly success and therefore discourages almost all effort leading to increased comfort of any kind, whereas Hinduism, about which I know nothing doesn't appear to have the same tenets). I was, no I still am, a little impatient with the inefficiency of every process, every activity, official or private

250. "run by ~~cathol~~ Franciscan nuns" appears in the original.

that is undertaken in Burma. But on the other hand, this same maaleish attitude also contributes to the overall enchantment that one experiences when one first gets here. Women with long black hair and flowered sarongs[251] lead horses through the streets, and smile when they see you looking at them; whether out of sheer good nature or embarrassment at oneself being caught 'staring' which is considered rude, almost insulting, I don't know, and it doesnt really matter. There is great admiration for the Israelis in Burma, there is an Israeli embassy in Rangoon, and hundreds of 'experts' assisting the Burmese in various projects. I like that. But things are not simple and charming everywhere, as again, I at first thought. But the Burmese are extremely polite, and the younger, educated ones, eager to learn, and above all to remain neutral in world affairs.

Our cook turns out to be a bit of a Mussolini[252]—power-mad, but without the drive and energy to be thorough about it. He thinks I am a little crazy to insist on using soap and hot water when washing up—I discovered only recently that the second boy (who is slow but a much better man) simply took the dishes to the well and scratched at them with his bare hands and well-water. now I carry out an inspection every morning—and feel idiotically British and like a sergeant-major. 'Power corrups' . . .

Now, please please tell what is happening to you—how you like Montreal, what you have found out . . how is Cilly, Arnie and Ronnie? if Ronnie remembers me, say that I love him very much, if he doesn't, just give him a kiss for me. But you are not lonely anymore—and perhaps you have met new people. How is your arm—Bubale?[253] are you much better? you <u>must</u> be . . .

It seems to take 6–8 days for a letter from here to Montreal—Please write soon—the postman comes so seldom, and I wait for him . . .

I love you both so much.
Assia

Give my regards to Cilly, Arnie.

251. See a photograph of AW in a sarong in Burma in Julie Goodspeed-Chadwick, *Reclaiming Assia Wevill: Sylvia Plath, Ted Hughes, and the Literary Imagination* (Baton Rouge: LSU Press, 2019), 145.

252. This is a reference to the Italian politician, journalist, and leader of the National Fascist Party, Benito Mussolini (1883–1945).

253. The rest of the letter, from "—Bubale" to the end, is handwritten.

TO PATRICIA MENDELSON

TLS,[254] Stanford

Wednesday, September 30, 1959[255]

September 30th

Dearest Pat,

Oh I am a pig for not having replied earlier, and for not saying what I thought when I read your letter: how glad, no, how delighted I am to hear about the baby. Never mind about the clothes—you can wear them for a long time yet, and when you must, you can have magnificent maternity clothes made—one afternoon I though about you and baby etc. and I thought how wonderful you'd look in a jacket[256] made out of iceblue, thick with pure silk satin all thickly unjudiciously embroidered in white and same iceblue—jacket with tabs at the side, and frog-closings at the back—rather like this appalling drawing fullstop.[257] Go out little and look magnificent at home all the time . . . I <u>know</u> you'll look elegant and splendid while you're pregnant . . .

I feel terribly guilty about the thought of you walking about Rangoon searching for the stupid pickup head . . . but thank you so much for doing it.

Later. We're having a rather harrassing time—though no doubt no more harassing than yours, which is probably nearer Purgatory than Harrass. Maung Maung is leaving tomorrow, and replaced by a 75 year old Indian . . . this appointment made in utter despair. We are sick of being here and want to go to Japan next year,[258] and all these negotiations are delicate and hazardous and slightly Machiavallian—this curve was unintentional but no doubt significant[259]

254. AW has drawn a woman wearing maternity clothes in the center of the page and typed her letter around it.

255. Date is supplied from internal evidence.

256. "look in a ~~materni~~ jacket" appears in the original.

257. AW is alluding to her drawing on the first page of the letter.

258. AW and DW are considering relocating to Japan; DW applied to work there through the British Council. However, AW's divorce from RL had not been finalized, and her marital status and relationship with DW are obstacles in their plan to move to Japan. According to AW's biographers: "Burma proved a problematic waiting room. There were whispers and frowns behind [AW and DW's] backs; the illicit liaison of one of Her Majesty's employees, living with a married woman, was unacceptable to Wevill's employers. Alton Becker recalled that Assia and David were very upset when the British ambassador gave them an ultimatum [to finalize Assia's divorce or leave Burma]. Assia tried desperately to prod Lipsey into action, but her letters had no effect" (Koren and Negev, *Lover of Unreason,* 75).

259. "and slightly Machiavallian" is typed at the bottom of the page and appears curved because of movement in the paper. AW's comment about the "curve" is handwritten.

J.S.[260] is still away, thank God. The whole affaire has subsided, in spite of the fact that J.S. attempted to revive it and some panic shortly before he left. Mandalay quiet and unruffled as the sewer in front of the house, equally stagnat. One guest for the last 2 weeks in the hotel. Owen[261] munching away at the Nation, Jack packing his treasures; tennis balls panting in the afternoon. Tea comes and goes, things get washed up, floors swept. No letters, only ominous things from the British Council.[262] Not a breath of cold, of fun, of new air. This would be unendurable for another year. It's rather awful to think, that for all purposes of survival one would be exiled from London for the rest of one's life. Today, for the first time, I feel a pang of hankering for London, if not for England. I envy you going, so soon.

David says that the thought of going to Rangoon horrifies him. At this rate I doubt that we shall come. Pity. I so wanted to see you both before you go. We may just possibly come towards the end of October.

I have lost your second letter and can't remember what you said about the Swiss pick up head—at any event we need the whole head. I think perhaps I ought to buy it myself, rather than irritate you with this any further, you've done quite enough.

Please write to us again—I so love hearing from you.

Love
Assia

TO PATRICIA AND MICHAEL MENDELSON — AL, Stanford

Monday, October 12, 1959

12/10/59

Dearest Pat u Michael,

Thank you, thank you so much for the needle—you are so incredibly nice . . . and kind, and . . . and . . endlessly.

260. This is probably a reference to John Slimming (1926–78), who was the British Information Officer with the British Council in Mandalay. His book *Temiar Jungle: A Malayan Journey* was published in 1958.

261. Possibly a reference to Arthur Elwyn Owen (1917–), Owen worked for the British Council and was a colleague of DW in the English Department at the University of Mandalay.

262. As the British Council itself explains, it is an international organization for cultural relations and educational opportunities. Founded in 1934, its headquarters are in London. The British Council established an office in Burma in 1946.

This in a Great hurry in order to get this cheque off, so that it is of use to you.

The needle, by the way is perfection itself, and a replica of the damaged one.[263] At least we can enjoy some music again.[264] Thank you.

How is Mike? I was, we were, distressed to hear about the illness, d'you think anything to do with drinking the miner-water? but you escaped, Pat.[265]

<The rest of the letter is missing.—Eds.>

TO LONYA AND ELIZABETHA GUTMANN

TLS, Emory

Friday, November 6, 1959–Tuesday, January 19, 1960

Nov. 6th 1959.

My dearest Vatinka,

I feel suddenly so sad this evening. The siberian womens' choir is singing inside my record-player; such a European, such a deep deep European song (but this of course is simply not true, this woman is wailing and dirging very asiatically, but the dirge has been through a kind of Europeanised mincer, and emerges tender and romantic in a way which turns my insides out).[266] All afternoon long I have thought and thought of you and Mutti. This often happens to me—I wake up from an afternoon's sleep, perhaps from a dream in which you both appear, and obsessed, I think of you longingly for hours afterwards—sometimes afraid that you are no longer there. Or perhaps I read a phrase in a newspaper, and bing . . . a bell rings and I spend a long time possessed by a very private day-dream. And I Play these records—and they make me cry . . .

263. "damaged ~~needle~~ one" appears in the original.

264. This needle is likely part of the components needed to fix the record player that was referenced in the two previous letters to the Mendelsons.

265. Tap water is unsafe to drink in Burma (Myanmar). Clean water was a major problem for Burma in both the twentieth and twenty-first centuries. In 2016, the Mandalay branch of the Food and Drug Administration (FDA) found that 40 percent of water bottled in Myanmar contained bacteria, such as *E. coli.*

266. AW had a penchant for folk songs. It is possible that she is listening to "Oh, You Dark Night (Oi, Ti Tyomnaya Noch)" as sung by the Siberian Folk Chorus (Women's Group). This song, with others, appeared on the vinyl record *Russian Folk Songs* (Monitor Records, 1958). "Oh, You Dark Night (Oi, Ti Tyomnaya Noch)" is track B2 on the record.

January 19th 1960

My dearest Muttinka und Vatile,

I began this letter, as you can see, 3 months ago—and lost it, as you can see from the wrinkles. It occurred to me, after I posted the letter in answer to your Christmas letter,[267] that I didn't puton it the extra 25 pyas[268] which are necessary for air-letters to North America, and unless by some miracle it has arrived by air all the same, it will take months by sea mail, and you will be there in Montreal wondering what has happened to me.

It is getting warmer again, not dangerously hot yet, but menacingly warm, as frightening as the first fierce cold days in November, in the real world. This will be a shortish letter, because in order to let you hear from me I must put this in thepost before 4 p.m. It is now 2 o clock, and we've finished lunch, and I have a bad cold, all because the temperature last week was down to the early 60's in the morning, and I sat out on the veranda reading . . . how quickly one becomes with the[269] momentary gentless of weather.

Last night we returned from a trip to Northern Burma, 130 miles from the Chinese Border. And what magnificence . . . we stayed with the local Sawba,[270] who is a real feudal Duke, Feudalism is still practiced in remote parts of Burma, and there on top of a mountain range which goes up to 6000 ft.[271] sat the palace with the dark-sun glassed Sawba, very benign, having invited practically the whole province to the Buddhist confirmation of his 10 grandsons. This really was the Orient most gorgeous, most fairy-tale like, unbelievable. Imagine this one fat man, who owns all the tea-bushes in Burma, who owns a town and an entire province, and does not feel the least moral discomfort . . . The town looked what I imagine the old Imperial Manchu towns in pre-war China must be like.[272] Clean, sitting on rock, are neat wooden house, covered with mats, and apple cheeked[273] Chinese children carry their brothers and sisters on sacks on the backs. There are many Chinese and Chinese women still have bound

267. The letter may not be extant.

268. A pya is a monetary unit used in Burma.

269. "one becomes ~~spiled~~ with the" appears in the original.

270. A sawba is a hereditary ruler; AW understands the sawba to be akin to the ranking of a duke in the British nobility peerage or system.

271. AW is describing the Greater Himalayan mountain range.

272. AW is likely referring to the last imperial dynasty of China, the Qing dynasty (1644–1912). It is sometimes referred to as the Manchu Empire.

273. "~~with~~ and apple cheeked" appears in the original.

feet. Minute, grotesque little triangles covered with socks, which support often a large peasant body. We ate a huge Chinese meal in a smoke filled Chinese peasant's restaurant, with strange animals and vegetables haning from the ceiling, to dry or smoke. Everything very dank and black, and the mist from the valley (which looks exactly like a Chinese landscape drawing) beautifully curling up into our very faces. I've never felt so remote remote. The river which flowed into the valley and which suplies the town with water, comes from TIBET . . . in the town walked the country women looking at pots and pans, wearing marvelous costumes made from a patchwork of Chinese brocades, I've never seen anything like that before—around therir padded hips they wear 20 brass rings. Oh lovely lovely. The country side is supposed to be full of bandits, but we didn't meet one. Ifeel very adventurous to have gone, though.

Please please give me news of Vati's luck. and write soon, as soon as you get this, so that I know you are not too unhappy. Give my love to Cillinka and to Ronnie. Be nice to Ronnie, I think he must be like me, a little, though don't tell Cilly that, she'll be upset.

Tell me what sort of people or friends you've made in Montreal, I want to know so much.

Eure[274]
Assia

TO PATRICIA AND MICHAEL MENDELSON — TLS, Stanford

Wednesday, November 25, 1959

8 University Estate,
Mandalay. Burma.
November 25th 1959.

My dear, dearest Pat and Michael,

How impossible to think of you walking up Baker St.—but there,you probably did it yesterday and today.[275] You lift up a telephone and dial things. Never

274. *Eure* is German for "your."

275. The Mendelsons were living at 164 Montagu Mews, Crawford Street, London, W.1., England, according to the return address on the envelope of this letter. They lived one-fifth of a mile, or approximately three minutes by foot, from Baker Street. More than a mile and a half long, Baker Street is a main artery in London; it connects Marylebone Road to Oxford Street. Earlier in its history, Baker Street featured affluent residences; now it is known as a commercial district.

mind. Are you well? was the journey heady? have you recovered completely? do morons on T.V. still cry "I wonder where the yellow went?"[276]

I do hope you are well, though. Both of you.

I feel as though I were writing from the Deserted Village.[277] Most tangible feelable things are precisely as they were. 80°– 84 in the afternoon, with a low comedy small wind in the mornings. The 3rd Man (British Council) arrived, installed with A.E.Owen, komisch,[278] guarded, a Super Elwyn, harrassing the original with superior gamesmanship, and mocking him mercilessly. Elwyn winking to Moodie[279] indiscreetly; to us he mumbles 'Charlatan.' But so, you remember, was Arnold Toynbee.[280] Elwyn harrassing us,mostly about the car, which he uses mostly now in order to save his own. Whole days without a car. Sillier and sillier notes flying across the fence. Really Elwyn is spiteful and malicious, with all the vices of a queer, and occasional grace also, I guess. Very bad. Last night David had a tremendous row with him. Very bad. How idiotic—Slimming vs. Wevill, Wevill vs.Owen, Owen vs. Slimming, Slimming vs. Clark.[281] Clark ignores Wevill. Wevills also ignored by Anderson,[282] Allan Sewage Taylor,[283] New Regime at U.S.I.S.[284] (stern, calvinistic, Burmese Only, vapours of International Studies). Mad mad Halliday[285] departed with the creme

276. "I wonder where the yellow went" is a Pepsodent toothpaste advertisement jingle. The commercial to which AW alludes was broadcast in the United Kingdom and the United States from the late 1940s to the 1960s.

277. AW may be referring to the poem "The Deserted Village" (1770) by Oliver Goldsmith, which invokes a village in physical decline (for example, depopulation, capitalist enclosures, and privatization) and moral decline (for example, the pursuit of decadence), among other themes.

278. *Komisch* is German for "funny."

279. Moodie is Professor John Moonie, who was head of the English Department at the University of Mandalay. He began his tenure at the University of Mandalay around 1947, retiring in 1967.

280. This reference is most likely to the British historian Arnold Joseph Toynbee (1889–1975), a professor specializing in international history and international affairs at the London School of Economics and the University of London.

281. Clark may be Sir Terence Joseph Clark KBE CMG (1934–), who served as an Orientalist and Middle Eastern expert and British diplomat with the Foreign Service (now the Diplomatic Service).

282. Anderson may be Dillon Anderson (1906–74), an American government official who wrote about the effects of mutual aid treaties on Burma in 1959.

283. David Wevill believes that AW is referring to a British couple, the Taylor-Allens.

284. USIS stands for the United States Information Service (1953–99), an American agency dedicated to diplomacy.

285. Halliday is likely a reference to Michael Alexander Kirkwood Halliday (1925–2018), born in England; he specialized in Chinese linguistics.

de la creme weeping crocodily at the Airport, wisps of Kashmir[286] shawls peeping out of attache case, and a bad case of Dobi's itch[287] driving him insane. He's gone to Korea.

All last week I had dysentry.[288] Our cook, fragile, lunatic, incompetently dishonest, serves lunch when the mood strikes him. It strikes him at odd intervals. Lunch at 4–5 p.m., dinner at 6. No tea. Breakfast cold and onioned of duck's eggs looking like diseased oranges. He goes to the bazaar at midnight, returns with nothing but a hair-cut. He, he alone gave me dysentry. Since we are[289] no longer invited to eat anyone else's food (we feel more amd more as though we lived in a 'restricted area' and were suspected of negro blood), it must be poor Samuel.[290] No other cooks in Mandalay.

Oh Pat dear, it is becoming unendurably horrible. No divorce until March. With rumors widening and gossip about us (generated we think largely by Elwyn) like smoke. Can't leave the country until the divorce. Not a word from Dick Lipsey of the L.S.E. No change. Impending Br. Council inspection from London, all will be revealed and maybe fired by January 27th.[291] David is pale and buffetted. And we miss you both so much. The same view the same temperature, the same sounds. 'Mohinga! ' witchy scream in the morning.[292] But you know all this. The hardest thing, though is the lack of a single friend. Pat dear, could you send me 3 pairs of nylon pants (white, non-frilly) I mean "Hoeschen"[293] from Marks & Spencer[294], and 4 for David, size small? we're both, embarrasingly, suddenly without, which is dangerous in a high wind. I wonder if you could

286. Kashmir is a northern geographical region of the Indian subcontinent. It includes territories managed by India, Pakistan, and China.

287. *Dobi's* is a reference to tinea cruris, colloquially known as "jock itch" or "Dhobi itch." It is a fungal infection of the groin.

288. Dysentery is an inflammation of the intestines. It spreads through contaminated food or water.

289. "~~Becau~~ Since we are" appears in the original.

290. Samuel is the Wevills' cook.

291. DW's contract was not renewed ultimately because AW had not been able to secure a divorce from RL in time.

292. Mohinga is a traditional Burmese soup, consisting of noodles, fish, and other ingredients. As a national dish of Burma that can be eaten at breakfast, lunch or dinner, it can be readily purchased from street food vendors and at grocery stores and can also be ordered at fine dining restaurants today.

293. *Hoeschen* translates from German to English as "panties."

294. Marks & Spencer is a major British retailer, based in London. It was founded in 1884 and continues to operate in the United Kingdom, selling clothes and other items.

send it through the bag? otherwise the postage would be ruinous and chance of arrival minute. If you can't[295] send it through the Bag, don't bother.[296] I'll make some, God knows how.

What a whining letter this is. I hate reading my whining letters.

Write me a long letter saying things about you, and whether you've found a house, and how you feel. And when Michael is coming.

My hair is very lank and dry—did your get dry here? what did you do? perhaps it's the dysentry. Have you bought marvelous cloth I mean clothes, of course. Have you seen snow? is it lovely cold?

Please tell me how much the pants are and I'll send you a cheque. I bless you about once a week for the record-head. We play Brubeck[297] over and over. USIS has run out of things. And all the other records seem stale, but Brubeck survives. Elwyn tells us, that U Chan Mya,[298] (our neighbour) is telling people that the Pagan slab which was deposited with David with the Hun American on the motorcycle, was really chiselled off by David himself, who, bothered by conscience decided to palm it off on U Chan Mya. Ho Ho Ho. Elwyn is in search of a "really valuable piece of Burma," antique he hisses, I wonder what he means . . he bought a sort of Burmese Landseer[299] view of Pagan,[300] in a pine frame 10" wide, hideous, but would look nice in the parlour in Penrith.[301] No doubt, no doubt. We really rather hate him.

But love you dearly. Goodbye.
Assia

295. "~~Is~~ If you can't" appears in the original.

296. AW may be referring to a mailbag or postbag. It appears that she is discussing the differences between sending a package through airmail versus sending it by boat.

297. This reference is probably to American jazz pianist Dave Brubeck (1920–2012).

298. U Chan Mya is a lecturer and the first head of the Department of Myanmar at the University of Mandalay.

299. AW may be invoking a dog breed with *landseer.*

300. Pagan is a village in central Burma; it is located ninety miles southwest of Mandalay. Pagan is known for its Buddhist shrines and ruins of other shrines and pagodas.

301. Penrith is a town located in Cumbria, England.

TO PATRICIA MENDELSON

TLS, Stanford

Saturday, January 16, 1960

16/1/60

Dearest Pat,

5 minutes ago the huge registered letter arrived.[302] Thank you so much—thank you also for the beautiful Christmas card, which hangs magnificenton the repulsive naval grey partition haughtily aware of two Burmese puppets . . . I have become so lethargic about writing letters that I'm beginning to lose the courage to write at all; but full of clammy righteousness I sit down after lunch, now, (temperature Ladies and gentlemen 73 in U Ko Lay's[303] refrigerator) to answer your letter written long, long before Christmas.

When I read that you were in Baden Baden,[304] the memory of you here in Zendel's cotton skirt getting out of the land-rover, vanished irrevocably. A new Patricia Mendelson drinks tea in an Edwardian greenhouse, a new Michel adjusts to a woolen suit, and pays for things in toy-currency, and everybody speaks German. . . . sorry, this slipped and it's too late to retract.

Things are happening to us. And they are happening at a vertiginous rate which frightens us a little. At the source of your reclining Buddha, du weist wer und wo, we kauften[305] another, ornate, unique, beautiful. But how to get it out? wir haben es bisher niemanded gezeigt.[306] and it sits slightly menacing upstairs, shrouded. . Also another, tall, cobwebbed, and delicate with the tunic[307] folds stiff and lovely as a European Gothic carving. This all overwhelms us. How can one get them out? Hal Brown is going soon, but one hesitates[308] to to impose things like this on him. Is that more or less what you did? or were you quite straightforward about these things or should one not ask you this at all. I now

302. See the letter from Nathaniel Tarn to David and Assia Wevill, January 12, 1960, held by Stanford University.

303. David Wevill thinks U Ko Lay might have been their neighbor.

304. Baden-Baden is a spa town in southwestern Germany.

305. This German phrase translates to "You know who and where, we bought" in English.

306. This German phrase translates to "We have not shown it to anyone yet" in English.

307. "delicate ~~and~~ with the tunic" appears in the original.

308. "but ~~would~~ one hesitates" appears in the original.

understand your state of mind while at the Chummery.[309] Can one insure things like this while here?

To other things. No Japan, irrefurtably no Japan. This depressed us for so long, that only with weeks of lunatic tennis playing did we finally get it out of our system. The council offered D another 2 year contract here, but we will talk to them, and with your advice about possibly doing post-graduate[310] work in Japanese in London, be able to settle things only when we reach London. When is the baby due? I have a feeling it will come in April, I hope it comes before we get there, because I want to see it very much.

Dear Pat—how are you? are you looking mlovely and serene as people say one should? have you found a house? is Michael pleased with the Institute?[311] have you made new friends? will you return to Burma within the next 2 years? if so then perhaps we would accept another 2 year contract, because then it will be lovely. We have a first-class cook now and a marvellous middle-aged Indian woman with twice my energy and solicitude. who looks after us and our guests the way no one else has since I was an infant. and so if you came you will, I assure you eat well.

Elwyn continues disgusting and Jeremiac[312] overshadowed and mocked (a little) by Number 3 he sits on his Pasha![313] (impoverished Pasha) pyjama'd broken spring sofas, piqued and plotting a hundred revenges. His nasty, petty

309. In India, a chummery refers to a bachelors' pad, a living arrangement with chums. Specifically, a chummery designates the living quarters of unmarried British army officers during the time of the British Raj. A well-known example of a chummery in Burma was the Candacraig, now known as the Thiri Myaing Hotel in Pyin Oo Lwin, which was built in 1904 and boasted seven acres of gardens. It was a chummery for the Bombay Burmah Trading Company in colonial times; one of its famous guests was George Orwell.

310. "doing ~~a pos~~ post-graduate" appears in the original.

311. In 1958, Michael Mendelson was awarded a Rockefeller Foundation grant, which was managed by the Royal Institute of International Affairs. This grant took him to Burma, where he and Patricia Mendelson lived for eighteen months, during which they were good friends of the Wevills. Following his time in Burma, Michael Mendelson worked as an instructor at the London School of Economics.

312. *Jeremiac* might be used here in an adjectival form of *jeremiad,* which is a lament that underscores sorrow, grief, disappointment, or complaint. It is often used satirically, suggesting that the person uttering the jeremiad makes the complaint tediously long and derives satisfaction from the utterance.

313. Historically, *pasha* is a title designating a high-ranking official in the Ottoman Empire or countries under Turkish rule.

little innuendos now make us laugh, because he seems to have emerged from his sinister cocoon into a kind of low-comedian, not intentionally on his part. H. E.,[314] now a knight, came here, and was shepherded around by Owen, as though he, Owen, were H.E.'s father's trusted old butler. Which of course is precisely what Owen will be in his next life, a butler to the Duke of Bedord,[315] sneakily reporting on guests' table manners in the kitchen.

David has had 2 lots of things published in the States, but nothing accepted in England. Are there any new magazines? perhaps Mike knows. Is Mike still writing?[316] I never had a chance to tell him that I cared for his voluptuous baroque very much indeed and please tell him as much.

Pat dear—I must go. I have photographed Him—and will send you a copy to ask for your opinion.

Write soon, detailedly about everything—and please ask Mike to write about what he's doind, and whether he'd seen Lorraine Lancaster[317] anywhere.

And thank you thank you again so much for the Marks and Spencer cornucopia.

Love love love
Assia

Will send you cheque for 10/- together with photographs as soon as they are ready.

A.W.[318]

314. The British honorific *H.E.* stands for "His Excellency," more colloquially known as H.E. or Excellency. *H.E.* typically designates a high-ranking official or head of state, such as the head of an international organization or an ambassador. The person alluded to may be Sir Richard Hugh Sedley Allen (1903–96), who was ambassador to Burma from 1956–62. In this role, Sir Richard was the head of the United Kingdom's diplomatic mission and its chief diplomatic representative in Burma.

315. AW might mean Duke of Bedford.

316. Michael Mendelson published *Old Savage / Young City* (London: Jonathan Cape) under his pen name, Nathaniel Tarn, in 1964.

317. Michael Mendelson pursued anthropological work for his doctorate and became an anthropologist. Lorraine Lancaster Barić was a sociologist who studied kinship and drew upon anthropological terminology and methods in her 1958 article "Kinship in Anglo-Saxon Society" in volume 9 of the *British Journal of Sociology.* In 1970, Barić became the first female professor of sociology in the United Kingdom when she joined the faculty at Salford University.

318. This last sentence and added initials are handwritten.

TO RICHARD LIPSEY

ALS,[319] Emory

Friday, March 4, 1960

Mandalay
March 4th 1960

My dear Dick,

This is instead of a telegram which I can't afford at the moment. The point is—what news of the divorce? has it been heard? what's the decision? Tomorrow I'm going to Rangoon—surrounded by the Embassy, which wants me out of the country immediately. Although I managed to get an extension of the Visa until April. The point is that[320] a Foreign Office inspector is expected, and everyone wants to wash their hands. Which amounts to this: the Burmese allow me to stay and the British want me out. So out I go. I don't know where though. The woman in Malaya has withdrawn her invitation to accomodate me there. I shall try and get a visa to Siam, and further, get a job in Bangkok. In the meantime, please cable any news you have about the divorce. I shall be in Rangoon until March 9th—if you get this by then, cable "Wevill, Britcoun, Rangoon." If not wire Mandalay, where I shall return to pack. I don't know where I'll be after that—but if you write to Mandalay, the letters will be forwarded.[321]

I haven't heard from you for 6 weeks. Did you feel that my letter was unanswerable? are you going to UBC? Are you well? I dreamt about you last night, and the night before—I dream about you every night strange, always marvelous good dreams. Please wire, and write in detail. I shall still be here if you write immediately.

Assia

319. The letter is not postmarked and presumably was never sent.

320. "The point ~~of~~ is that" appears in the original.

321. AW and DW are married in Rangoon on May 16, 1960, the day after AW's thirty-third birthday. AW and DW left Burma two days after they were married, heading to England via Ceylon and the Suez Canal. They had planned to arrive in Vancouver in September but settled in London instead.

TO PATRICIA AND MICHAEL MENDELSON ALS,[322] Stanford

Saturday, May 21, 1960

on the Glorious Worcestershire[323]
May 21st 60

Darling Mendelsons,

We received your letter[324] hairs before embarking—congratulations on Andria[325]—may she be gorgeous! What an exciting letter to read, thank you, thank you so much for writing in spite of our swinishness in not replying for so long.

David has been "withdrawn" from Burma on the recommendation of H. E.—rather a shock when it came, and regretfully we left. He is to finish his contract in London, after which we have neither destination nor anything much firm in mind. The reason is obvious—me. A Foreign Office inspector is due in Rangoon this week and I guess the old coward felt weaker than ever in spite of his earlier protestations of concern. Aunt Elwyna (Owen) is jubilant. She has made the 1st female Representative to Aden (incredible, isn't it?) and is of all extraordinary facts, here, right here on the ship with us—and last night the Chief Steward sent her to our table . . . David revived me with orange juice.

I'm sorry we can't help you with photographs. Your letter went to Mandalay and therefore took another 8 days to reach us. I'm so sorry—had we written this wouldn't have happened.

We left Rangoon on the 21st—and are therefore due in London 5—weeks from today. Do you think you could possibly find a large cheap (not over £4) room for us in Hampstead?[326] We are both rather frightened of arriving in London with nowhere to go and mountains of luggage in tow. Please don't go to any discomfort for this—we could stay in a hotel for the 1st 2 nights and look

322. The letter has two postmarks: June 9, 1960, from Paquebot, Aden, Yemen; and June 12, 1960, from London.

323. AW and DW are on the MV *Worcestershire*, owned by Bibby Brothers & Company, and they disembarked at Tilbury on the River Thames in Essex, England, on June 24, 1960.

324. See the letter from Nathaniel Tarn to DW and AW, May 10, 1959, held by Stanford University.

325. Andrea Rose is the Mendelsons' daughter. She was born on April 9, 1960.

326. In the early 1960s, the Mendelsons lived at 21 Kidderpore Gardens, London, NW3, in Hampstead, an affluent residential area in London. Historically, it has been associated as a place that attracted liberal intellectuals, artists, and writers.

around after that, but if you happen to hear[327] of a room at about June 21st–30th please take it for us.

Is there anything we could get at Aden for you? if so, wire the ship at Aden—or at any rate write to us at Suez: Wm Stapleton u Sons, Port Said.

Oh how wonderful to think that we shall see you again soon—very soon. Kiss Andria for me.

Love
Assia

TO CELIA CHAIKIN

ALS with envelope, Emory[328]

Tuesday, June 7, 1960

May 7th 1960[329]
200 miles South of Aden.

My dearest,

As I've promised, I'm writing from Aden. I have nothing new to tell you. I turn over in my mind the words in your letter about Australia. It still seems dreadful to me—I feel instinctively that it would be wrong and foolish of you to leave Canada—however inviting things look in Australia. I wish again that you would tell me exactly what Grisha[330] proposes for you—and whether he knows all about your situation. Above all—I cannot reconcile myself to the possibility that I may not see you again if you go to Australia.

I wonder if there will be a letter from you at Aden tomorrow.

I shan't be able to send you any more fresh news until we reach London on June 24th—over 2 weeks from now.

327. "happen to ~~find a ro~~ hear" appears in the original.

328. AW offers 19 Hans Place, London, SW 3, as her return address on the envelope. Today Hans Place is a highly desirable and exclusive residential area that features a private garden square. The garden square is listed on the Register of Historic Parks and Gardens. Hans Place borders a high-end shopping district; AW's address is south of Harrods, where she liked to shop. Located within the Royal Borough of Kensington and Chelsea, Hans Place is also close to important museums, universities, and embassies.

329. Based on internal evidence, AW misdated the letter. It is more likely the letter was written on June 7, 1960, instead of May 7, 1960.

330. Grisha Gutmann is the uncle of AW and CC. He resided in Australia.

We are utterly bored and weary with this ship and its dreadful passengers.

Vatik—I have brought you 100 Burmese cheroots from Burma—I hope you like them. They are the best cigars made in Burma.

We are both slightly depressed with the heat and boredom. The heat is expected to be 125° in the Red Sea. Tonight we shall sleep on the deck.

Oh I'm so tired of travelling!

Please write to me and tell me your news. We've got a little beautiful white mouse with us with eyes red like rubies. The mouse lives in a drawer—perhaps she will survive all the way to Canada.[331] Tell Ronny about her. How is Ronnie? I've brought him a Jungle slingshot, the kind with which the Burmese hunt very seriously in the jungle—I hope he likes it. Also a Chinese toy. You never mention him—only his brother.

Please write write. I dream about you often. Oh God I wish I could see you immediately.

ever liebes kind,[332]
Assia

TO CELIA CHAIKIN

TLS, Emory

Thursday, September 22, 1960

10 Addison Gardens,
London W.14.
September 22nd 1960.

My dear Cillinka—

I have not forgotten your birthday. Many happy returns my dear, and may this be a good year for you. Also congratulations on Tamara—a lovely name, she should, with you as her mother and name like that be a beauty.

I have written Ronny a long letter, but forgot to put the name of the house on it, I just wrote 'Palmer Avenue' I hope he gets it, it was such a large letter that I sent it by sea-mail. I meant to write to you earlier this week—but I have been so harrowed during my working day and so dead tired at night that I never

331. DW recalls that the white mouse was a gift from an Israeli scientist; it survived the trip back to England in 1960 in a drawer and lived with the couple for a few more years.

332. *Liebes kind* is German for "dear child."

got round to it—until now, i.e. after office hours, on office typewriter. Then I thought of sending a telegram, but that would have meant missing lunch for 2 days—and since I don't eat breakfast either nowadays, that would have been too hungry-making.

The flat we negotiated for earlier, has fallen through. We found, on reading the leases, that the lease amounted to exactly half the time that the owners said it would. We've found another flat—address above with garden, overlooking park, with Central heating. Not cheap.[333] Not at all cheap, but I cannot endure the squalor of Knightsbridge very much longer. At last, after years, after dreaming for years, they have taken me on as a copywriter trainee script-writer at Notleys.[334] Training for six months, and after that I shall be able to make real money.[335] All my accounts will be fashion accounts. I'm pleases though I wish this had happened several years ago . . .

I think, just in case anything unwarranted happened, that perhaps you'd better address your letter to Notley's: i.e.

"NOTLEY ADVERTISING LTD.,

15 Hill Street, London W.1.

Not a word from Mutti and Vati—and I wrote so promptly last time . . . are they well?

Are you well? I do hope you're not overtired—which I'm sure you will invariably be. Dick has just been presented with a son, although the son is a bastard. It will be very difficult for him to get a divorce now, because he has

333. AW and DW's new address (10 Addison Gardens, now Lower Addison Gardens) is approximately three miles from the flat they expected to lease at 19 Hans Place. Almost sixty years later—in November 2018—it cost £20,450 on average per month to rent a flat at 10 Upper Addison Gardens, London, W14, and £2,100 on average per month to rent a flat at 10 Lower Addison Gardens.

334. Notley Advertising Limited is a London-based advertising agency that was acquired by Saatchi & Saatchi in 1972. Acquiring Notley caused Saatchi & Saatchi to double in size. Many promising and ambitious writers worked in advertising in this era. Among AW's coworkers at Notley was poet Peter Porter (1929–2010), whom AW helped to secure the job. According to Koren and Negev, "Notley's advertising agency was famous for employing poets: Peter Redgrove, William Trevor, and Edward Lucie-Smith were all working there at the time. Assia joined them for a drink at the pub, with David [Wevill] and other copywriter-poets who worked in nearby agencies" (*Lover of Unreason,* 65).

335. AW's salary as a trainee was five hundred pounds for the year. In 1961, she accepted a copywriting job at Colman, Prentice and Varley, which offered her double the salary she was making at Notley (Koren and Negev, *Lover of Unreason,* 77).

perjured himself in the divorce application, and he may be slapped into jail if he proceeds with it. His mistress is furious.[336] Ho ho ho.

It is ironic that his child was born at the time that I had my miscarriage.[337] I'm all well now—now—though I had an infection after I left the hospital. Winter is here. Grey, bloody and cold. I like the world now. I'm happy.

I hope you are. My love to M & V. and several long kisses for Ronny.

Assia

TO LONYA AND ELIZABETHA GUTMANN

ALS with envelope, Emory

Friday, November 4, 1960

10 Addison Gdns.
London W.14
November 4th 1960

My dear Muttinka u Vatile,

Thank you very much indeed for your letters. I was so delighted to read that you are comparatively well, and uncomparatively happy with most things.

I missed a heart-beat when I read that you were thinking of coming to Europe—My God. are you really? but why not this summer? by next summer, Europe may be less Europe and more America, or not Europe at all but part of the Western Chinese Empire . . . come this summer, come please, those ships may never be built, and God knows if I shall see you then. If I am still with Notley's after the next 5 months, I shall be earning more money, if I'm not with Notley's, I would be earning much more money somewhere else, and could probably help you with the fare.

I'm in hospital again. Unbelievably, I have had another miscarriage, another curetáge.[338] Next week I shall see a gynaecologist (privately). Apparently my

336. RL welcomed a baby with his partner, who was married at the time.

337. AW and DW were expecting a child. According to her biographers, AW was looking forward to this pregnancy, as were her parents. See Koren and Negev, *Lover of Unreason*, 75–76.

338. *Curetage* is French for "curettage," which is the medical practice of removing tissue by scraping or scooping.

womb was titled sideways. In hospital, they all believed me to be unmarried, and an attempter of my own abortion.[339] The nurses were marvelous—all Catholic, some nuns—the sisters must have been the pick of sisters in England. Discipline not so military, and the atmosphere consequently much improved. The misery of old old patients, 80–101, indescribable. I was very depressed and cried all yesterday afternoon.

Please thank Ronny for his letter. I shall write him soon.

I'm sorry Ronny behaves badly, but please don't tell Cilly, but I think, being her 1st child he was inconsistently treated, confused, and now, as in the textbooks, abominably behaved. But never mind—be kind to him, very kind, on my behalf, and he will I'm sure behave better. Somebody must have started the bribery business, otherwise he would not be as intractible as he appears to be now.

David is working at the Japanese.[340] He is getting more and more poetry published, with requests from Vancouver for poems. He will one day be recognized for what he is, a very fine poet—I know this does not impress you much, but it would make me very happy.[341] I think he is about ready to bring out a book next year.

He writes superb things—and I know and I can help him and I do.

I'm very tired. The weeping was so tiring.

Please write soon.

My love
Assinka

339. Abortion was illegal in England until 1968, when the Abortion Act of 1967 legalized it in some circumstances.

340. Born in Yokohama, Japan, to Canadian parents, DW and his family relocated to Toronto, Ontario, Canada, before World War II.

341. In 1963, DW would win the Eric Gregory Award, a British poetry award; he was selected by the Society of Authors and was the first Canadian to be awarded the prize.

TO SYLVIA PLATH[342]

TLS, British Library

Tuesday, May 22, 1962

May 22nd

My dear Sylvia,

Today I got the tapestry for you, or rather the materials for it. The pattern can only be had directly from the Sunday Times[343] now. According to your descriptions of roses and ribbon, it looks as though the one you had in mind is called the Sunday Times Rose Bouquet, and was published about 2 years ago.[344] I rang the Sunday Times, but the girl who deals with it was out. Harrods assure me that the pattern can still be had.

Tramming: that's when you stretch the thread across 5 or 6 inches of the canvas, and then work over it diagonally. I couldn't remember the word, d'you remember? but you'll see it clearly illustrated in the pattern. I bring it up again, because for tramming on this canvas use half the thread (quite easily divided) because otherwise you will overseed the stitches and everything will be too bulgy and fibrous.

Rather than encourage you to wander in the wastelands of trying to match the shading on the diagram with whatever you can find in the way of wool, I bought the whole shooting match, this will make things much easier for you, at least on your first tapestry. However, if you hate some of the colours (I thoughtactually that entirely white roses shaded with grey would be prettier) you could easily change them at Harrods, or send them to me, and I'll change them. On the little card you'll find certain substitutions in wool numbers,[345]

342. The recipient of this letter is American poet and novelist Sylvia Plath (1932–63). SP attended Smith College (graduated in 1955) and Newnham College, Cambridge (graduated in 1957). She is the first wife of Ted Hughes and mother of Frieda Rebecca Hughes (1960–) and Nicholas Farrar Hughes (1962–2009). SP posthumously won the Pulitzer Prize in Poetry for *The Collected Poems* in 1982.

343. Founded in the 1820s, the *Sunday Times* is an influential London newspaper known for its high-quality reporting on politics and the arts.

344. The *Sunday Times Rose Bouquet* was printed in "Mainly for Women," *Sunday Times Magazine,* January 17, 1960, 19. The tapestry was designed by Anita Skjold. SP started but did not finish the tapestry. After SP's death, Elizabeth Sigmund discovered and completed the tapestry; however, over the years it eventually "crumbled and disintegrated into nothing." See Elizabeth Sigmund and Gail Crowther, *Sylvia Plath in Devon: A Year's Turning* (Stroud: Fonthill Media, 2014), 70.

345. "in ~~number~~. wool numbers," appears in the original.

this is because Harrods had run out of the one manufacturer's wools, and substituted with another manufacturers who uses a different numbering system. I hope that at least some of this makes sense. I am writing in a tremendous hurry.

Let me warn you again that you can become seriously addicted to tapestry, and you might find yourself staying up too late at night doing it, or stop eating, or mending and baking and working[346] Please, please don't let it possess you . . . But I hope you'll enjoy it.

Much love,
Assia

TO TED HUGHES[347]

ALS, Emory

Circa Thursday, August 15, 1962[348]

Thursday

for the first time, I wonder which Hughes reads this—Ted. I've bathed you out of my skin and I smell safely of Harrod's best soap[349]—

I've been at home all day—with my effulgent bladder (alright?) reading The Devil,[350] drawing all day. All day. Sometimes I read The Wound.[351]

The bottle-opener has left a small rosy map-lake on my wrist. Bring a postcard with you, and on it a short manifesto and a razor-blade—and we'll celebrate your birthday so fabulously—there won't ever be another like it.[352]

Where have you banished me to this time?

A.

346. This word runs off the page and only "worki" is visible.

347. The recipient of this letter is English poet Edward James "Ted" Hughes (1930–98). TH attended Pembroke College, Cambridge (graduated in 1955). He is the first husband of SP; they were married from 1956 until her death in 1963. AW and TH began an affair in the summer of 1962. TH went on to become the poet laureate of England; he was appointed to the position in December 1984 and served until his death on October 28, 1998.

348. The date is supplied from internal evidence.

349. "best soap—~~and it's just like flushing your letters down the CPV lavatory~~." appears in the original.

350. *The Devil* is a Russian novella by Leo Tolstoy. It was published posthumously in 1911.

351. TH's play *The Wound* was first broadcast on the BBC on February 1, 1962; it was rebroadcast on February 17 and July 14, 1962.

352. TH's birthday is August 17.

TO CELIA CHAIKIN

TLS,[353] Emory

Tuesday, December 18, 1962

14 Highbury Place
London N.5.
December 18th 1962.

My dear Cillinka,

Thank you so much for your letter. That was very generous of you, considering that piggishly I hadn't written first. Bloody Christmas I do hate it, really, it's all like a school prize giving, when you know in advance that you're not going to get the worthwhile prize anyway. It's never really been Christmas since I left home.[354]

We've moved into a new flat, as you can see from the address.[355] It overlooks a park, it's centrally heated; it's an old Georgian house which has been completely modernised.[356] It has a huge living room and a small bedroom. I shall take pictures of it, when it's finished, and send them to you.

353. A square cutout of an angel is affixed to the left-hand side of the letter. AW drew a speech bubble that reads: "WHO's speaking? speak up, I can't hear ya." A drawing of a bull to represent Taurus is taped to the bottom right-hand corner of the letter, and AW drew a speech bubble with the following: "hello? hello? hello? Are you there—Cillik you angel you? It's me your bewildered loving Taurus. (Kind, steadfast, forever loving, broad shouldered) it's me wishing you a happy New Year. And to the children joyful, tearless New Year. And to Arnie customers with honest hearts and lots of it. And to you lots of sleep and black cashmere and an iron nervous system." Apparently, AW intended the angel graphic to represent her sister, Celia, and the bull graphic to represent her speaking to Celia. AW's astrological sign was Taurus the bull.

354. With the strong encouragement of her parents, AW left home and was sent to London in 1946 for the express purpose of marrying John Steele. In order to obtain a British passport for AW that would ostensibly allow her family to join her in England, her parents expected her to locate Steele in his home country after he returned and marry him. Assia married Steele on May 17, 1947, when she was twenty years old. Independently of marriage plans, Assia applied, was accepted, and enrolled as an art student at the Regent Street Polytechnic School of Art in London, where she planned to specialize in art and interior decorating. By 1950, Assia's father, mother, and sister had settled in Canada, initially following her move to Canada with Steele in 1948.

355. AW and DW recently moved from a flat at 3 Chalcot Square, London, which was sublet from SP and TH beginning in September 1961. SP and TH had taken a three-year lease of Chalcot Square in February 1960, but SP and TH decided to move because of the small size of the flat and their growing family. In December 1962, the Wevills moved to the flat at 14 Highbury Place, London.

356. The residences in this area are Georgian and Victorian townhouses to this day. AW's flat would sell for more than one million pounds in today's currency. Where AW lived overlooked Highbury Fields, which comprise twenty-nine acres of cultivated green space.

I'm enclosing a little cheque for Ronny—for him to buy himself whatever he likes. Encourage him to spend it, rather than save it. A happy birthday to Ronny.

Other things. Other things come on another page.

Muttinka wrote me a sweet letter this morning—sending back the cheque I sent her. Cillik—could you, if you have the time buy Vatik the full recording of Boris Goudeonov[357]—this is my birthday present to him. If I send him a cheque he will only send it back, I know that now. Cillik, I must go now, little Cillinka. Have a happy Christmas. I shall write you more fully, the next time you write to me. I'm sorry Tamara has tonsil troubles, poor little darling. If I were richer, I'd have bought everybody presents. But this moving entails new carpets and all kinds of little things and the overdraft at the bank is killing me. But I'll certainly buy you something good at the sales.

And a happy new year to you all.

Assia

£5 is for Vati
£1 " " Ronny
O. K. ?[358]

TO TED HUGHES

AL, Emory

Circa 1962–63

As I was sealing this envelope I heard the key turning. I quickly pushed the envelope under the sofa, but he caught the quickness of my moving. There was a short, sad, scene. I was furious at my clumsiness—at my unintentional tormenting of him.[359]

357. *Boris Goudeonov* refers to *Boris Godunov,* the title of a famous Russian opera by Modest Mussorgsky (1839–81). The opera is based on content from Aleksandr Pushkin's play *Boris Godunov* (1831).

358. The instructions to distribute funds are handwritten by AW.

359. AW writes about DW returning home and discovering AW hiding a letter to TH under the sofa in the home she shares with DW. AW is caught between DW and TH. According to Koren and Negev, "In matters of the heart Assia always took her time. She was not an initiator; she was a responder" (*Lover of Unreason,* 110).

Now I begin to think, superstisiously—that when I'm possessed with you, you magically have dispossessed me—and vice versa. When I feel free of you—then surely you want me most—if only there was a way of testing it:. It's Thursday—8:$^{\underline{30}}$ p.m. and you are in total possession.

Now—now—have you forgotten me?

TO JANNICE PORTER[360]

ALS, *Lover of Unreason*

Circa Wednesday, March 20, 1963

Wednesday.

Darling Janice,

I tried to phone you today—but half-way through the 12th ring realized that you'd be out.

Tomorrow is the day. I found a very old Pole in Maida-Vale.[361] It should be alright. At least he was kind and human. I had to go and see a succession of Harley St. bastards. Oh Janice. At least it'll be over by noon tomorrow.[362]

Could you come to visit me on Friday, or Saturday in the ghost-house?

23 Fitzroy Rd. N.W.1.[363]

(It's just round the corner from Chalcot Sq.)

And please burn this note.

Love
Assia

360. Shirley Jannice Henry Porter (1933–74) had married Peter Porter (1929–2010) in 1961, and they considered AW a close friend. In addition to being AW's friend, Jannice Porter was a nurse by occupation.

361. Maida Vale is an affluent residential district in West London.

362. AW is alluding to a scheduled abortion.

363. SP lived at 23 Fitzroy Road from December 10, 1962, until her death by suicide on February 11, 1963. Following SP's death (hence AW's reference to it as a "ghost-house"), TH relocated to 23 Fitzroy Road, and AW both recovered from her operation and lived there with TH, Frieda Hughes, and Nicholas Hughes when DW was away from London.

TO OLWYN HUGHES[364]

ALS, British Library

Monday, May 20, 1963

23 Fitzroy Road[365]
May 20th 1963

My dear Olwyn—

This is the cover of the New Statesman envelope,[366] all there is within reach. I'm bloody well sick again with cystitis so virulent, I can't move. And again, at the worst possible time! Hilda is home, not speaking to me, is choking with public shock.[367] Difficult to retaliate from bed. Poor Hilda—it is dreadful for her—but she can't change anything at the moment, and her censure is sad, and unmeaningful to me. By an enormous leap of the imagination, I can, just about, put myself in her place as Ted's aunt and demi-guardian; i.e. see how excruciating my existence to her must be. But this is about the limit of my charity. I can't stop to be for her sake.

Never mind.

The nanny. Ted described her—she's vain, unhappy, and longing for unqualified approval. She's been too strict at first, but letting up now. She's also in her menaupause. Worse luck. As Ted said—the outrider of death. Quite obviously she won't stay. I'm giving my notice at the end of the month, and on July 1st I'll be free.[368] I'll look after the children.[369] In the meantime, we'll look for the

364. Olwyn Marguerite Hughes (1928–2016) is TH's sister.

365. AW and DW decided upon a six-month trial separation to assess the state of their marriage, and so DW went to Barcelona, Spain, to write. After DW left the country on May 5, 1963, heading to Spain, AW joined TH, thereby making 23 Fitzroy Road her home too.

366. The envelope may have been related to SP's poem "Child," published in the May 3, 1963, issue of the *New Statesman*.

367. TH's aunt Hilda Annie Farrar (1908–2003) is the sister of TH's mother; Farrar disapproved of the affair between TH and AW and held AW partly responsible for SP's death. She also disapproved of AW's three marriages and what she termed AW's "gypsy looks." According to Jonathan Bate, "Aunt Hilda was the main problem [for TH in making future plans with AW at this time]: she was horrified by Assia, jealous, angry, panicked, afraid of what people would say, anxious about the effect on Ted's reputation" (*Ted Hughes: The Unauthorised Life* [New York: HarperCollins, 2015], 223).

368. AW may be referring to putting in a notice to quit her job at the Colman, Prentis and Varley advertising agency, which is where TH first approached AW about his romantic interest in her, on June 26, 1962.

369. AW means that she will assume primary care of SP and TH's children, Frieda and Nicholas Hughes.

House. When we find one, pray God—by July 1st—by all means please come. Yes, please please come. We've decided not to go to Yorkshire because my presence, Hilda says, would pain your people. Stupidly, I hadn't thought of that.[370]

Your mother[371] is movingly sweet—and self possessed—and altogether very impressive. I'm sorry I had to be the cause of so much misery for her. Alright—this is the last apology I make.

Nick walks about, feeds himself and chants "Dada," dada dada. Frieda is butted between Theresa's[372] discipline and Ted's shortening knee-slide. We've decided to enforce Theresa's edicts, rather than contradict them by going to the other extreme. Oh—the incredible relief of living without a nanny and constantly accommodating a stranger's psychological strains.

When had you thought of coming?

Olwyn—I'm a lousy correspondent.

love
Assia

TO DAVID WEVILL[373]

AL, Emory

Undated, circa 1963[374]

Thursday

My dearest, my sweet.

I saw your note today. I was chilled when I saw that for the first time since we've known each other you addressed me like that. A. like sleet.[375] You're beginning

370. AW did not consider herself to be responsible for SP's death initially. When Julia Matcham, a colleague of AW, approached her about SP's suicide, suggesting that AW must feel guilty, AW reportedly replied: "Why should I? It had nothing to do with me." See Koren and Negev, *Lover of Unreason,* 115.

371. TH and Olwyn Hughes's mother is Edith Farrar Hughes (1898–1969).

372. Theresa is a nanny, or au pair, who had been hired to mind Frieda and Nicholas Hughes.

373. An unpublished love poem (presumably about AW) by DW is on the verso. He refers to the woman about whom he is writing as a princess and his bride, remarking on her black hair, green eyes, and "indifferent body." The short poem ends in the speaker's declaration of love for the woman.

374. DW believes this letter was written in 1963 and was never sent to him.

375. DW would sign his letters to AW using the first initial of his name, as can be seen in his letters at Emory University. However, in the extant letters to her, he would address her with a loving salutation. Apparently, in the letter to which AW responds, he must have addressed her as "A," which is a practice TH employed also.

to hate me. Perhaps no wonder. I went there today.[376] Couldn't stand it. I'm staying with Julia.[377] Some warm comfort. I was sickish this morning. Alright now.

Chalcot Sq. dead as the heater. It's with you I want to be. Yes, with you. Darling—I walked past Langland Gdns.[378] Thinking. Dearest Sweet. David. If you still want me after this—you might hate me too much by then—will start again.[379] Oh David this is so awful. But necessary. Yes, necessary. I think of you almost constantly. Wondering where you might be. Where.

The manuscript looks wonderful in every way. The poems are superb. I read and re-read them finding you over and over again.[380] David. Dearest, my darling. I dread the weekend for us.

TO OLWYN HUGHES

ALS,[381] British Library

Undated, circa spring or summer 1963

olwyn oh Olwyn—

Forgive my not writing.

What d'you think? I feel cautious, but optimistic—and it might solve all kinds of problems. Anyway—please come over. We'll eat anyway, and draft crafty contracts.

Love
Assia

376. It may be that AW is relating her experience of visiting the flat she shared with DW at 3 Chalcot Square. The visit could have taken place after AW and DW decided on a trial separation.

377. This reference could be to Julia Matcham, AW's colleague in advertising. Matcham lived at 346 Bedford Gardens, London, in the Holland Park area, near AW and DW's old flat at 10 Lower Addison Gardens.

378. DW recalls that Langland Gardens is where Liliana Archibald, a friend of DW and AW, lived.

379. They did start again: after DW returns to London on November 2, 1963, he and AW reconcile, eventually settling at 25 Belsize Park Gardens by summer 1964.

380. AW values reading and responding to DW's work, prizing her role as a reader. DW explains that this manuscript is what became the poetry collection *Birth of a Shark* (Macmillan, 1964).

381. AW's letter is at the end of a letter begun by TH. In the letter, TH and AW ask Olwyn whether she would like to go into business with them and a couple, Suzette and Helder Macedo; the proposed company would act on behalf of publishers, offering the work of English-speaking authors for translation.

TO TED HUGHES

AL, Emory

Wednesday, January 22, 1964

22.1.64[382]

My mood has changed about 6 times today. And this is only 5 p.m. I find it very difficult to accept that I shan't see you again. That my future is blanked, with you—that you're no longer in my life. I want to wind everything up, sell everything I possess, move. Start from scratch. I'm surprised at the anger I feel towards you. I'm convinced you've mayhemmed my life. You've left me with a rubbishy life—with nothing to salvage. Absolutely nothing. The only revenge I can take on you is to go to bed with any attractive man who asks me. To hurt your sensations out[383] of my body, if not out of my mind, or blood.[384] And I shall never draw again.[385] I allowed you to go on about seeing you again in 2 weeks because it was intolerable at that moment, to think that it was the last time we touched each other, ever. But that's exactly what it was

TO CELIA CHAIKIN

ALS in greeting card,[386] Emory

Circa September 1964
Printed greeting: HAPPY BIRTHDAY

25 Belsize Park Gdns. NW3

Cillinka.

my pockets, I regret to say—are comparatively unabundant at present. We're moving house—and as you may already have heard from M u V (from whom

382. This letter was written on a narrow strip of a section of what looks like the back of a card.

383. "To hurt ~~you out~~ your sensations out" appears in the original.

384. AW is upset because TH invited Susan Alliston and Tasha Hollis to Court Green to celebrate Christmas in December 1963. Though AW is with DW in London at the time, apparently AW becomes jealous and angry when the gossip reached her after Alliston's return to London. In a January 25, 1964, letter to AW, TH attempts to pacify AW: he informs her that she is all he has, all he ever wanted, and that his plans are pinned to her. He suggests that when he has more money, they should leave England and live a different life together. This TH letter is archived at the Stuart A. Rose Manuscripts, Archives, and Rare Book Library at Emory University.

385. In a January 31, 1964, letter, TH compliments AW on her drawings and urges her to keep sending them to him, even when she cannot post a letter; this letter is held at Emory University.

386. Content of the letter is in a birthday card designed by June for the Gordon Fraser Gallery, Bedford.

I have not heard for what seems ages).[387] I'm expecting an infant child in February.[388] The new address is: 25 Belsize Park Gdns. NW3.[389] I feel marvelously well. Tell me how you are. My love to the children, double love to Ronny. And a birthday kiss for you.

Assia.

TO LUCAS MYERS

AL, Emory

Saturday, March 13, 1965

March 13th 1965

Our dear Lucas[390]—

Thank you three-fold: for the cards particularly the one at Charing +, and the charm-flint which worked, Which Worked, Which Worked!!!

There is of course no way of telling what is worse or less bearable to other people in the way of pain—and I therefore don't know whether this was "easy" or not—it lasted for 9 hours, and except for the last 45 minutes was not unbearable. I emerged whole, ecstatic (in which condition I have been for 10 days) and so did my daughter Schura (to rhyme with Jura) whose full name is Alexandra Tatianna Elise.[391] Miraculously unwrinkled with black hair, very long, and North Sea blue eyes—skin fair as sweet briar. Very equable, tactful, grave, very touching. Above all very touching. Thank you for all your goodwill and luckwill, because it must have worked. Thank you.

387. "M u V" is AW's shorthand for Mutti and Vati, her parents.

388. AW is anticipating the birth of the baby. The baby's father is TH.

389. Belsize Gardens encompasses many thoroughfares, including Belsize Park Gardens, and is considered an expensive residential area.

390. Elvis Lucas "Luke" Myers (1930–2019) first befriended TH during their days at the University of Cambridge, England. They launched *Saint Botolph's Review* together, which was named after Saint Botolph's Church in Cambridge, England. Myers lived in the rectory of Saint Botolph, and the church also was the place the other *Saint Botolph's Review* poets—TH, Myers, Daniel Huws, David Ross, and Daniel Weissbort—considered their spiritual home. It was at the launch party for *Saint Botolph's Review* that TH met SP, on February 26, 1956, at Falcon Yard.

391. Alexandra "Shura" Tatiana Elise Wevill (SW) was born at 9:55 p.m. at Charing Cross Hospital on March 3, 1965. According to AW's biographers, SW was named after Tatiana from Alexander Pushkin's *Eugene Onegin* (1833) and AW's mother, Elizabetha "Elise" (or Lisa) Gutmann (Koren and Negev, *Lover of Unreason*, 146–47). SW is the half-sister of Frieda and Nicholas Hughes.

She was born on the 3rd—there was a snow-storm; both moon and sun were in Pisces with Libra rising.[392] What does that mean? 5 days later when I left Charing +, a gentle almost scented spring grazed England. My hand writing has changed. Very odd.

What are you writing? You sound elated—it must be Good—you are too severe with yourself for spend thrift elation.

David's written a marvelous, long poem called "Our Lady of Kovno"—but he only made one copy and I'm too weak to type it out, but I will, and I'll send it to you.[393]

Dear Luke—be kind to your digestive system—ruthless to distraction and please be bored with Africa! Continue to tell us where you are.

Assia

TO LUCAS MYERS

TLS with envelope, Emory

Thursday, July 15, 1965[394]

Dear Lucas,

We got a controller boy heea what comes from Kingsport,Tenn.[395] I was intolerably desolated to find that he did not know you.

Ted and I went to Spoletto for a paid holiday.[396] And we lived like Americans. And got fat and brown.

392. TH produced an astrological chart for Shura that is housed in the Rose Library at Emory University.

393. "Our Lady of Kovno" was published in the journal *Ambit*, no. 26 (1965–66): 34–35, and in DW's poetry collection *A Christ of the Ice-Floes* (Macmillan, 1966).

394. The letter was mailed in a J. Walter Thompson Company envelope, addressed to Myers in Paris, France, and postmarked July 15, 1965.

395. Myers hails from Sewanee, Tennessee.

396. Jonathan Bate describes AW and TH's trip: "In June, leaving little Shura with the long-suffering David Wevill and a nanny, Assia accompanied Ted to the Festival dei Due Mondi (Festival of the Two Worlds) in Spoleto, an ancient town on a foothill of the Apennine Mountains. Stephen Spender had asked Ted if he would like to travel with him, but Ted explained that he was going with 'a friend'. . . . Founded by the composer Gian Carlo Menotti in 1958, the annual Spoleto event had become one of the great arts festivals, in which Europe met the Americas and practitioners from every field of the creative arts came together. . . . The world's top poetic talent was there" (*Ted Hughes*, 242–43).

It has been raining in England for 11 weeks. Feels like a bog of soda water. My father is going to Russia tomorrow. He said that of all our friends he liked you best. Which I suspect is his way of saying that he liked none of our friends except you.

I met Allen Tate in Italy and assured him of your industry lately.[397] I am impressed by his poetry which I had never read before. And a long childhood reminiscent poem which is his latest and excellent. Also there was Ezra Pound.[398] He didn't speak but looked hand-dressed and about to die like a new magnolia.

Kim is still insane and we haven't seen her. Only Philip who's given her all his money and looks after her devotedly. I feel guilty about not visiting her. Should I visit her?

Other news are outstanding, but more tenuous.

Come back soon.

Assia Wevill[399]

TO LUCAS MYERS

ALS with envelope, Emory

Saturday, September 24, 1965

JWT

Dear Lucas

Thank you for the card. And for the enquiries.

There is really little news. We've found a Spanish Girl with a child to replace Joan Wilson. She'll come in 2 weeks from now. My father returned to Canada.[400] David has won the Arts Council Triannual book prize together with Philip

397. John Orley Allen Tate (1899–1979) is an American poet and critic associated with the southern poetry group the Fugitives and New Criticism. Elaine Feinstein observes that Tate was a relative of Lucas (*Ted Hughes*, 37–38).

398. Ezra Pound (1885–1972) is an influential American poet and critic associated with modernism. He resided in Italy and was seventy-nine years old at the time AW encountered him.

399. AW's name is signed in blue and purple colored pencil.

400. AW's mother passed away on March 18, 1965. Following her death, AW's father went on a three-month tour of Europe, and he took the opportunity to visit AW and SW in London before he returned to Canada.

Larkin.[401] David Ross's childrens' book has been accepted by McMillans.[402] He looks extremely squashed, is silent. Stephanie is more chipper—bears an eerie resemblance to Jill, dusty water. Swallowing Ross in dainty mouthfulls, but not enjoying the meal. The quail died this morning.

London is full of Africans. Dancers, juju men, naked ladies dancing in Trafalgar Square.[403] Witch-dentists, Totem repairmen. It's the absurd, unapt Commonwealth Festival, with queens, receptions, £750,000 budget and no glamour[404]

I'm delighted about the Levy-Strauss arrangement.[405] Now you should meet a lady/girl with a beautiful shed in a quiet suburb, to avoid the winter lice of the Londres. Yesterday David mentioned wanting to go to Paris for a week. But he forgot about it by today. Matters with Ted are precisely at the point they were when you left. I'll let you know if anything changes.

Be well. What a beautiful card you sent.

Be well. And eat meat.

Love
Assia

401. The 1962–65 Arts Council triennial prize of £175 was awarded to DW for his 1964 poetry collection, *Birth of a Shark*. The citation for the award explains that the prize is awarded to "the best first or second book of original English verse published within the three-year scope of the award." British poet Philip Larkin (1922–85) was awarded an Arts Council prize of £250 for *The Whitsun Weddings*. DW and Larkin were the only two awardees of the 1962–65 Arts Council triennial poetry prizes.

402. David Andrews Ross published several children's books with Macmillan, including *Crack the Ant* (1968), coauthored with his second wife, Stephanie, and *Birdfight* (1968).

403. Trafalgar Square is an iconic public square in London.

404. The 1965 British Commonwealth Arts Festival was the first of its kind; events and displays occurred in London, Liverpool, Cardiff, and Glasgow. Maori singers performed in Trafalgar Square, and the Nigerian Duro National Theatre staged performances in all four festival cities. See "The Commonwealth Festival 1982," *The Round Table: The Commonwealth Journal of International Affairs* 72, no. 286 (1983): 182–85. In retrospect, this inaugural festival was an important moment of "postimperial engagement." According to Radhika Natarajan, "Britain hosted visual artists, musicians, dancers, poets, and writers representing national cultures, who together presented a diverse Commonwealth assembled in terms of egalitarian multiculturalism" (705). See Natarajan, "Performing Multiculturalism: The Commonwealth Arts Festival of 1965," *Journal of British Studies* 53, no. 3 (July 2014): 705–33.

405. AW may be referring to Claude Lévi-Srauss (1908–2009), an influential French anthropologist associated with structuralism. He chaired the department of Social Anthropology at the prestigious Collège de France in Paris, where Myers was living at the time.

TO PATRICIA MENDELSON

ALS,[406] Stanford

Sunday, circa December 12 or 19, 1965

Sunday Dec. 65

My dear Patricia,

You seemed so embarrassed by my thanks for all the beautiful things, that I never had a chance to say how immensely grateful I am truly. Ever since she was born I wanted to buy her some really pretty things to wear and the money never stretched that far.[407] So I gave up.

Women are utterly irrational about these things. Indeed, it is a sort of awful conspicuous consumption—in my case, quite fraudulent—but the pleasure they gave me today was quite out of proportion with my whining Puritan conscience's needle pricks.[408]

This evening, she sat there like a real child, no longer just human sea-weed, her small feet dangling between the seat and the 1st step, and she ate real bread and butter and egg, for the first time. And immaculately. Like a real child.[409]

I am ashamed now, to think how ignominiously indifferent I was to Andrea's infancy, and how I let you apologise for your doting. I was a stupid, seriously flawed bitch-woman. Anyway, you are 3 times the person I am.

Assia[410]

406. This letter was written on the inside of a card with these additional handwritten words, in AW's hand, on the verso: "Here's a home-made Christmas gift / Eat it, mes amis with thrift. 1965 AW + D.W."

407. Patricia Mendelson sent clothes as gifts for SW.

408. AW's mother was a Protestant, and AW uses "Puritan conscience" in this sense: "a strict individual conscience requiring high moral standards" (*Oxford English Dictionary,* s.v. "Puritan conscience," special uses). A Puritan is a "person who practices or who is characterized by extreme strictness or austerity in religion, morals, etc. A use arising from the fact that the early Puritans were known for the prominence which they attached to personal religion, for strictness and gravity of behavior, and for plainness of dress and manners" (*Oxford English Dictionary,* s.v. "puritan," A2).

409. SW is nine months old at the time of this letter.

410. After AW's signature, "WEVILL" was added by an unidentified hand.

TO PATRICIA AND MICHAEL MENDELSON

ALS, Stanford

Undated, circa late 1966
Tel. North Tawton 447

Court Green
North Tawton,
Devon.[411]
Thursday.

Dear Pat u Michael,

We did not go to Germany. Neither did we go to Yorkshire.[412] But are here in a nettle Emporium.[413] So are mama u papa.[414] Also many "friends of the family." It is difficult, almost impossible. But not quite.

But my papa is arriving on Sunday. And so I must pick him up at London Docks.[415] If I do not presume on your hospitality too much may I spend the night in your house? alone. Everybody else stays here. If this is not convenient, please phone and reverse the charge.

Love
Assia

411. AW and SW are living with TH, Frieda Hughes, and Nicholas Hughes at Court Green as a blended family unit.

412. TH's extended family hails from Yorkshire.

413. According to SP, Court Green was rampant with actual stinging nettles (*The Letters of Sylvia Plath*, vol. 2: *1956–1963*, edited by Peter K. Steinberg and Karen V. Kukil [New York: HarperCollins, 2018], 644). AW also may have used *nettle* in the sense of it as a verb: sting, irritate, vex, provoke, annoy, incite, and rouse (*Oxford English Dictionary*, s.v. "nettle [v.]"). With *Emporium*, she probably meant "a place where a specified thing is present in abundance," one of its lesser-known definitions (*Oxford English Dictionary*, s.v. "emporium [n.]," 2).

414. AW refers to TH's parents, who lived with TH and AW and their children at Court Green. In 1966, TH and AW were living in Ireland, and Olwyn Hughes requested that TH and AW return to Court Green because, as Jonathan Bate explains, Olwyn Hughes "had finally had enough of domestic duties" and "was off to London to start her agency" (*Ted Hughes*, 246).

415. AW's father is on his way to England from Canada, hoping to relocate so he would be closer geographically to his daughter and granddaughter. Upon arrival, he joined the Court Green household. However, he left Court Green because he was "unable to stand the squabbles" and, subsequently, lodged in a hotel, but a "few months later he returned to Canada, his hopes frustrated, and Assia lost a vital ally" (Koren and Negev, *Lover of Unreason*, 158).

TO TED HUGHES

AL in a handmade card, Emory

Tuesday, February 14, 1967[416]

FOR THE HEART INSIDE THE HEART OF THE DRAGON
FOR CERTAIN FEATHERS IN CROW'S WING, ON THE LEFT THERE
MY BEST
HEART
MY VALENTINE
FEBRUARY 14TH 1967

TO CELIA CHAIKIN

TLS, Emory

Saturday, March 11, 1967

March 11th 1967

My dear Cillinka,

I can't tell you how touched I was by the contents of your parcel, which arrived on Saturday. There were great oohs and xx and ahs from Shura, who inspected every item, pausing at the petticoat with ecstatic "Oh 'OOk, pee-teey!"—Frieda has one which was sent from America which Shura had clearly secretly admired and coveted for months—and here, at last, was one of her own. They dance in it. Shura has been dancing for 9 months now—her head tilted to one side in acute concentration. She dances most successfully to either Bach Cantatas or pop. I played a cantata this morning (Wachet Auf!)[417] and hummed with it—she was alarmed, and then enraged and said: 'Shuddub.' It was awful. She sings very interesting songs at night—and now talks. She's still in nappies, since training which I began gingerly about 10 days ago induced nothing but alarm and constipation. I enclose a recent phyotograph taken of her, and an earlier one, taken at Christmas which I meant to send you ages ago.

416. The card is drawn on paper taken from a small spiral-bound notebook. It features a tree with branches extending to the top of the page, and the roots dissolve into rainbow colors with a heart in the center. Three silhouettes of birds, soaring in the distance, are drawn underneath the branches on the left-hand side of the card. AW's text wraps around the roots and heart.

417. Johann Sebastian Bach (1685–1750) is a German musical composer and musician; he is celebrated for his instrumental and church pieces. His cantata *Wachet Auf, ruft uns die Stimme* (*Awake, Calls the Voice to Us*) was first performed in 1731.

I was also more than touched by Mutti's picture in the frame. That was very generous of you. You can take back the spoon and anything else you may like when you come to visit me. Please come to visit me. I cannot tell you what pleasure and re-assurance that would give me. We may never see each other again unless you do—now—this year. This summer. I have been, literally suicidally depressed during the past week, and am only just emerging out of it. I hereby appoint you as Shura's legal guardian, should I not outlive you. I also hereby bequeathe you, or to you to bequeathe to Shura when you see fit, all my worldly goods, manuscripts, etc. I have made a will which is in a sealed envelope in my desk. Should I ever (I don't really expect to, and certainly never consider it, except at times like this) inherit any money from Vati, I hope you will keep it in trust for Shura, invested in the Montreal Trust.

I am clearly ill. The last four years have been a strain simply too hard to bear.[418] I think, I'm probably paranoid. In fits, not continuously. But when I'm in them, as in the last one, I have packed two trunks for you (they are still in this room, as I write, packed and closed) with a cheque for $1200 to pay for Shura's fare and initial necessities. The continuing presence of Ted's mother, the strain that engenders, the isolation, the hostility and to me, fine contempt of Ted's friends here, are sometimes unendurable. Upt till now I always thought, when in despair that I would leave, return to London with Shura. But I must dismiss that now. I don't have the self-confidence for advertising anymore, things are very difficult in advertising now.[419] I couldn't bear some bloody woman looking after Shura. She is all I have. I adore her, as only I adored Mutti. This is in a fit. When I recover, all these speculations seem nonsensical. I see little of Ted. He works in the morning. We used to lunch with his father (strain) now I lunch with Shura, and he eats with his father alone. I go to my room for the early afternoon, sleep and read for two hours. Then it's tea time. Blackout of food and bath for 3 hours. Twice a week he goes to play snooker with his father and two nits. The rest we spend desultorily

418. The difficult events over the last four years to which AW gestures include the suicide of SP and AW's separation from her husband DW. AW had an affair with TH while he was married to SP. To complicate matters, AW is living in Court Green, TH's residence, with SW, TH himself, Frieda Hughes, Nicholas Hughes, and TH's parents. AW had given up professional success and a lucrative career in advertising to live with TH as a family unit in Ireland (February–May 1966) and then Devon, England (February 1966–spring 1967), before moving to London with SW and taking up her work in advertising again.

419. AW established her reputation in adverting with the acclaimed "Lost Island" Sea Witch commercial in 1965 and with the award-winning "Wood Nymph" commercial in 1967. Both advertisements feature hair coloring products.

in the library. There is no one I care for around here, and I have cold-shouldered his dearest friends, a couple whose presence bores me and with whom in am in fiendish black secret battle. The man[420] is alright, a drama teacher, communist, the woman is my real enemy. An ex-social worker, ex religious maniac but with the looks of an emaciated Marylin Monroe (Brenda, Vati knows her) I beat her hollow in intelligence and experience but she feels that I have usurped her place as the rightful soul of Court Green.[421] Ted spends many afternoons there (she is now pregnant again) and insists that I invite them to dinner. (At the end of the last dinner, she very pointedly did not thank me for quite an elaborate meal.) She hates me, has clearly hated me right away, but is either, or was, rather, too stupid or too cocksure to bother concealing it, as Vati will testify. Ted insists that it's all my fault. I retort that she bores me with her minute accurate reports of the progress of the drainage. She is a bore, Earth Mother, mean, acutely mean. Never mind.

Please come, Cillik. Somehow arrange it, before either of us dies. If you could come alone, that would be better. I am assming Ted's parents will still be here. I could put you up easily in my study, but couldn't put anyone else up, much as I'd love to have seen Ronnie. Perhaps Ronnie could sleep with Shura, or something, there is another bed in her room, but the room is tiny. Please come. I am very seriously asking you to.

Love,
Assia[422]

TO YEHUDA AMICHAI AND HANA SOKOLOV-AMICHAI[423]

TLS, Yale

Tuesday, July 18, 1967

18.7.67

My dear Yehuda, my dear Hannale,

To hand, this morning your letter and The Collected Works. Thank you. I received a missile from Tarn on Monday about 4 contributions to some student mag-

420. AW is referring to Trevor Hedden.

421. Brenda Hedden had an affair with Hughes while he was AW's partner.

422. The name was typed and then written again, over the typed letters, in black ink.

423. German-born Israeli poet Yeduda Amichai (1924–2000) is an acclaimed Israeli writer who was nominated for the Nobel Prize in Literature. His poetry appeared in *Modern Poetry in Transla-*

azine which he edits—and I sent off four. No pay. But copies of the magazine.[424] (What kind of shirts does he wear to write missiles in? what sort of socks?)

What an insane week that was. I seem to remember us there in P.Grady's 7th Salon like the publicum[425] in the Colisseum watching ourselves being watched, the gladiators being our secret selves . . . Neither of you two is guilty.[426]

Here are some of the pictures Helga[427] took. Her unspeakably dreadful husband is here. He's wooing her and appalling Ted. All the things which you were meant to be entertained by (Devon Tea in Chagford,[428] the monsters in Exeter Cathedral,[429] the meat in the refrigerator, The Times in the news agents, Churchill's bodyguard,[430] The Blonde) are all here curious about you. Ted's back is

---

tion, no. 1, a literary magazine that TH and Daniel Weissbort (1935–2013) founded in 1965. TH had encouraged AW to translate Amichai's poems, and Amichai and AW are working on a book together at the time of this letter. On September 22, 2000, the *New York Times* described Amichai as "Israel's most important and influential poet" (https://www.nytimes.com/2000/09/22/continuous/amichai-israelacutes-most-important-and-influential-poet-dies-at.html). Hana Sokolov-Amichai became the wife of Yehuda Amichai.

424. Four of AW's English translations of Amichai's Hebrew poems—"It's a Long Time since Anybody's Asked," "You Also Were So Tired," "Farewell," and "The Place Where I've Not Been"—were published, with the translator's name listed as Anastassia Gutmann, in *Afrasian* 1 (1968), which was a student magazine affiliated with the School of Oriental and African Studies at the University of London. Tarn served as the editor of the special issue dedicated to poetry.

425. AW may mean *publican*. In Roman history, a publican was a tax gatherer, someone "generally regarded as traitorous and impious on account of their service of Rome and their extortion." It also signifies a "person who owns or manages a public house or tavern" (*Oxford English Dictionary*, s.v. "publican," 1a, 3).

426. The Colosseum in Rome was completed in the year 80 CE. It could accommodate fifty-five thousand spectators and was the site of brutal physical contests. Roman gladiators generally were slaves, prisoners of war, or criminals.

427. Helga is the wife of Daniel Huws (1932–), a friend of TH from Cambridge. Daniel Huws is a poet and became a leading authority on Welsh manuscripts, receiving an honorary doctorate in 2017 from the University of Wales in recognition of his work. Helga Huws also served as a confidante to SP. SP confided in her about TH's affair with AW in the summer of 1962 (Bate, *Ted Hughes*, 191).

428. Devon tea is Devonshire tea, a cream tea, typically made up of scones, clotted cream, jam, and tea. Chagford is a market town in Devon in southwestern England. Chagford borders Dartmoor National Park, with the River Teign nearby, making it geographically noteworthy and of interest to tourists.

429. Exeter Cathedral is an Anglican cathedral known for its Gothic architecture. It is located in Exeter, Devon, England. One can take a virtual tour of Exeter Cathedral on its website.

430. AW may be referring to Walter H. Thompson (1890–1978), who served as the bodyguard of Sir Winston Churchill (1874–1965) and published a memoir entitled *I Was Churchill's Bodyguard* in 1951 that brought name recognition to Thompson in the United Kingdom.

miraculously and suddenly better—both he and I suspect that the reason for the estrangement between Ted and his spine was the awful[431] premonition about the Festival.[432] Simply not his natural role in life.

Be well. Be wary. Come back to Devon. And thank you for coming in the first place. You were the most agreeable guests we've ever had.[433]

Ted said he will phone you this evening.

Assia

P.S. I'm devoting an hour every morning and an hour in the afternoon to the translations—at this rate I should be able to send Maschler[434] the lot by the middle of August. That should meet a September publication.[435]

A.

431. "and his spine ~~is~~ was the awful" appears in the original.

432. AW probably means the first Poetry International Festival, which took place July 12–16, 1967. TH invited Amichai to read his work as a featured poet, alongside Bella Akhmadulina, W. H. Auden, John Berryman, Yves Bonnefoy, Hans Enzensberger, Allen Ginsberg, Robert Graves, Anthony Hecht, Patrick Kavanagh, Hugh MacDiarmid, Pablo Neruda, Anne Sexton, Stephen Spender, and Giuseppe Ungarett. Bate explains that the festival was TH's "brainchild, hatched in collaboration with the theatre director Patrick Garland" (*Ted Hughes*,252).

433. According to Koren and Negev, "Assia instantly fell for Yehuda Amichai and his wife Hannah who, like her and Ted, had experienced the joys and torments of an illicit affair; the 43-year-old poet had left his wife a few years earlier, after falling in love with Hannah, a young fellow teacher. They had been waiting impatiently for Amichai's much-delayed divorce to come through." AW wrote this letter "to her new Israeli friends after their overnight stay at Court Green. She found common ground with Amichai, who had fled Nazi Germany as a child with his parents, just like her" (168).

434. Thomas Michael Maschler (1933–2020) is the head of the London publishing house Jonathan Cape, which was founded in 1921. In 1967, Jonathan Cape acquired Goliard, forming the imprint Cape Goliard; Tom Maschler and AW's friend Nathaniel Tarn were instrumental in the merger. Cape Goliard published Amichai's *Selected Poems* (1968); these poems were translated by AW under the name Assia Gutmann, the name she employed for most of her translations of Amichai's poetry. By 1987, Jonathan Cape had merged with other leading British publishing groups and was acquired by Random House. Jonathan Cape was considered a prestigious publisher; see Edwin McDowell, "Random House to Buy British Group," *New York Times*, May 8, 1987, 29.

435. The postscript is handwritten.

TO ANNE SEXTON[436]

ALS,[437] University of Texas

Wednesday, August 9, 1967

Dear Anne—

Thank you for your letter. It was delightful to have you here, and Lois.[438] Disassociations or no, come again.

To my enormous amazement I find Aurelia[439] both touching and totally admirable. Really a remarkable woman—a kind of near-genius knot herself, coupled with a generosity of spirit which makes me feel humbler than I have ever been.[440]

Oh—and bless your mother in law![441]

Keep well.[442]

Assia.

436. Anne Sexton (1928–74), a confessional poet, was good friends with SP. Sexton won the 1967 Pulitzer Prize in Poetry; the announcement was made in April, four months before this letter from TH and AW.

437. AW's portion of the letter was written at the end of a letter started by TH, which has not been transcribed.

438. Lois Sisson Ames (1931–) is SP's Wellesley High School and Smith College classmate, who also attended the University of Chicago; she married Robert Webb Ames (divorced in 1969). Ames was a friend of Sexton and was the authorized biographer of SP but failed to produce a book.

439. Aurelia Schober Plath (1906–94) is SP's mother and TH's former mother-in-law.

440. "feel humbler than ~~for years~~ I have ever been" appears in the original.

441. Sexton's mother-in-law is Wilhelmine (Muller) Sexton (1903–86).

442. Sexton, who had broken her hip in late 1966, is recovering from the injury at the time of this letter. She also continues to struggle with her mental health.

TO TED HUGHES

TL/AL in a handmade card,[443] Emory

Thursday, August 17, 1967

Apple, apple
on the Tree,
I love Ted
Does he love
Me?[444]

Apple, Apple
In the bowl,
Say I'm cold
In my South
Pole![445]

Apple, Apple
On the hood
Tell how I'm
Trying to be
good . . ."[446]

For sweet Ted on his birthday,[447] some apples: August 17th 1967[448]

443. The card features three flaps that open upward. The first flap is decorated with an apple tree; the second illustrates a bowl filled with two apples; and the third presents a dandy with a heart on his plumed hat and an arrow racing to meet it. A flower, partly shaded, decorates the verso.

444. AW typed these lines under the first flap of the card.

445. AW typed these lines under the second flap of the card.

446. AW typed these lines under the third flap of the card.

447. TH turned thirty-seven.

448. Underneath the vibrantly colored and cheerful images drawn on the flaps are these words in the center of the card; they are written in calligraphy.

TO YEHUDA AMICHAI AND HANA SOKOLOV-AMICHAI

TLS, Yale

Saturday, August 19, 1967

Court Green,
North Tawton, Devon.
August 19th 1967

My dear Yehuda, my dear Hanna,

There you are in an unknown building, unknown weather surrounded with barely remembered smells (aired mutton entrails? something like that) and here I am in the library thinking very intensely of you, and the rats are scrabbling amongst Ted's papers: How amazing that you were here a whole season ago, and everything seemed punctuated and more important and more vivid. I do miss you so much, and the thought that you are no longer even in some oblique address in London really pains me.

I have no news except of all kinds of declarations of intent on Olwyn's[449] part—how Penguins should have been offered the manuscript and how you'd have got £ 250 for it—and that she's doing just that, and writing to you. . . . and sending a copy of the letter to me—but so far, none has come. I have now translated 14 of the 21 poems on the list—which leaves 7—I should do them within a month, completely—completely enough to send to Maschler.[450]

I have applied to Texas—or[451] rather I have finally typed out that terrible school-essay type letter where I say how important and splendid you are, Yehuda, and what my incredibly impoverished qualifications are to translate you. And they are, (the letter, the poems) in an envelope—waiting for Ted to wait for the world to stop spinning long enough for him to find the address.

He is hiding in the hut writing a childrens' play[452] for which the deadline was last month. The tomatoes are ripening. We have printed a set of rules for

449. Olwyn Hughes became TH's agent and worked in that capacity for other important literary figures, including Jean Rhys, beginning in late 1963. See Bate, *Ted Hughes*, 235.

450. AW began another sentence beginning "Ted re" but struck through it.

451. "Texas—~~Ted noted that I shan't get a grant if a publisher~~,or rather" appears in the original.

452. AW is likely referring to what became TH's *The Coming of the Kings and Other Plays*, which is considered a book for children. It was published by Faber and Faber in 1970. Jonathan Bate observes that *The Coming of the Kings* is TH's "homage to T. S. Eliot's 'Journey of the Magi'" (*Ted Hughes*, 322).

the children to annoy us less by. They blow soap bubbles in the yard,[453] and Shura's profanities grow daily more amazing.

—we'd so love[454] to see you—is your festival still serious? is it really possible that we might see you next year?

Please write to me Channa.

Assia

TO PATRICIA MENDELSON

ALS, Koren and Negev

Thursday, August 31, 1967[455]

Thursday

Dearest Patricia,

I'm writing this in a very solemn mood. But to thank you with all my damaged heart for all your sweetness and patience with me in London and your endlessly thoughtful kindness. How could I ever begin to compensate you?

Shura wants "to go by train" again. She's sleeping in a real bed now—sneaking about in the corridors. What a marvelously wholesome atmosphere you seem to live in—and clearly will continue to do all your life.[456]

I'll have to go all theological and say Bless you, darling, marvelous Patricia.

Love to Andrea u Mark.[457]
Assia

453. "in the ~~yeard~~ yard" appears in the original.

454. "~~This is so brief~~—we'd so love" appears in the original.

455. The date is supplied as a result of the postmark (September 1, 1967).

456. "to do ~~so~~ all your life." appears in the original.

457. "Mark" is Marc Mendelson; he was born on March 15, 1963. He is the son of Patricia and Michael Mendelson.

TO MICHAEL MENDELSON

ALS,[458] Stanford

Undated, circa summer 1967

Court Green

Dear Michael,

Here they are—4 of them. I hope you like them—they are not the best Amichai by a long shot. Farewell is one of the best in the book, however.[459]

It was lovely to see you and Pat—I wish I was there on Sunday to eat the cakes.

Please persuade Pat to come down here. I can't bear to think of her alone in London.

David's telephone number is: 794–3350.

love
Assia

TO PATRICIA MENDELSON

TLS, Koren and Negev

Tuesday, September 12, 1967

Court Green
Sept. 12th (Ithink)

Dearest Patricia,

Your parcel arrived and its lovely contents. Thank you, for going to so much trouble on my behalf. The cheque is attached.

Things here have reached a pitch of mild disaster, culminating in a feverish rush to London of mine to try and find a job within 3 days. Through some kind of miracle, I did find one—waiting for the contract to be signed/. The idea being that I spend weekends here, and work for four days in London. That seemed the only working compromise. Ted is exhausted with the war between parents and me, and I seem to be the most expendable factor.[460] Terrible on the children. Insufferable for Shura. She wept throughout the two nights of my

458. Letter is written on the Poetry Book Society Ltd. letterhead.

459. This poem was collected and published as "Farewell You" in Amichai's *Selected Poems* (London: Cape Goliard, 1968) and as "Farewell, You" in *Poems* (New York: Harper & Row, 1969).

460. AW moved out of Court Green as a result of the animosity TH's parents showed her. According to Bate, TH's parents "could not stand Assia. Their constant complaint to Trevor and Brenda Hedden was that [AW] had seduced Ted; because of her three previous marriages, they

absence almost throughout. I didn't ring you, because I couldn't possibly have come to see you in the fever of dashing from interview to interview—at nights I took a sleeping pill and just collapsed into bed.

I feel unendurably sad.

The garden is beginning to wilt—it will never be again—I'm sorry that you've never seen it. All that remains are some photographs. Is this all there is to life? just photographs and passports?

Mike will be back soon. You have all that to look forward to.

Do you know of a flat at around 500 a year, with 2 bedrooms—I don't expect you to know of one for an instant, but should you come across anything, would you let me know?

All my love, to you, and to the children, and to sweet Hoohoo.[461]

Assia

TO PATRICIA MENDELSON

TLS,[462] Koren and Negev

Undated, after fall 1967

To Patricia,

How's this on the right?[463]

I know it doesn't sound right, absolutely.

But it's a starting point of sorts.

Thank you for the Sunday Treat—it made Shura's week.[464] And weren't you sorry you didn't let us wash up?

My God, that poor Madeleine.[465] But he loves her. Why didn't we pick a man

---

called him 'Edward the fourth.' There was a perpetual bad atmosphere" (*Ted Hughes,* 246). AW moved away from Devon and back to London in mid-September 1967 (255).

461. *Hoohoo* is a reference to Patricia Mendelson's mother-in-law, Yvonne Suchar Mendelson, whose nickname is "WhoWho."

462. Letter is typed on Ogilvy & Mather Ltd. letterhead. AW is employed by Ogilvy & Mather of Brettenham House, Lancaster Place, London, WC2, from the fall of 1967 until July 1968.

463. "on the ~~left?~~ right?" appears in the original. AW refers to a clipping affixed to the letter; the clipping addresses volunteering for the National Hospital Service Reserve, which was constituted under the Civil Defence Act of 1948. The program ceased on August 1, 1968.

464. Patricia Mendelson recalls that AW and Shura had lunch with her and her family.

465. Madeleine is a school friend of Patricia Mendelson.

like that for a husband. Those are the only kinds which work. You don't have to answer that. It's them bloody artists what bash up womens' souls. I'm telling you.

Anyway, I love you.
Assia

TO YEHUDA AMICHAI

TLS, Yale

Tuesday, October 31, 1967

Flat 14
51 Marlborough Place,
London N.W.8.
Oct. 31st 1967

My dear Yehuda,

Thank you for your letter. I'm delighted at the vertiginous volume of things which you're bringing out—how excellent for you! Also bravo bravo bravo for the 3rd edition—that pleases me; it's such a sweet revenge on time! on Them.

As for Penguin: this is by no means completely out—it's stammering rather than singing. But don't write it off.

As for Denis Silk:[466] Of course, I shall ask Maschler to put his name under Silk's version of Ibn Gabirol.[467]

As for Nova:[468] I rang them five minutes ago. Moraes[469] is no longer on their 'permanent staff'—however the issue into which your article is to go has not been assembled yet, but will be within the "very near future." They are (Nova, that is) writing to you.

466. Dennis Silk (1928–98) is an English poet, playwright, and translator. Born in London, Silk died in Jerusalem. Silk edited *Fourteen Israeli Poets* (London: A. Deutsch, 1976), a collection of Israeli poetry in translation, and *Retrievements: A Jerusalem Anthology* (Jerusalem: Israel Universities Press, 1968). Amichai described him as "a subtle and powerful poet. Every poem is a small drama—very strong and powerful and unforgettable" (Oliver Bernard, "Obituary: Dennis Silk," *UK Independent,* August 15, 1998, https://www.independent.co.uk/arts-entertainment/obituary-dennis-silk-1171685.html).

467. "of ~~The~~ Ibn Gabirol" appears in the original. Solomon Ibn Gabirol (ca. 1022–[1058–70?]) is a medieval Hebrew poet. The first poem in Amichai's *Selected Poems,* co-selected and translated by AW, is titled "Ibn Gabirol."

468. *Nova* is a British monthly periodical in print from March 1965 to October 1975.

469. Dom Morales (1938–2004) is an Indian writer and poet.

As for King Saul: Of course, straw makes sense, mud doesn't, I have duly altered it.[470] I am excruciated with sorrow.

I have not received the new poem you said you had sent. Could you send me another copy. That's very bad to have missed that.[471] I should point out though, that since the book will be coming out in January, I doubt very much whether we can still add or subtract or change poems. If you like I shall add these two, or talk to Maschler about it. But I feel he will be angry. Could you send me the other poem in both Hebrew and English?

I have transmitted all your alterations to Cape, which they have apparently faithfully attended to. Now comes disagreement: In King Saul and I: I pondered long about "trained" as compared to exercised, I consulted Ted, and he agreed that exercised is more interesting, ambiguous in a desirable sense, whereas if one used trained one would have to qualify it, i.e. trained to do what? 'exercised' arouses no questions as to purpose. However, if you're unhappy about it, I shall change it to trained.

Ted is well and has just finished an Opera Liberetto[472]—he looks well and has all kinds of new and splendid clothes, he looks rather like a darker, bigger more threatening version of Patrick Garland.[473]

My love to Channa,
and to you a warm goodbye
Assia

470. AW translated "King Saul and I" for Amichai's *Selected Poems.* She and TH highlighted it in their presentation of Amichai's work on the BBC program "Yehuda Amichai," which aired on Radio 3 on December 12, 1968. AW introduced the poem, and TH read it.

471. In the original letter, AW typed a sentence but struck through it. The editors believe it reads: "And thank you for Tom's."

472. The opera libretto is *The Story of Vasco,* which is based on the play of the same name by the French writer Georges Schehadé (1905–89). TH translated the play from French to English; he was commissioned by the Sadler's Wells Theatre in 1965 to transform the play into a libretto. He spent two years drafting and rewriting the libretto. Parts of TH's work were performed by the Sadler's Wells Opera at the London Coliseum in March 1974. Director Adam Barnard pieced together TH's *The Story of Vasco* from TH's archive at Emory University, and the result was produced at the Orange Theatre, Richmond upon Thames, in March 2009. See Bate, *Ted Hughes,* 322; and the article "Undiscovered Ted Hughes Play Set for Premiere," *Guardian,* March 2, 2009.

473. Patrick Garland (1935–2013) is an actor, writer, and English director. As the *Guardian* reported in his obituary on April 22, 2013, Garland founded Poetry International with TH and Charles Osborne (1927–2017).

TO YEHUDA AMICHAI AND HANA SOKOLOV-AMICHAI

TLS, Yale

Undated, circa November 17, 1967[474]

My dear Yehuda and Channa—

Look, here it is! the contract! yes, yes. And a crackling letter from Olwyn accompanied it—please sign it and return it to her.

Oh Yehuda, surely Murray Mindlin[475] can send you books or records or hypodermic needles with Nova's fees, thank you for your sweet offer, which, of course is absolutely out of the question. But thank you infinitely all the same,; if there is any shopping I can do for you Channa, please let me know.

As for Penguin, now turns out that nothing of real consequence has come of any negotiations yet—Olwyn wants a copy of the translations for Penguin to see—I'll have to type out another copy then. It would be nice, wouldn't it?

Texas[476] don't want anything translated by way of verse which has been published in the last 5 years, which means 'no.' They'd like me to do some prose—no thank you.

I'm sending this off in a great hurry. And much love,

Assia

474. The date is supplied by internal evidence because the date on the letter was torn from the page. Visible text reads "17." The letter would have been written on the seventeenth of the month.

475. M. (Meir) Murray Mindlin (1924–87) is an author and editor who also worked for the publisher Frank Cass. He wrote favorable reviews and discussions of Amichai's work in various outlets. Associated with editorial and other service work for the journal the *China Quarterly,* Mindlin wrote poems, too, and his *Dead Reckoning and Other Poems* (London: Faustus, Menenader) was published in 1974. Amichai's section 6 of "Names, Names, in Other Days and in Our Time," from *Open Closed Open* (1998) and collected in *The Poetry of Yehuda Amichai* (New York: Farrar, Straus and Giroux, 2015), is about Mindlin's wife, Andrea. They had a daughter, Miranda Juliet (1964–), and a son, Jeffrey Michael (1968–).

476. AW may mean the *Texas Quarterly,* a journal that published poetry and ran from 1958 to 1978. Alternatively, she may be referencing the University of Texas Press, which published translations of poetry, such as English translations of Rubén Darío's poems, in 1965.

TO YEHUDA AMICHAI AND HANA SOKOLOV-AMICHAI

TLS, Yale

Tuesday, November 21, 1967

Flat 14,
51 Marlborough Place,
London N.W.8.
November 21st 1967

My dear Yehuda & Channa,

First, to thank you for your letter. And for the poem, and for the corrections, which I have long ago submitted to Maschler from which direction there is a busy silence.

However, there has been no silence from Olwyn, from whom you may have heard by now. She had sent the book to Alvarez[477] at Penguin, who liked it very much, and would like to publish it as a half-Penguin with another 21 poems from you.[478] At a hair-raising guess, I would say that the other half will be someone as sympatisch as Rokeah.[479] But this is guessing. Anyway, would you like to send me 20 poems from your new book, or from your old book, as you like, with a rough English translation. Or, more practically, send me 5 poems at a time. I would like to see the Hebrew originals first, though, because that's where the real magic lies, which stimulates me.[480]

Two weeks ago a battle of mammoths was fought between Maschler and Olwyn about the American rights. Tom was being sly and underhanded, contravening the clause in the contract which gave you and me the American rights. This came out in the open in error. Maschler said that if he doesn't have the American rights, Olwyn can have the manuscript back. In the meantime she had sent Alvarez another copy, returned to Maschler and said "O.K., I'll have the book back." Maschler then suddenly softened and said that if she can find

477. Al Alvarez (1929–2019) is a British critic and writer.

478. This work in progress became Yehuda Amichai's *Selected Poems,* translated by Assia Gutmann [Wevill] and Harold Schimmel, with the collaboration of Ted Hughes (Harmondsworth, England: Penguin Books, 1971). AW died in 1969, which necessitated an additional translator.

479. David Rokeah (1916–85) is an Israeli poet.

480. "magic lies, ~~and~~ which stimulates me" appears in the original.

an American publisher for the boook within 3 months the rights are ours. If she can't, the rights are his.[481]

VERY STRANGE.

Anyway, there's this Penguin once I finish translating the other 21 poems, which I should be able to do quite quickly now. In this office. Publication will take place about a year after they receive the manuscript. Is that alright with you?

We saw Patrick Garland last night with a box full of the most marvelous pictures from the Festival,[482] mostly of Paz's wife,[483] and you and Channa. And Ann Sexton looking like Mrs. America.[484]

On the same evening, after emerging from the ice-blown underground at Gt. Russell St.,[485] a face, familiar, reddish, ecstatic, surrounded by fur, was suddenly linked to[486] Mindlin and child, and up again, to Mindlin's wife, whose name I can't remember. Mindlin was a little cool. Why was Mindlin cool? His wife was sweet. The child was also furred. Perhaps Mindlin was tired. He looked angry.

Ted sends his love.

When is your American novel coming out?[487]

Hannale, you must write to me. Goodbye to you both,

Assia

481. The first American edition of *Poems* by Amichai and translated by AW was published by Harper & Row on June 18, 1969; the copyrights were assigned to Amichai, with translation copyrights assigned to AW.

482. The Poetry International festival in London was founded in 1967 by TH.

483. Octavio Paz (1914–98) is a Mexican poet and diplomat; his wife is Marie-José Tramini. Paz received the Nobel Prize in Literature in 1990.

484. Earlier in her life, Sexton worked as a fashion model.

485. Great Russell Street is located in Bloomsbury, London.

486. "was suddenly ~~surrounded by~~ linked to" appears in the original.

487. AW is referring to Yehuda Amichai's *Not of This Time, Not of This Place*, translated by Shlomo Katz, published by Harper & Row in 1968.

TO AURELIA SCHOBER PLATH

Excerpt from *American Isis*[488]

Thursday, January 4, 1968

Ted told me that I was no use to him as an invalid (this was during my post-flu depression and sinus and bronchitis and things),[489] and I thought that was the most brutal thing he'd ever said to me, when I nursed him and his mother for three weeks of his slipped disc. I thought suddenly that that degree of brutality would slowly dement me. That I must perhaps think of living without him completely.[490]

TO YEHUDA AMICHAI AND HANA SOKOLOV-AMICHAI

TLS,[491] Yale

Thursday, January 11, 1968

January 11th 1968

My dear Yehuda and Channa,

I can't tell you how horrified I am to have discovered that I seem to have ignored your last three letters. The pressures at work are largely responsible.[492]

488. The letter is quoted in Carl Rollyson, *American Isis* (New York: St. Martin's, 2013), 240, and it is sourced to the University of Maryland in his notes. The excerpt could not be located by archivists there.

489. Irish poet Richard Murphy (1927–2018) recalls: "I had seen Assia in Middlesex Hospital, where she had gone for tests in February 1968 because she feared she had cancer. In fact she was suffering from depression and anxiety, but looked well, reclining on pillows, surrounded by flowers, beautiful as ever" (*The Kick: A Life among Writers* [London: Granta, 2002], 275). AW was treated for cystitis (*Letters of Ted Hughes,* 278).

490. AW and SW are living in London as their own family-household unit at the time of this letter. Although TH was interested in mending his relationship with AW in early 1968, Bate records that AW's growing "bitterness came from the fact that at the beginning of the month [April 1968], his star sign in eclipse, Ted had vowed to make a final break with her" (*Ted Hughes,* 266). AW and TH's relationship was a fraught one in 1968; in April 1968, AW wrote the version of her will and testament that is archived at Emory University and included in this volume. See pp. 266–67.

491. Typed on the second page of the letter is "1st Chorus / A lofty raceforgets its fa."

492. AW is working as a copywriter at Ogilvy & Mather. DW's former advertising supervisor Royston Taylor secured a job interview for AW that she passed "with flying colors" (Koren and Negev, *Lover of Unreason,* 169).

A feeling of last ditch panic seems to fill the whole of England, and advertising always feels it most immediately and most acutely. We've been working like slaves until 9, ten o'clock at night all in order to grab some £1,000,000 account from another agency—but the sensation is that if you don't do it, you're out. We have a Rumanian Gauleiter[493] as Chairman (with an Etonian accent, of course) and in the past 6 weeks 27 people have been fired. The survivors are treated to little cocktails parties in the evenings, where our brains are then further picked. It all feels a bit like Scott FitzGerald's[494] accounts of Hollywood in the 1940's.

Anyway, that's why I have not written to you. I return home exhausted, and can no longer write or anything in office hours.

Encounter has taken 3 poems[495] and another newspaper 2 more (The Scotsman.)[496] Mindlin[497] wrote to ask for some, which I shall send him when I finish writing this letter.

I have not begun translating any of the things you've sent me. Much as I'd love to, I feel[498] that I won't do you justice as far as time is concerned—unless, of course the office panic stops within the next three weeks or so, which might well be the case. If Dennis Silk would like to do the other half of the Penguin I won't feel offended. Though I'd so love to do it myself.

Ted is re-writing Seneca's Oedipus for the National Theatre.[499] Which sounds very grand, but judging from the rehearsal which we attended looks like an exhibit in the Greek Pavilion of Expo '67. Golden cubes revolving in searchlights,

493. In World War II, a Gauleiter was a leader of rank in the Nazi Party.

494. Canonical American writer F. Scott Fitzgerald (1896–1940) is best known for his novels and short stories, but he also was a Hollywood screenwriter. AW refers to Fitzgerald's Pat Hobby stories (1940–41), which were published in *Esquire* magazine, some of them posthumously, and which were collected and published as a collection in 1962.

495. *Encounter* is a literary magazine, founded in London in 1953 by Irving Kristol and Stephen Spender. In 1968, it published Yehuda Amichai's "Mayor" in February (59); "My Father Fought Their War . . ." in March (47); and "To My Mother" in May (43). The poems were translated by Assia Gutmann [Wevill].

496. The *Scotsman* is a Scottish newspaper, founded in Edinburgh in 1817.

497. Mindlin was familiar with Hebrew, having translated James Joyce's *Ulysses* (1922) from English into Hebrew.

498. "I'd love to ~~do so~~, I feel" appears in the original.

499. TH worked with the director Peter Brook to produce a new English translation of the Latin *Oedipus* by the Roman Seneca (ca. 4 BCE–65 CE). According to Bate, "In early January 1968, Ted asked Brook if he could be joined in the rehearsal room by a friend 'who helps a lot in these things.' This was Assia" (*Ted Hughes*, 257).

the actors space-suited and a pink phallus 20 feet tall descends properly Deus ex Machina ready for an orgy in the last act. Ugh.[500]

Months, months ago Avigail[501] brought your lovely presents, for which I didn't have the ready grace-time to thank you for your sweetness in going to all that trouble. Please, please forgive me. If you can, please please do. The ear-rings are quite beautiful. And Ted is delighted with his dagger.

God's ways have been very mysterious with me lately. I don't know what God is up to. The Devil reminds me that I'm no housewife, that I shall fall into the kitchen sink one day[502] and drown in steak-bubbles and detergent. The garden is frozen and dead. We shall never live in Court Green again. Ted's father is still there, Emperor of the Barn.[503] Should he go back to Yorkshire . . .

Write to me and tell me your news. Both of you. And while it is still only the 11th of January please, both of you have a splendid New Year.

Much love from me and Ted.
Assia

TO TED HUGHES

TLS, Emory

Friday, February 2, 1968

Friday Feb. 2/68

Dearest love, sweet Ted. Those were two of the best days for what now feels like years. Thank you. We've allowed so much scum to come between us. So much irrelevance, they now look like irrelevances. Most miraculous of all is that we

500. The phallus was golden (rather than pink) and seven feet tall, according to Bate (*Ted Hughes*, 260). The production was staged at the Old Vic and opened on March 19, 1968. The playbill for TH and AW's *Oedipus*, held at Emory University, contains this inscription by TH to AW: "Asseeke [AW] sat in white, on this opening night, she was the best sight."

501. *Avigail* may reference the daughter of Harold Schimmel (1935–). Amichai dedicated "The Sweet Breakdown of Abigail" to Schimmel's daughter, which TH translated and which was published in *TriQuarterly* 39 (1977): 249. (See the notes accompanying chapter 5 in Adriana X. Jacobs, *Strange Cocktail: Translation and the Making of Modern Hebrew Poetry* [Ann Arbor: University of Michigan Press, 2018]). Harold Schimmel immigrated to Israel in 1962 and was a translator of Amichai's poetry, including poems published in *Selected Poems* (Harmondsworth, England: Penguin, 1971). Schimmel also translated Amichai's *Songs of Jerusalem and Myself* (New York: Harper & Row, 1973) after AW died.

502. "into the kitchen ~~skin~~ sink one day" appears in the original.

503. "Emperor of the ~~yard~~ Barn" appears in the original.

have somehow survived—this week was excellent proof to me—I don't know what it looks like to you.

I went to see 'Hunger' this afternoon. A Swedish film by one Carl Neilson.[504] The 1890's in Christiana, a poor philosopher cum poet cum Kierkegaard is in his third day without any food or money. One isn't sure whether he's mad or not. He warns his shoes, on a park bench deep in autumn leaves 'I'm not going to talk to you today, you'll have to talk to each other.' He pawns his vest and gives his money to an unemployed shoe-maker. He says to a policeman "Should you thank God today, give him[505] my thanks while you're about it." Only one piece of real dialogue in the film, and that with an icy perverse beauty (the dark girl in Silence)[506] who may or may not be a nymphomaniac. The rest are tiny snippets of talk. He dreams he's a dog vying with another for a bone. His teeth are half rotten. A very chaste film, and marvelous. Towards the end, his landlord points out a crack in a door where he (the landlord) sees his wife a fat woman with high boots on, copulating with the newest lodger, watched impassively by the husband's father, a paralysed old man with a quilt for a coat. The atmosphere is more like 20 pages of Kafka's diaries,[507] than anything else. So spare and excellent. I sat next to a dark man who followed me out and asked if I would like a drink half a block away from the cinema. There must be thousands of aimless people like that in London. When I left the film it felt as though it was the early 1920's—very odd and vivid sensation which lasted for 30 seconds. On the bus I recognised and sat in front of two women whom I'd seen on the same bus before. Both beautifully dressed and sad, impossible to tell how old, in their thirties perhaps. Hard women both in their own way. I listened to them talk—this was obviously their first intimate conversation—the one telling the other she would be a fool to marry, and pointing to the thousands of miserable looking women around who marry second choices, marrying for the sake of marriage. They congratulated each other on how sweet each was, and what bastards of men they seem to attract. At a very interesting point one of them left the bus.

504. *Hunger* is an acclaimed 1966 Scandinavian (Danish-Norwegian-Swedish) social realist film directed by Henning Carlsen and featuring Per Oscarsson. The film is based on the 1890 novel by Knut Hamsun, who won the Nobel Prize in Literature in 1920.

505. "thank God today, ~~thank~~ give him" appears in the original.

506. Probably AW is alluding to the Swedish film *Silence* (1963), directed by Ingmar Bergman.

507. Franz Kafka (1883–1927) is an influential German-language Bohemian writer; his book *The Diaries of Franz Kafka, 1910–1923* was first published in 1948.

What impressed me about Hunger was the slow and patient way in which the milieu was set, the sexual extravagance which occurs twice makes a genuine point, and is treated with the same graveness as the dog-dream, both were absolutely shocking. I'd love to see it again with you.

I tidied the top drawer in my bedroom and came across the colour slides which Jane Bown took in Cleggan[508]—how young and vulnerable Frieda and Nick look—Nicky was only just four! Soon it will be 2 years ago. There isn't a single, safe anniversary between us. I've often thought of that. How are you and you and you. How sweet you are. How sweet.

A.

TO YEHUDA AMICHAI AND HANA SOKOLOV-AMICHAI

TLS, Yale

Wednesday, March 6, 1968

Flat 14,
51 Marlborough Place,
London N.W.8.
March 6th 1968

My dear Yehuda. And Channa—

This will be very brief—mainly to acknowledge your letter, which reached me in hospital[509] (I'm out now, thank God) to say that I have begun, am in the midst, in full steam of translating what I like best in your newest batches. I think they're terrific—infinitely more varied, and with[510] fine steel backbones, and I enjoy doing them. I have received your November batch. Some I began translat-

508. AW and TH lived with their children (and Teresa Manaion Reilly, a local who helped with the household chores) at Cleggan Farm in Cleggan, Connemara, Ireland, in 1966. They lived less than two miles from the poet Richard Murphy, who had known SP and DW as well as AW and TH prior to their relocation to Ireland. Though living in a remote part of Ireland, AW and TH received visits from painter Barrie Cooke (1931–2014), in addition to Murphy. By all accounts, AW relished her time in Connemara.

509. AW checked into Middlesex Hospital in London as a result of a cystitis flare-up.

510. AW inserted a word by hand that is illegible.

ing and found that they[511] lost too much, so rather than quarrel with the words I abandoned them[512]—promiscuously thinking that I'll find lots more magic mushrooms . . . which so far, I have done. I love 'If I forget thee Jerusalem'—it's like a Talmudic Raga,[513] I hope I haven't damaged it too much, I played with it for a long time. And Tourist is splendid and full of your best spleen.[514] Ted says that he'll append a note and try them on the New Yorker.[515]

Congratulations on your prize! I mean you just can't help it, there they come like wild mink in Devon, all these prizes and all the people loving you and nodding their heads and claiming you as theirs. Theirs. Poor Channa. Remember me Channa!

I saw a BBC film on Jerusalem last night[516]—I sat there trying to remember the smell of the buses and the dust-smells, and nothing came, only the Indian food smell of the tenants below.[517]

How tantalizingly familiar and entirely out of reach Jerusalem looked—that's how I remember it. Every one being everyone else's pie-dog.[518] The melancholy, glossy hotel proprietor grieving about loss of business since the war. The voices like quarrels. Dried out quarrels without end. Please write to me Channale.

love
Assia

511. AW originally typed *they* but changed her mind, typing *that* instead. In the original, it appears as *theyat* where the *a* was typed over the *y*.

512. "rather than quarrel with the words ~~too much~~ I abandoned them" appears in the original.

513. From the Sanskrit, *raga* means "color" or "passion" and is used in classical music from India and other countries to denote a melodic framework for composition and improvisation.

514. Amichai's "If I Forget Thee Jerusalem" and "Tourist" were both translated by AW and published in *Poems* in 1969.

515. Two poems by Amichai and translated by AW appeared in the March 22, 1969, issue of the *New Yorker*. They are "My Mother Once Told Me" and "Song of Resignation." These appear to be the first poems by Amichai published in the magazine.

516. The film *Jerusalem the Golden: A Portrait of a Reunited City* aired on BBC 2 on Monday, March 4, 1968, at 8:35 p.m. The summary, provided by the BBC, reads: "For three great religions, a sacred city. For 3,000 years, a city of bloodshed and conquest. Is Jerusalem now one city in any terms other than those of military conquest? Will the Israelis and the Arabs ever learn to live here in peace?" In 1967, from June 5 to June 10, a brief war—variously named the Six-Day War, the June War, and the Third Arab-Israeli War—was fought.

517. "below. ~~Nothing has changed~~" appears in the original.

518. An Asian stray or wild dog, the pye-dog, or "pie-dog," frequently roams in packs in and around villages and settles near human communities.

TO TED HUGHES

AL,[519] Emory

Circa late March 1968[520]

This is the ancient steel nib with which I used to write you those broken nervous letters years ago. I wrote you a business letter this morning—through my throat. I'm writing this through my aesophagos, my throat a huge and growing wound. I'm writing to your big hands, to the lovely inside of your wrists, to your best-tempered eyes, to your brain not at all. And I'm not writing from my brain[521] but from well below my aesophagus.

I want to know whether you want to mend us because you still love me, because you still feel the animal thing between us (the sight of me in that awful bed must have been pretty unappealing)[522] or whether you want me as your child keeper only.[523]

I still have ABSOLUTE HOPES that we can build a happy, loving life together. I know that I can still love you fully with all my faculties and my body and my life—my darling Ted.

Open up—again—open out to me, as you used to—my love. And I will flourish under you, and care for you and give you everything I have. If you secretly feel that you can't, then I shall go away to Canada within two months of Monday, April 8th. Let me know <u>fully</u> by Monday. Please let me know!

So far, everybody but you and I have been dictating our lives—we <u>need</u> to be alone, to recover from our Intolerable. I feel so full of love for you at your sweet best, I admire you and I am frightened at the power you have over me. No man has ever had this power over me as a woman.

Reassure me. My lovely tiger. Love me back—and if you can't, then say so, and let me go with whatever peace I can salvage.[524]

519. Yellow crayon scribbles are on the letter. Likely these markings were made by SW.

520. The date is supplied from internal evidence. The letter was most likely written at the end of March 1968 or possibly on Monday, April 1, 1968.

521. "And I'm not writing ~~to~~ from my brain" appears in the original.

522. AW alludes to her hospital stay the previous month.

523. AW is the head of her household and is the sole provider for SW.

524. A horizontal birdlike figure sporting a unicorn horn and holding out a paper, presumably meant to be a letter, is drawn at the bottom of the letter. Koren and Negev describe it thus: AW "drew a dying bird, with outspread wings, looking like a woman who had jumped from a roof and was flattened on the ground" (*Lover of Unreason*, 176).

TO TED HUGHES

TL in a handmade card,[525] Emory

Thursday, April 4, 1968[526]

Please God send Ted a happy year—send him the Year he has waited for for so long. And may he have more money than he absolutely needs, so that he won't ever again worry about ending up without any. And please God make him feel truly well and in full control of his body—and make his spirit fiery and splendid as ever, and, if you can spare it, God, more so than ever. And Please heal all his bruises and his many wounds. Please make him utterly whole again because he is one of your best creatures.[527]

And please make him forget our awful tribulations of the last year—and please restore him his heart wholly. And please ask him to forgive me my pride and its consequences. Look after him God, because he is rare and marvelous and you spent so much love in creating him. And if it's the last thing I ever ask you God, send him back to me loving and sweet as he was before our sorrows.[528]

525. The card features artwork with two female angels, side by side, each holding a scroll with a typed script with handwritten words.

526. Date is supplied from the postmark on the accompanying envelope.

527. This paragraph is the text on the scroll that the second angel displays. It is marked with a "1," indicating it should be read first. "One of your best creatures" is handwritten.

528. This paragraph is the text on the first scroll.

TO DODO AND ERIC WALTER WHITE

TLS, University of Texas, Austin

Monday, April 15, 1968

Flat 14,
51 Marlborough Place,
London N.W.8.
April 15th 1968.

My dear Eric and Dodo,[529]

I'm writing to thank you, hugely, for the pleasant evening last Wednesday. To apologise, also for our absence at the supper later—but as we said, we were both exhausted, and I had to face I.C.I. fairly early the next morning.[530]

Eric, I was perplexed by the Marriage;[531] it had so many interesting elements in it, but not enough surgery, for my tastes. And since these are low, primitive, and ignorant, I should not have brought them into this letter at all.[532] But thank you so much for taking us, all that glamour is irresistable.

I got in touch with the National Trust[533] who inform me that they have splendid houses in Surrey[534] at splendid rents—which was dismaying news.

529. Eric is Eric Walter White (1905–85), and his wife is Edith Dorothy "Dodo" Swinburne (1909–77).

530. AW may have been working on an advertising account with Imperial Chemical Industries (ICI), which was a successful British chemical company in London. It was founded in 1926.

531. Probably AW is alluding to Sir Michael Tippet's opera *Midsummer Marriage,* performed at Covent Garden Opera on Wednesday, April 10, 1968.

532. "this letter ~~in~~ at all" appears in the original. AW appears to be dismissing her "tastes" and sensibility in connection with the opera because Eric Walter White was a notable opera critic. White worked as an assistant secretary and literature director at the Arts Council of Great Britain in London and authored several books throughout his life, including *Stravinsky: The Composer and His Works* (Berkeley: University of California Press, 1966); *Benjamin Britten: His Life and Operas* (London: Faber and Faber, 1970); and *A History of English Opera* (London: Faber and Faber, 1983).

533. The National Trust for Places of Historic Interest or Natural Beauty, known as the National Trust, was founded by Octavia Hill, Sir Robert Hunter, and Hardwicke Rawnsley in 1895. It is a nonprofit in the United Kingdom that is dedicated to heritage and environmental conservation, and within its scope is the preservation of English country houses.

534. Surrey is a wealthy county in England. Historically, the cost of living has been relatively very high and contains some of the most expensive properties outside of Inner London.

Is there any uncompromising way in which you, Eric, could touch the strings which Mr. Betjeman[535] might[536] care to pull?

Love,
Assia

TO YEHUDA AMICHAI

ALS,[537] Yale

Wednesday, May 8, 1968

May 8th 1968

My dear Yehuda—

I'm delighted that you like them.

As for the corrections:

(1) Quick and Bitter—I have substituted "sensible" <illegible—Eds.> <other> wise I feel though that the meaning of move<ment> <illegible—Eds.> love is exactly what I tried to convey.

<illegible—Eds.> multiply—but it feels clumsy in <illegible—Eds.>

(2) <illegible—Eds.> I've substituted "turns" <illegible—Eds.> so sinned in <illegible—Eds.>, or forgetfullness <illegible—Eds.>

(3) <illegible—Eds.>

(4) Tourist—<illegible—Eds.>

(5) Indian Summer—I think under-exposed is right—i.e. is not exposed sufficiently to light and dark.

535. English poet and broadcaster Sir John Betjeman (1906–84) served as poet laureate of the United Kingdom from 1972 to 1984.

536. Before AW struck the *d* in *cared* and inserted *might* by hand, the letter read, "which Mr. Betjeman cared to pull?"

537. The letter has significant water damage, marked as "<illegible—Eds.>." Supplied text appears in <angle brackets>.

(6) In My Time, In Your Place: amended

(7) National Thoughts: I really knew about *a Mitzvah dance*[538]—that by simply using Hassid dancing the meaning would be clear to anyone who knew anything about it, and for those who don't I would have to add a foot-note.

(8) Song of Resignation—corrected

(9) My Child—I used magic-spell instead.

(10) The heart is a corrupt dictator—I've added a foot note.

(11) In my worst dreams—I've made the 2 corrections.

(12) <illegible—Eds.>: you never sent me the fig-tree stanza however I inserted it just before the last stanza—it didn't seem to fit anywhere else.

I've lost touch with Abigail—forgotten we translated 4 poems from Ibn Gabirol, and I'd like to publish them. Do you know where she is.

I'm writing a T.V. play at the moment. Or trying to.[539]

Did you like the look of the Cape-Golliard book?[540]

Love to you and *Hannale,*
Assia.

538. The Hebrew is difficult to read because of water damage to the letter. As such, the translation may not be exact.

539. See Koren and Negev, *Lover of Unreason,* 179–80, for an overview and discussion of the television screenplay AW was writing and directing. After submitting an outline of her project to the creative director at Ogilvy, AW was granted eight thousand pounds from the advertising agency to fund it. Her colleagues served as actors, and another agreed to head photography. Set in 1914, the play focused on a love triangle: the female main character, a young woman, is courted by her piano teacher but loves her boyfriend, who is killed in World War I. The woman marries the piano teacher, though she does not love him.

540. AW asks Amichai about his *Selected Poems,* which she translated.

TO TED HUGHES

Telegram,[541] Emory

Tuesday, May 14, 1968[542]

Thursday morning alright stop
reorganized work load. stop
please confirm

Esther[543]

TO YEHUDA AMICHAI

TLS, Yale

Wednesday, May 29, 1968

Flat 14,
51 Marlborough Place,
London N.W.8.
May 29th, 1968.

My dear Yehuda and Channa,

Thank you for your last letter.

This morning I received 3 measly copies of the Cape/Golliard book. It looks very beautiful—pause—but I must apologise for the cover. Ages ago I said vaguely, why not over-print[544] the cover with the Hebrew version of Ibn Gabirol and they said yes, yes. Then 3 days before the press date, they rang me and said, what about it? and that afternoon I sat down in the office, supervised by the Gauleiter, and wrote it out. It was a shambles, uneven, ugly-archaic. So I tried again. And later in the evening, again. In my hurry I entirely overlooked the 3rd stanza, and didn't notice it until I closed the envelope. An appalling mistake, for which, I hope you will forgive me. I do apologise.[545]

541. The post office telegram was sent to "Ted Hughes N. Tawton Devon." It was handed in at 11:24 a.m. in London via Telex service and was franked by the North Tawton Post Office.

542. AW's birthday is the next day, and she and TH are making plans to celebrate her birthday after the fact in London, according to her biographers (Koren and Negev, *Lover of Unreason,* 178).

543. As her middle name, Esther may have been used in the telegram to preserve privacy.

544. "why not ~~typ~~ over-print" appears in the original.

545. The Cape Golliard Press book was published with a blue cover with the Hebrew script for "Ibn Gabirol" featured in lighter blue.

The contract date for the Penguin edition is on Friday—I have finished translating 22 of the new poems. I translated many more, but some of them simply didn't work in English, and I abandoned them. By the same mail today, I shall send you off the 22 poems, but they may take a little longer to reach you. I have not translated the Queen of Sheba, as you suggested in your last letter; rather I stuck almost entirely to the new poems you sent me. Since the contract was quite strict in stipulating the date of delivery, it seemed rather late to begin translating it. However, once the book is published, I'm sure it will be taken by one of the magazines. I re-read it, it's an enchanting poem, and I'm now full of regret for not having translated it earlier.

Here is the list of the poems which will reach you:[546]

1. In my time, in your place
2. National Thoughts
3. The end of Elul
4. Song of resignation
5. My child
6. Two songs of peace
7. To summon witnesses
8. If I forget thee Jerusalem
9. Luxury
10. Tourist
11. Eye examination
12. God's Fate
13. Indian summer in Princeton
14. My mother once told me
15. The heart is a corrupt director
16. She knows
17. It's a long time since anybody's asked (from the Book)
18. I was the moon
19. Quick and bitter
20. In my worst dreams
21. Poem in an orange grove
22. Two Bedouin poems

546. Of the following numbered poems, most numbers are circled: these are 1–5, 7, 10–12, and 14–22. The ones left unmarked are 6, 8, 9, and 13.

Ted has seen all these translations and combed them a little. I hope you are not too disappointed with them. A friend of mine, Myra Coopman,[547] is in Jerusalem at the moment training producers in Television. She knows about you, please look her up. You'll find her at Television House, ? *Jerusalem, neighborhood?*[548]

She has directed some excellent short films—she is quite marvelous. Someone else, one Brian Robertson[549] who has a house near Natanya (for the life of me I can't remember the name of that ignominious, gaol ridden, beautiful town, north of Haifa)—oh yes, Acco.[550] He's the director of the Whitechapel Gallery in London.[551] Again, I asked him to look you up. Are you always being looked up?

It is now almost a year since you were here. What a generation ago it seems. Ted is battling on alone in Court Green with his father and Frieda and Nicky. He's under great strain. I'm looking forward to the Harper Row edition.[552] Has your novel come out yet?[553]

Is there anything you want over here which I could send with Brian Robertson, or some Israeli friends who are returning quite soon?

We're half expecting the Revolution to cross the channel. The French are worrying the world again.[554] You get these sensations of ominousness with

547. AW refers to filmmaker and artist Mira Hammermesh (1923–2012). Hammermesh married Richard Coopman in 1962, and in 1968, at the time of this letter, she was in Israel setting up Israel Television and working in documentary film, the genre for which she became acclaimed as a filmmaker.

548. The neighborhood to which AW refers is Romema.

549. English art gallery director, critic, and author Bryan Charles Francis Robertson, OBE (1925–2002), is referenced here.

550. Netanya and Acco are cities in Israel. Acco is commonly referred to as Acre, but locals call it Akko or Akka.

551. The Whitechapel Gallery in London was founded in 1901 and is renowned for its modern and contemporary exhibitions, including work by Picasso and Jackson Pollock.

552. The Harper & Row edition of *Poems* (1969), translated by AW, is the first collection of poems by Amichai to be published in the United States.

553. *Mi Yitneni Malon* (1971) is Amichai's second novel.

554. Much civil unrest erupted in France in spring 1968, to the point that many thought there would be a revolution or civil war.

monstrous vividness on television. Wait till you get your Televisia . . . The communication lark will be the death of all of us yet. Hail illeteracy. Guthenberg was as much as the world can take.[555]

Has Marshall McLuhan[556] struck in Jerusalem yet?

love
Assia

TO YEHUDA AMICHAI

TLS, Yale

Tuesday, June 18, 1968

Flat 14,[557]
51 Marlborough Place,
London N.W.8.
June 18th 1968

Dear Yehuda,

Thank you for your letter and your poem.

Alas, it's too late. Both firms have already calculated their "costings" and it's all rigidly at the printers.

But it's a splendid poem—and why don't we do another selection in 2 years time perhaps—and we could use it. Do send me the Hebrew of it. I find it so difficult from a literal translation.

If you write to Patrick Craigh c/o Jonathan Cape, 38 Bedford Sq.,WC1—it will reach him.[558]

555. Johannes Gutenberg (ca. 1400–1468) is a German engraver, inventor, and printer who ushered in the printing revolution in Europe with movable type printing and his innovative printing press.

556. Canadian philosopher and public intellectual Herbert Marshall McLuhan (1911–80) is a key figure in media theory. His famous expression "The medium is the message" was published in *Understanding Media: The Extensions of Man* (New York: McGraw-Hill, 1964), which also explores his concept of the "global village."

557. "~~Flat 5~~" appears in the original.

558. AW likely means John Patrick Brasier-Creagh (1930–2012), who went by Patrick Creagh. He is a British literary man: a poet, academic, and translator, celebrated for his Italian translations. AW may have known him through Al Alvarez; Creagh married Alvarez's ex-wife, Ursula Barr. AW would have certainly encountered him in 1967 at the Spoleto literary festival, the Festival dei Due

I'm—or rather, a colleague and I are making a film to begin shooting this week-end.[559] I'm silly with the excitement of it.

Love
Assia

TO YEHUDA AMICHAI

TLS, Yale

Tuesday, June 25, 1968

Flat 14,
51 Marlborough Place,
London N.W.8.
June 25th 1968

My dear Yehuda,

Thank you for your letter.

1. 3 soft cover Cape-Golliard books had been sent off to you about 3 weeks ago—you should have received them by now.

2. I haven't yet received your novel from Harper-Row—I'm enormously flattered that you asked[560] them to send me one in the first place.

3. The poems.

a. Quick & Bitter. YOU'RE right. But it's too late to change it. They've gone off. I will check their having gone off, though.

b. Altogether, both Harper and Penguin will have 42 poems. Which is the normal length, and in Harper's case the specified length.

c. In My Time in Your Place. I translated the last stanza originally, quite literally. I was displeased with it—and Ted confirmed that it sounded clumsy. He suggested the revised version you have—and I felt much happier with this version, although of course it transmutes your lovely metaphore.

Mondi, where she accompanied TH and where Creagh served as an interpreter for Allen Ginsberg and translated his work.

559. After this sentence, "~~I suppose these last days will be the bes~~" appears in the original. AW is probably alluding to Martin Baker, the art director at Ogilvy and AW's colleague and friend at the advertising agency. He worked with her on the film she was directing. Shooting took place over two weekends (Koren and Negev, *Lover of Unreason,* 180).

560. "flattered ~~by your kindness~~ that you asked" appears in the original.

d. Again, I agree with you about 'inevitably' in In My Worst Dreams—this line troubled me for ages, and again, with Ted's co-operation we decided that this worked best of all the alternatives. But you're right, it does muffle the effect.

4. Your mate in the Penguin is very likely to be Haaviko.[561] This is, however, not settled yet.

5. Yes—I shall translate the 4 additional poems you suggested, they're all splendid, and have all appealed to me.

But Yehuda, we won't be able to change anything after that. They're such a cross and irritable lot, these publishers, these agents.

I've had a note from Myra Coopman, saying that she'd lost your address—she is at Television House—Schechunat (Something or other, which I can't remember)—could you phone her there, and tell her that I've lost her address. Please ask her to send me another beautiful post card with her address on it.

Tell her I'm making a film—shooting began on Sunday. Tell her that I miss her valuable presence in London. Tell her that that it's all gooey and sentimental, and that I miss her.

And you, and Channa.
love
Assia

TO TED HUGHES

TL, Negev and Koren

Tuesday, July 9, 1968

Tuesday Morning of July 9th/68

My sweetest Teddy, dear love—you're all gone again. I left the house at 9.30, just as you caught the train. What a game of Scrabble we are. How I want us to live together, the 5 of us, to make a family again, instead of running our separate nut-

561. Finnish poet, essayist, and publisher Paavo Haavikko (1931–2008) shared a selected poems volume in the Penguin Modern European Poets series with the Swedish poet Tomas Tranströmer (1931–2015): *Selected Poems* by Paavo Haavikko (translated by Anselm Hollo) and Tomas Tranströmer (translated by Robin Fulton) was published by Penguin in 1974. Amichai's *Selected Poems* in the Penguin Modern European Poets series was published in 1971.

houses. These long absences feel so dangerous—they show me that I could live without you, but once I make contact with you again, the total independence seems worthless. Is this the nature of women, or only my own?

God, I look forward to August.[562]

Teddy—sweet, go easy on the awful Truths—because knowing it only curdles oneself. I don't want to know the last-ditch condition of things or persons, I wish I could somehow regain meaningfully that glazed innocence I once had. Ridiculous. But I do like my friends—I want them as I think they possibly are. Knowing any more is more than I can take. I think all the puss should come out in writing—but in real life, I want the people with my glaze.

Oh Teddy—I see things very clearly at the moment. Clearer than ever before, ever. For us to continue[563] living separately feels fundamentally wrong, the reasons for it, are abstractions. We're meant to be together. And the children need both of us. And we need both of us, and it's worth the effort. Yes, the whole effort. No man's an island, which you're pretending you are, and I am persuading myself that I am. I don't want to be. I want to be with you. Don't leave it long, dear love, otherwise there will be no means of return to you. I shall have turned into a salt pillar.

And I love you.

This is before being fired . . .[564]

562. AW, TH, and SW went to Germany on a holiday in August 1968. Frieda and Nicholas Hughes were visiting their maternal grandmother in the United States.

563. "~~We~~ For us to continue" appears in the original.

564. This last sentence is handwritten by AW. As AW's biographers explain: "Later [on this] day, Assia was summoned to the office of her boss, Dan Ellerington. He had sacked scores of employees at Ogilvy that year—and now he told Assia that he was not satisfied with her output. The campaign that she was working on did not result in enough sales and she was fired. It could not have come at a worse moment. In a profession that had become more aggressive and flashy, with most copywriters in their twenties, her experience and age were working against her. She had the rent to pay, a daughter to bring up—and she was well aware that Ted was not going to support them" (Koren and Negev, *Lover of Unreason,* 181–82).

TO YEHUDA AMICHAI

ALS (picture postcard),[565] Yale

Circa Thursday, August 8, 1968[566]

What a wonder, what a wonder We are here. German rain keeps falling. Where did you live, Yehuda.[567]

On the train here I spoke to a round robin of a man who was in the Waffen S.S.[568]—yes, he knew Wilna[569] backwards. My spine is still partially contracted. I cannot, no, I cannot imagine where you could possibly have lived here . . .

and I, half-German? no, no, no. Suddenly Germany disgusts me.

Assia

TO MARTIN BAKER

ALS (picture postcard),[570] Koren and Negev

Thursday, August 8, 1968[571]

Ah, this is the true country of Dan Dare—I haven't managed to forget him, in spite of breakfasting on a geranium-balcony overlooking the Rhine. but I can't quite remember what it feels like to enter the O u M lift.[572] Bless O. Bless M. Or <u>some</u> of them.

Assia

565. Text is written on a postcard depicting "Blick von der Festung Marienberg" (View from Fortress Marienberg); it is postmarked from Würzburg, Germany.

566. The postcard is dated from a comment in AW's journal for August 8, 1968: "We posted cards to Amichai." See p. 190.

567. Würzburg is Amichai's birthplace; he moved to Palestine in 1936, later becoming an Israeli citizen.

568. The Waffen-SS was the military branch of the Schutzstaffel (SS), which was the Nazi guard. The Waffen-SS committed war crimes without concern for legal restraint.

569. AW means Vilnius, Lithuania.

570. The postcard bares identical markings as that to Yehuda Amichai. Text is written on a postcard depicting "Kolorierter Holzschnitt aus dem 'Buch der Chroniken.' Von Hartmann Schedel, 1493. Original im Mainfränkischen Museum, Würzburg."

571. Date provided by the postmark.

572. Martin Baker explains that "Dan Dare" is a 1950s comic character in the United Kingdom and that AW is alluding to Dan Ellerington, the creative director at Ogilvy & Mather. Baker emphasizes in his communication to the editors that "Assia had extreme concern about this trip

TO ERIC WALTER WHITE

ALS, University of Texas, Austin

Wednesday, September 11, 1968

MAC 8396

Flat 3
OKEOVER MANOR,
North Side,
Clapham Common
S.W.
Sep. 11th 1968

My dear Eric,

Here is the resúme you asked for during our lunch, a month ago.[573]

I'm sure that in the waiting rooms of Hell, there are thousands sitting at little tables, writing resúmes of their lives.

What did you finally do with Lois Ames; the biographer?[574]

My love to you, and Dido.

Assia

Assia Wevill

I'm 36. I'm half Russian, half German, and half Jewish. My education consisted of 8 years in an Israeli State school,[575] a Church of Scotland Missionary school,[576] and 3 years at the University of British Columbia in Vancouver.

---

with Ted to Germany, she had very real fears of all things German" (personal correspondence on July 18, 2019).

573. White responds to AW on October 4, 1968, apologizing for the delay; he and his wife, Dodo, had been on a vacation in Malta. He informs AW that he has written to his contact at the BBC on AW's behalf and will let her know when he has advice to share. In a letter, dated October 1, 1968, White writes Huw Weldon, controller of programs at Television Centre, asking for guidance about landing a job with BBC television on behalf of AW. White praises AW's abilities to Weldon. In his October 8 reply to White, Weldon advises that AW talk to two people: the head of the BBC Features Group and the appointments officer at Broadcasting House. He explains that AW may not have luck with the first contact because the Features Group is fully staffed, and landing a position with it is a very competitive process. As for the second contact, he affirms that many BBC employees found jobs at the BBC after working at the Broadcasting House, which is the path he himself took.

574. White explains in his October 4, 1968, letter to AW that he had a long talk with Ames about SP, much to Olwyn Hughes's agitation, and that Ames may return in a year.

575. AW attended Balfour Elementary School, Tel Aviv, Israel.

576. AW attended Tabeetha School, Tel Aviv–Yafo, Israel.

I came to England in 1955 and worked as a supply teacher in the East End (The Isle of Dogs, the Lansbury Estate, West India Docks.) I married David Wevill, the poet in 1959, and with him went to Burma. We were there for two years.

On our return I worked as a secretary in an advertising agency (C.D. Notley)—and persuaded the chairman to allow me to write copy. He did, and I became a copywriter. I moved to Colman, Prentis & Varley, and from there to J. Walter Thompson.

At Thompson's I became interested in television. I named and wrote the script for a 90 sec. cinema commercial called Seawitch, which at the time, 1966, caused a mild commotion in the trade. Another 90 sec. commercial, Woodnymph, won the 2nd prize in Cannes, 1967.

I am now a senior copywriter at Ogilvy & Mather. I feel frustrated and constricted by the narrow scope of operation in television commercials.

With an art director at Ogilvy & Mather I'm directing and producing a private 25 minute colour film which won't be ready until late in November.

In July, Cape Golliard published a book of verse by the Israeli poet Yehuda Amichai, which I translated from the Hebrew. A larger selection will be published by Penguin and Harper Row (New York) in the spring.

I would love to work in the bowels of real television. I'm full of energy and ideas which are wasting in advertising. Ideally, I should like to be apprenticed to a budding Ken Russell[577] for a while, make a film about Georg Grodeck,[578] about the North West Indians, about a Western Canadian suburb, about Kafka, about fading brigadiers in Devon.

TO PATRICIA MENDELSON

ALS,[579] Koren and Negev

Undated, circa summer–fall 1968

Wednesday

Dearest Pat,

Thank you so much for your note.

I feel a bit silly now, to have told you, in the first place . . .

577. AW refers to English film director Henry Kenneth Alfred Russell (1927–2011).

578. AW refers to German-born physician and writer Georg Walther Groddeck (1866–1934).

579. The letter is written on Charles, Hobson & Grey Limited letterhead. Charles, Hobson & Grey was active in advertising from 1965 to 1996.

And I haven't a card as magnificent as the one you sent . . . Where did you buy it?

Why? Why don't you learn to play the recorder—it gives me such immense pleasure, and the repetoire of music written for it, is very large. We could play duets?

Why don't you—honestly. You're so musical—it would be a pity to waste it. D'you remember talking about doing a job?—learning music is equally demanding and twice as satisfying.

Tell me what you think.

And thank you so much for having us on Sunday. I so look forward to seeing you.

love
Assia

TO RICHARD GILBERTSON

TLS, Emory

Monday, September 16, 1968

3 Okeover Manor,
North Side,
Clapham Common,
London S.W.4.
16.9.68

Dear Richard,[580]

Thank you very much for the charming book[581]—it really is one of her delights (if it weren't for her obligation-verse). How kind of you to have thought of me.

I hear that La is infinitely better—and that you escaped the floods. I wish you'd send me your catalogue—or come and see me when you are in London.

My love to La.

Assia

580. Richard Gilbertson is a Devon-based publisher of TH's work, including *Animal Poems* (1967), the nine-page *Five Autumn Songs for Children's Voices* (1968), and two editions of the eight-page poem *The Martyrdom of Bishop Farrar* (1970). Gilbertson also published limited editions of works by Charles Causley, Thom Gunn, Seamus Heaney, Kathleen Raine, and Peter Redgrove. Gilbertson also is a poet.

581. Probably AW means Kathleen Raine's *A Question of Poetry* (1969).

TO YEHUDA AMICHAI AND HANA SOKOLOV-AMICHAI

TLS in greeting card,[582] Yale

Undated, circa December 1968[583]

My dear Channa & Yehuda,

Since Rembrandt[584] was demonstrably not anti-semitic, I chose him. Ignore the Christmas bit, unless it doesn't infringe on you—and have another, spectacular year—on ALL FRONTS.

You seem remoter and remoter and remoter. We are water-logged with Zoress of one kind and another. But a huge photograph of you and Channa stand on Olwyn's mantelpiece. Have you been paid yet? You are owed something like £250 sterling. If you've not been paid, then ask for it gently. Otherwise, you will, may,[585] not be paid at all.

Couldn't the Israeli Government need Ted's presence in Israel next spring say—it would be so splendid to go there—and see you.

Have an excellent year.
A.

582. The card depicts Rembrandt's *Procession with the "Star of the Kings" on the Feast of the Epiphany,* published by the Trustees of the British Museum as Christmas card number 31. Inside the card, underneath the manufacturer's message "With Best Wishes for Christmas and the New Year," the card is hand signed "from Assia u Ted."

583. The date is supplied from internal evidence. It is possible the royalties owed to Amichai are for *Selected Poems* (1968).

584. Rembrandt van Rijn (1606–69) is considered the most important artist of Holland's golden age.

585. "you will, ~~many~~ may," appears in the original.

TO PATRICIA AND MICHAEL MENDELSON

ALS (picture postcard),[586] Stanford

Undated, before 1969

Much love to you all—Assia[587]

TO LONYA GUTMANN

TLS, *Lover of Unreason*[588]

Circa January 1969

My Dearest Vatinka,

If you ever receive this letter, you will know that I have not taken this decision lightly.

The prospect before me is so bleak, that to have lived my full life-span would have entailed more misery than I could possibly endure.

It is the life alone, dependent on an au pair to look after my little Shuratchka properly—dependent on the sort of people for whom I work—a very bad, 3rd rate agency who would fire me in case of illness. No husband. No father for Shura.

I've often thought of this—but the pain it would give you, and the criminality perpetrated on my little Shuri—these thoughts often stopped me at the last sane moment, in the past.

I have lived on the dream of living with Ted—and this has gone kaput. The reasons are immaterial. There could never be another man. Never.

Believe me, my dearest Vatinka, my friend, my colleague in exile and disaster, that what I have done was necessary—you wouldn't have wished another 30 years of hell for me—would you?

586. Postcard of *January* from a Flemish calendar of the early sixteenth century depicting "Domestic life; sledging." The postcard is not postmarked and may have accompanied a gift.

587. Beneath AW's signature, in pencil, is written "Wevill-Hughes" in an unknown hand, suggesting the card may date from 1964 to 1968.

588. The text of this letter is taken from Koren and Negev, *Lover of Unreason,* 204–5, as the original has not been located.

Thank you for all your kindness to me throughout my life. I did so love you, my dearest father—and don't grieve for me. Believe me, I have done the right thing.

Please don't grieve for me, my darling Vatinka—life was infinitely worse—infinitely. I lived a full and comparatively long life. It is necessary to know when there's no more life to live.

Perhaps there is another world—and if there is, we shall meet—Mutti, and you, and I. You were excellent parents—and you both did everything you could for me. Please don't think that I'm insane, or that I have done this in a moment of insanity. It was simple accountancy. And I couldn't leave little Shura by herself. She's too old to be adopted.

Goodbye Lonya. Father. My past protector. I miss you very much. Goodbye my dearest.

Assia

II. JOURNALS

Editors' note: AW recorded her journal entries in two notebooks and on loose-leaf papers. The arrangement of AW's journals within this volume represents a chronological ordering for the ease of the reader, and brief notes in angle brackets identify the source document. The first journal is a red exercise book with "AW" and "October 1962" written in AW's hand on the cover and consists of handwritten entries with some typewritten pages tipped into the journal.

MONDAY APRIL 8TH '63.[1]

In GALWAY, driven here in a small fiat and increasing waves of thick, serious downpours. I'm waiting for an order of bacon and tomatoes in the D.B.C. café and ices—all pastel-Green mottled freshly, 3 daffodils per table, and tables covered with embossed white plastic. There's a dark waitress in a black uniform and starched apron (this would be practically extinct in London) and many smiles. Prices are high—"tea" for two will amount to 12/-. The town is dour—smug, catholic-clean and bereft, utterly bereft of joy. There was a que of miserable "young people" at the cinema. We followed a red-cheeked girl and a boy who held hands, confidently. They're probably engaged, although she cavorted self-consciously on heels. Most Irish women are next to plain, most over 25 look ugly. They look to be without spirit, and suffer from piety. Piety makes plain women. The men though, shine with something, sex maybe, or dissatisfaction, or good looks. The red, blue and black looks they have are masculine, women fade with it, because their hair is coarse, and unaccustomed, like all European peasants' hair.

It smells of peat, looks like all the Isles of Wight, only with deeper, blacker alleys. The same Goods in all the shops, Cadbury's[2] Easter bunnies and Yardley 4/9 talcum powder[3] repeated a dozen times in every street.

1. AW and DW took an evening ferry to Dublin, Ireland, on Saturday, April 6. They rented a Fiat and traveled to Galway. According to Nathaniel Tarn, AW confided in him about the trip and considered it a flop (Nathaniel Tarn Papers, M1132, Department of Special Collections, Stanford University Libraries).

2. Cadbury's is a British confectionery company, founded in Birmingham in 1824. It changed its name to Cadbury in 2010 and is still famous for its chocolates.

3. Yardley is Yardley London, founded in London, England, in 1770. It is famous for its fragrances, cosmetics, and toiletry products. It provides toiletry items to Queen Elizabeth II.

The Irish have no sense-of-looks whatsoever. Their villages are ugly; there are no gardens, their clothes are ugly, their food is unspeakable. Only the country[4] is beautiful, bereft, untouched, like Tinker[5] children.

APRIL 11TH.[6]

Back in Dublin. Dublin is buried in Good Friday. Abysmal and anticlimactic. The best part of these 6 days were the one evening in Cleggan. I suppose I set out from Dublin with the idea of visiting Richard Murphy.[7] We made our way to Galways—the looks of Ireland improving with every mile. Galway magnificent to look at from the distance, like a town in the Dolomites,[8] sheer brown town-wall over cliffs dropping into the bay, and the town itself mean and smug and rechérche[9] for 19/4.[10] As is suitable. The road to Cleggan was marvelous. The end of Europe and the real beginning of the American Atlantic coast. No ruins, no villages, a modern church. Peat fields, and men, neither old nor young wearing long overcoats, a leather belt and Wellingtons rutting about in front yards. The cottages out of stone, sometimes with a smoking chimney, thatch roof, and sheep and dung-clung cows going about their business. I wonder why lady-type travellers always write about their journeys in such an ill-tempered

4. "Only ~~their~~ the country" appears in the original.

5. A contested term with respect to origins and meanings, one meaning in British English is associated with itinerant traveling groups, such as Irish Travellers and Romani people (historically called Gypsies). It is considered an offensive label when used in this way. Another meaning of *tinker* in British English is a "mischievous child."

6. April 11, 1963, was a Thursday.

7. Irish poet Richard Murphy recorded his meeting with AW and DW in his memoir *The Kick:* "A few months after Sylvia's death, Eileen O'Malley surprised me in the Pier Bar by introducing me to Assia and her husband, the poet David Wevill. I assumed that they had come to find out what happened in Cleggan to Ted and Sylvia" (229). According to DW, however, "no footsteps were being followed. My mother's family was Irish, and with her failing health, I was curious to see the country. We both needed a break" (qtd. in Koren and Negev, *Lover of Unreason,* 122). As AW's biographers recount, "The Wevills drove to Cleggan and waited in the grey building of the Pier Bar for poet Richard Murphy. David went out to speak to the fishermen and Assia drank ginger ale" (Koren and Negev, *Lover of Unreason,* 121–22).

8. The Dolomites refer to the mountain range in the eastern section of the northern Italian Alps.

9. *Rechérche* (French) means (in British English) "choice, rare, or refined and elegant."

10. "smug ~~abandoned by~~ and rechérche for 19/4" appears in the original.

way. To wit, Ethel Mannim[11] on Burma.[12] She sounds as though she had dysentery throughout Asia. I sound as though I had tooth-ache. Well, I have tooth-ache. And Ireland in April is bitterly cold and uncomfortable. And I wish I liked fishing or sailing, or knew some Irish history, or some people who owned a country-house without a roof, or who could sing, or at least cook.

In some ways Ireland is still pre-1920 England. There are enough people who are poor and frightened enough to work as servants. But they look so infinitely more ambiable than the best paid English. The country has not been raked over by speculators yet, and enormous high tracts of it are untouched by chemical fertilisers or TV aerials or tractors. Dogs look useful and intelligent. They lack the obscenity, the public sexuality of highly bred English dogs. In Ireland they are animals who earn their keep, and look as wistful as donkeys.

In a cottage in Blessington,[13] turned into a rough tea-room, Mrs. O'Honas—the crude mantelpiece was hung with a ½ yd. width of best English cotton tapestry and wooden bobbies, curtains to match. This was in fashion between the 1870's and 1890's. I doubt if anything of the sort survives in England. Every window, with the exception of the smartest houses around Merrion SQ.,[14] are hung with new lace curtains. All this is at once slightly sad (but why?) and greatly endearing. click, dry bread for a minute, and you're in 1910. Ireland is wounded in a tea-rose world of white flannels and well-connected curates.[15]

But Guinness[16] is ⅓ a pint—and Murphy's peat bill for the winter was £30—which must be bitterly lopsided for a 1910 economy.[17]

Cleggan has about ten houses in all,[18] an impressive Government-built pier and an empty bay. One of Murphy's boats was in the bay, and there were two men

11. British novelist and travel writer Ethel Mannin (1900–1984) wrote *Land of the Crested Lion: A Journey through Modern Burma* (London: Travel Book Club, 1955).

12. "Mannim ~~about~~ on Burma" appears in the original.

13. Blessington is located in Wicklow, Ireland, about thirty minutes south of Dublin's City Centre. It is known for being the center of Ireland's Ancient East; among other attractions is Glendalough's sixth-century monastic site.

14. Merrion Square is a Georgian square, designed in 1762, located in Dublin. Oscar Wilde and W. B. Yeats lived in residences that are part of Merrion Square.

15. "curates. ~~But this is not so.~~" appears in the original.

16. Guinness is a beer that has been brewed in Dublin since 1759.

17. "economy. ~~Return to Cleggan. Time~~" appears in the original.

18. "ten houses in all ~~together~~" appears in the original.

clambering over it, and a boy watching from the pier. I looked unhappily about. I hate approaching people for unoffered hospitality, which any approach to Murphy must have implied. We were careful to find a hotel in Galway before we left. Cleggan looked marvelous, as yet eager for tourists, virgin, swept with no pretensious aside from the presence of Murphy and the expensive sailing boats. Murphy is a famous man in Ireland—"The Last Galway Hooker"[19] was displayed in every small hotel and bookshop in Connemara, even the barman at the Ballynahinch Castle[20] was faintly rustled when we said we had come from seeing him.

We walked into a tall plain grey house which read the Pier Bar[21] in enormous letters. Inside was an old travel-nosed man, 4 seats which could have furnished a bus once, or a very expensive American church pew, a large wooden counter, a living peat fire and 50 odd cut-out sea-birds stuck on the wall. There were Sweet Afton cigarettes,[22] there was guinness and two apologetic, sad middle aged people and their dog. The dog was part retriever and many other parts, and very old it was, and moved like a woman with a recent hystorechtomy. It was exactly like its owners.[23] Its enormous size displaced it in the pub, and its complex ancestry was too pretensious on the one hand, and too shadowy on the other to merit the kind of canned feelings which get discharged towards normal old dogs. We said we were looking for Murphy. "You wait here" the red-travel man said "I'll get him for you." We stopped him. Couldn't have the thought of Murphy hurrying down from tea, from his fire, from tourist accounts or poetry to meet two unknown and unexpected smart looking non-Alecs. The two sad looking people were about to go. Men with a sea-gull's nose and a big belly with a pullover starched over it, and a pretty grey haired woman and a frightened smile and big hands. "There's an article in the Sunday Express,[24] Eileen, about the Prime Minister of Northern Ireland[25] who's a personal friend of ours—would you keep it for us?" Ah. Shame. It was partly for our benefit. The voice

19. "in Ireland—~~his book~~ 'The Last Galway Hooker'" appears in the original. Richard Murphy is the author of the fifteen-page poetry book *The Last Galway Hooker* (Dublin: Dolman Press, 1961).

20. Ballynahinch is a castle located in Connemara; it became a luxury hotel in 2018.

21. Pier Bar is only a two-minute walk from Richard Murphy's residence at the time, the Old Forge in Cleggan.

22. Sweet Afton is a brand of Irish cigarettes.

23. "like ~~the people~~. its owners" appears in the original.

24. The *Sunday Express* is a British middle-market newspaper that was founded in 1918 and continues to be published today.

25. The prime minister of Northern Ireland is Terence O'Neill (1914–90).

was tinged with Middle-class/gentry Irish, but the voice had travelled in Pullmans[26] and ordered somewhere, expensive meals and engaged servants. Eileen, stood them a drink on the house, for which they were inspiredly grateful. They sat down again. No sign of Murphy. I drank ginger ale and looked out into the bay—David was talking to them. I heard words: Vancouver—Benson's[27]—my wife in advertising. I couldn't bring myself to turn round.

Two men walked past the Pier bar door.

APRIL 12TH. GOOD FRIDAY.

We arrived in Cork at $5^{\underline{30}}$. I asked the general very carefully at what times the Boat to England leaves. "There's one at 6 tonight and none other until Tuesday." Oh God. There's the end of Co. Cork, and the vague speculations about putting about Kerry. Our money very low—about £17 left. At roughly £2 a night plus food plus cigarettes this would have left us

<u>May $19^{\underline{th}}$.</u> 10:15 in Fitzroy Rd—4 days after my 100th birthday and 14 days after the end of my $3^{\underline{rd}}$ and sweetest marriage. <u>David</u>—my sweetest husband, my most always favourite, my best and truest love. What insanity, what methodically crazy[28] compulsion drove me to sentence him to being alone, and myself to this nightmare maze of miserable, censorious, middle aged furies, and Sylvia, my predecessor between our heads at night.[29]

Theresa, the nany, is to be fired. I offered, and Ted accepted the offer to look after the children. I can't help feeling that I'm inviting Sylvia's doom on myself. With the enormous difference that she had a million times the talent, 1000 times the will, 100 times the Greed and passion that I have. I should never have looked into Pandora's box, but now that I have I am forced to wear her love-widow's sacking without any of her compensations.

What, in 5 years time will he reproach me for? What sort of woman am I? how much time have I been given? how much time has run out? What have I done with it? have I used myself to the hilt, already? am I enough for him? AM I ENOUGH FOR HIM?

26. AW refers to railroad parlor or sleeping cars.

27. DW worked for the advertising firm Ogilvy, Mather & Benson.

28. "what ~~in~~ methodically crazy" appears in the original.

29. "~~between our heads on the pillows.~~ at night." appears in the original.

Last night, in the half dark, as he lay naked—and the thick hair on his chest and stomach formed a diffused, moving monster's face—like a tattooed snake—I came into a panic fear, like the kind I had when I was 4. Was that the black, manic, Negress-eater, the killer, who was quite formally showing himself like a harmless photograph, for the first time. That's crazy.

MAY 20TH.

In bed. Excruciating cystitis, on the wave now, after sulpha,[30] and fear that there must be an ulcer there by now, which is incurable. If we can't make love properly again, I'd just as soon not live. I seem to have stupefied since I've been here. I can't think of anything funny or interesting or clever to say. Ted in whirlpools of disaster, which grow and mutate like cancers. They steal his writing time, and my sickness makes me a total loss. He's far too ready to accomodate anything, and everybody's whim. Soon he'll break out—he must. If only I could make him time. The sickness puts me into a position of demands—all movement brings on a bout of pain, and his constantly having to bring me things—cigarettes, fruit. Oh Ted—Ted—Ted. I'll bring him presents of peace once I'm well, I will, I will, I will. I MUST BE WELL.

Where are the vast populations of adorering admirers? is my presence discouraging his friendships? Why has Redgrove[31] vanished? the proof of his 3rd book[32] arrived on Saturday. Unsurprising—impaled on the same old cold, watery wines of "awarenesses" of his other two books. Hint at Ted saying[33] that David u Redgrove use words too experimentally. Perhaps I misunderstood. Probably misunderstood. Can't bear the thought of any kinship between DAW and Redgrove. Remember David tying his shoelaces on the chair in the Chalcot SQ. kitchen—the sun behind him—the absolute grace of him and his beautiful head in profile, straight pale hair massed across his forehead.[34] The sun is in ashes.

30. AW may be referring to sulfamethoxazole-trimethoprim, perhaps what she calls "sulpha," which is used to treat cystitis.

31. British poet Peter Redgrove (1932–2003) befriended TH at Cambridge; he and TH were lifelong friends. Redgrove was a founding member of the Group, a gathering of poets in the 1960s in a salon-workshop style setting in England, where he met DW.

32. AW refers to Peter Redgrove's *At the White Monument* (London: Routledge and Kegan Paul, 1963). Before this book, he wrote *The Collector* (1959) and *The Nature of Cold Weather and Other Poems* (1961).

33. "Hint at ~~the~~ Ted saying" appears in the original.

34. "hair massed ~~on~~ across his forehead" appears in the original.

I'm sure that when I return to CPV[35] tomorrow I shall be fired. My absences have been too absurdly frequent. That's the last link Gone. David gone. my independence over—I'm immersed now in the Hughes' monumentality. Hers and his. The weak mistress, forever in the burning shadow of their mysterious seven years. I'm getting weaker and weaker. I have no will. No talent. A slight, decorative intelligence—and Cystitis. Not enough Vanity. No husband.

Oh—it's all because I'm sick. I'll be alright, maybe.

Ted writing: He sits cross-legged, sideways, against Sylvia's black desk (too small for him) a mug of tea on it, sugar bowl, Theresa's sandwiches in one hand, pen in another, writing voraciously, poring through paper-obstacles, breathing through them, his nostrils flared, his hair feathery and leaping forward like a peacock's back-train in reverse, swaying a little as he writes. Rather like a great beast looking over an enormous feast, dazzled and confused by the variety. Frieda's in the bedroom, playing with my trinkets, her blanket with her, sometimes leaning on Ted's knee. Murmuring to herself; saying the "light hurts"—"Make the room brown." "Nicky coming"—exciting herself by hoarding all her possessions into a mound. Ready to protect them against Nick. Ted completely immune to all the noises. My getting up, Frieda's clickety-click presence. He's in a wild fever, in the most absolute concentration I've ever witnessed.[36] He's possessed.

8 P.M.

changed into my pale blue dressing gown. Felt like Mme Barov—in bed with her rotting heart for a whole year, and her silk scarves around her black black head. But her cycle was complete and satisfactorily expended. The 2 children, the perfect mourning, the perfect falling away from life. One long pain—death—and a box of jewels.

Went downstairs. Ted tender and Solicitous and wonderfully sweet—sweet—sweet dangerously self-less. Theresa with her nylon ski pants and golden slippers was hinting that her Pekingese needed its nails clipped. We looked—the claws[37] were almost complete circles their ends growing back into the ani-

35. AW alludes to advertising agency Colman, Prentis and Varley, then located at 34 Grosvenor Street, London.

36. "the most absolute ~~self-~~concentration" appears in the original.

37. "the ~~nails~~ claws" appears in the original.

mal's pads. "Poor Susie, she can't walk" The little dog totters about sound-less, life-less, its height of pleasure being carried around the park in a carrier-bag. Theresa told us about an unwanted lover in the hotel she lived in—he spent days in bed with bottles of whiskey. The request for the nail-clipping followed immediately. Ted clipped them, the animal howling with rage and surprise. We were both almost sick with the obscenity of it. Poor Theresa is hollow with lovelessness, she's transparent, as though she were wholy made of layers of bland cellophane, exposing her drying entrails and her watery heart. The pain returned, suddenly. Theresa suggested it was psychosomatic—how could it be? My God—what if it never went. On whose bed shall I Krapienen[38] slowły—not this one—the cost is too high.[39] I'd rather die, suddenly than continue like this. The idiotic doctor didn't come today, although he promised to.

10:00 I know the wallpaper by heart. Grey never-been roses posy column after column. A biro with a long feather in a toy ink well with Berlin's coat of arms. The half moon of flesh between Ted's black socks and shoes. His pen tapping on the table, and the mosquito whine of the nib. Holbien's[40] silver point Henry VIII on the floor, the glass spattered with something white. My tartan bag with the B.E.A.[41] Düsseldorf tag,[42] and the Burma customs permit on the underside. My silver baby-brush, Ted's Hercules' candlestick (is this the candlestick of "Nick u the Candlestick?")[43] the tulips fainting into the lilac corpses. Bottles of pills. The bed's becoming uncomfortable. My face teary and watery with mascara. There's a bruise on my right bosom. Ted inspects it with pleasure. Like a P.I.D.A.[44] sheep stamp. It's dutifully purple. The pain's slowly going.

I've got about 25 sleeping pills left. I'll guard them. I've still got Highbury

38. AW probably means *Krepieren,* which is German for "to die miserably."

39. AW may be referring literally and figuratively to SP's bed, which she was using.

40. AW references German painter and printmaker Hans Holbein the Younger (ca. 1497–1543). He was the King's painter to King Henry VIII.

41. *B.E.A.* stands for "British European Airways."

42. AW and DW visited Germany, including stops in Bingen, Boppard, Düsseldorf, Heidelberg, and Mainz, in the autumn of 1962.

43. The Hercules (or Atlas) candlestick is featured in two Plath poems: "By Candlelight" ("the little brassy Atlas— /. . . / At his heels a pile of five brass cannonballs") and "Nick and the Candlestick." Plath recorded "Nick and the Candlestick" for the British Council on October 30, 1962. In this recording and in lines later excised, Plath directly referred to the candlestick: "The brass Atlas you inherited / Is hefting his milk-pillar. / He kneels // Head bent."

44. Probably AW means the Pig Industry Development Authority (PIDA).

for the next 10 days.[45] If the sickness doesn't go—I'll go to Highbury and take the pills there. Nobody can get in. It's mine. My poor love. DAW.

On and off, I've looked at his face[46] today for about 6 hours. I've discovered that he really does consist, even physically, of above easily 4 different men. His right profile, discounting the deeply set eyes is Holbein's Henry VIII. The left hand side, looks much younger and hansomer. In full face, with his eyes fully on one, one loses track and is either dazzled or dismayed. His mouth is grim—it's a sandy ditch. When he's angry, or suspicious, his face actually turns black, or a dark brown /grey and the cloud colour and amorous impact[47] of his eyes disappear, and become camouflaged and as significant as his nostrils. The weight of his chin must account for 1/8 of his total weight, and bears heavily on his neck—he has 2 of them.[48] Basically, he's a prim, rational (self-admittedly) highly-charged puritan, with whole Versailles[49] of virtues beautifully landscaped through his brain. He's busy espalliering Sylvia.

May 23rd—10:30 a.m. Still in bed. *Chaos.*[50] Five changes of plan between yesterday morning and now. We looked desultorily at houses in Wiltshire[51]—or really only one house. The children are to be sent to Yorkshire to Hilda, while a house is found. Ted will stay in Yorkshire. The nanny is fired. I'm to look after the children henceforth.

Feelings of immense alienation between Ted and I. Ted dreamed of Sylvia's hair having turned white, and of shooting a cat (which they had in Boston)[52] which wouldn't die. All began yesterday when a new Malcolm Brinnin[53] sleek

45. In December 1962, the Wevills moved from 3 Chalcot Square to a flat at 14 Highbury Place, London.

46. "I've looked at ~~him~~ his face" appears in the original.

47. "and amorous ~~eyes disap~~ impact" appears in the original.

48. "has 2 ~~chins~~ of them" appears in the original.

49. "whole ~~Babylons of~~ Versailles" appears in the original.

50. Koren and Negev write that this word is Hebrew for *Tohu Vavohu,* from the Book of Genesis.

51. Wiltshire is a county in southern England. The distance by car between Wiltshire and Yorkshire is approximately four and half hours and about two hours from London.

52. SP and TH lived in a sixth-floor apartment at 9 Willow Street, Boston, from September 1958 to June 1959. Their cat, Sappho, was a descendant of a cat owned by German writer Thomas Mann.

53. John Malcolm Brinnin (1916–98) is an American critic, poet, and biographer who edited several poetry anthologies; he also was known for working with Welsh poet Dylan Thomas on American speaking tours.

paper-back, The Modern Poets arrived.[54] In it was a quintessential photograph of Sylvia which he had never seen before. She looks tense, slightly reproachful, and very young. There's a picture of Ted (1958) very young, laughing, very handsome. A cruel juxtaposition of them both that's exactly[55] how they were: dour, paining, puritanism bleaking her face—and he, innocent of the Boulder in him. He's aged like weather—boarding, she like a young girl after terrible strain. After an illness. He wants a house in the North—in Cumberland, in Lancashire, in Sutherland.[56] The North terrifies me. Big Boulder smashing me. I feel devoid of substance, of self. I feel swallowed up by those 2 pictures, by his dreams. Very near to wild hysteria all morning. Sylvia growing in him, enormous, magnificent. I shrinking daily, both nibble at me. They eat me.

Lipsey—resentment at him. I don't want to make love again for ages. Ghastly duplication of feeling. He is Lipsey. Abrupt preoccupation with (rightfully) Other urgent matters, leaving me unsatisfied, untalked out. Fantastic—the way children (not even my own) have finally surrounded me. The children I like, very much. I shall like them even better, I think, when they're a little older. Lipsey: Genius—myth. As remote and utterly superiour as Lipsey's.[57] It was never like that with David's writing. He always let me in, was touchingly unsecretive. Always talked about it.

I hated him all night. Couldn't bear his arm under my head. Pretended it was a wooden bar.

May 24th. 10:30 a.m. Suddenly looked at the empty mirror and saw it reflected the raining-rose wallpaper swimming in white wine. A tall rose is[58] in it also, and lillies of the valley. The sun's bright. It's summer—one of the zoo lions is roaring.[59]

54. John Malcolm Brinnin and Bill Read edited *The Modern Poets: An American-British Anthology* (New York: McGraw-Hill, 1963). The photographs of SP and TH in it are by Rollie McKenna, taken in Boston, 1959. Plath and Hughes were both published in the collection: Ted Hughes, "Hawk Roosting" and "View of a Pig" (170–73); Sylvia Plath, "Black Rook in Rainy Weather" and "The Colossus" (255–58).

55. "both ~~when~~ that's exactly" appears in the original.

56. Cumberland and Lancashire are counties in northwestern England. Sutherland is a county in the Highlands of Scotland.

57. "superiour ~~and~~ as Lipsey's" appears in the original.

58. "A tall ~~red~~ rose is" appears in the original.

59. The ZSL London Zoo is 1.2 miles away from 23 Fitzroy Road.

"The sickness" is vengefully back. Yesterday was one of the most, dreadful, bleakest, dullest days of my life. All day felt nothing but a patronising resentment. Trapped. trapped. trapped. Joanna came—says I must go away; can't let them trap me like this, let's go to Italy! Joanna free as a Tulip—what she said felt unreal, had relevance to a photograph of me, a gossipy story—not to me. The lion is groaning horribly.

What a revenge! I had absolutely no feeling for Ted; a bleak,[60] grim sense of duty to look after his children. Image of cold stone house in the North—hands chapped and red, tired, children chattering like monkeys, Ted locked in a small icy room, coming out 3 times a day furaging for food like a bear. Great monumental disorders.

We all look unkept, unkeptable. Patronising visitors come from London. I'm their mother. The thought of ever marrying him utterly repugnant. Let him continue to be her God.

May 25th. Halifax.[61] We took the children up to Hilda. A mid-summer day. I unaware of the details of it. My insides raging. Anger and a silly flapping spite. Children docile and touching. I kissed Nick's neck over and over again. It kills me when he gurgles with it. The sinister Theresa is left behind in the flat. Is she burning my clothes?

May 27th Hebden Bridge.[62] Morning. Snap snappy morning. Crackling mood of E.J.[63]—I feel undocile. Endless idiotic conversations. Or rather, not conversations but retorts. "Have you ever thought," he says "that if you made a £1 every time you made love, you'd be very rich by now." The car's parked near a garage, near Hilda's liverish brick house. Door painted yellow. We saw Frieda purposefully walking towards—Ecstasy of welcome must be in full session now.

60. "Ted; ~~just~~ a bleak" appears in the original.

61. Halifax is located in West Yorkshire, England.

62. Also in West Yorkshire, Hebden Bridge, is located eight miles west of Halifax.

63. AW presumably means TH in using his initials.

<The following entry, for May 30, 1963, is typed and handwritten and is tipped into the journal.—Eds.>

May30th. Upstairs. 3 p.m. The window wide open on the first summer day absolute. First day of fearless welching[64] on CPV. First day with Theresa and her dog and her smell and her bag-fulls of silver gone. The telephone working. Otherwise as before. As before. Daisy-chains of ache, cottoned to is she going? is he there? is this a bed-sitting room house for two? Woke early with a headache, and the tranquiliser failing to send me back to sleep talked for hours, couldn't sleep, finally got up at 2.30. Talked about title for play.[65] He finished it yesterday, and woke up transformed, almost guilt-less for half an hour. He is almost incapable of performing one word wrong—play of its Noh-kind[66] perfect. Bang bang bang go[67] the clover and cruel and kisses and death, and Mexborough[68] un-immurred and I bawdy-lady shame . . . The whole man glitters. The whole man is ferocious with such intelligence and magic I am afraid to occupy the space next to him.

Letter from David. The saddest ever. The saddest. He sounds ill. Can't sleep at night with coughing. Fevers in the next paragraph. He goes to Barcelona airport on the crazy dream off chance that i might get off the plane. I'll go and visit him. I'll go and blank the wall—both of us can stand there together in the sun, and wait. But I'll go. Today I'm occupied with the boulder. 2 days ago, I'd have sold my venice molecule to go at once. Why can't I be more consistently loyal? Every day is a new film, with new heroes and new beasts. Only resentment on the same plane, every day. Nothing satisfies it, nothing lessens. And it used to not be there. It amounts I think, simply to jealousy of his preoccupations. At the forefront is Sylvia, and after that the Grand Scheme, the Genius, the children,

64. According to the *Oxford English Dictionary*, *welching* or *welshing* is that which "defrauds or cheats a person; that fails to honour debts or obligations; that reneges on agreements." According to the *Merriam-Webster Dictionary*, it is a term that is now sometimes considered offensive.

65. AW may mean *Gaudete* (London: Faber and Faber, 1977; New York: Harper & Row, 1977); TH was working on it as a filmscript in 1963–64. Christopher Reid notes that AW "seems to have contributed ideas" to it (*Letters of Ted Hughes*, 230).

66. The *Oxford English Dictionary* explains that *Noh*, borrowing from Japanese, is a "traditional Japanese masked drama with dance, mime, and song, evolved largely from Shinto rites."

67. "Bang bang bang ~~he shoots his cruelties and murders and kisses and clover~~ go" appears in the original.

68. Mexborough is a town in South Yorkshire, England, where TH lived from 1938 to 1951.

the fixity of the sun, the millions of hawks and fishes owls and nightshade that I neither see nor hear. Is he kind? what's 'kind'? "I'm dumb"—he says. That's her word. "Dumb" means unkind. He means blind, deaf. I'm twice as deaf, blasphemously blind. And I'm writing this aware that it's all censored. But he has genius, easily and innocently. He is magnificent. He doesn't cultivate it. He is easy, easy superb. Unwormed. I should be pleased that he appears to love me, love him back—wholly. Make it whole. Please make me whole.

Monday May 30th. 9$^{\underline{00}}$ Evening. Bright dusty evening. White abyss under the typewriter keys. Dangerous words trapped between £ and @. Ted typing "The two days of Man."[69] My puny suggestion. I thought The Espalliered Man—Ted says too cute, too many curlicues. Atmosphere again at total deadlock this afternoon. He came bouncing up from the midst of his typing this afternoon—I was re-folding sheets and things "What are you doing?"—what's he suspect me of? Terrible red silence. And then from bad to worse.

We went for a walk on Primrose Hill.[70] Bought cigarettes, chewing gum, matches—looked absently at the Listener,[71] vaguely hoping that David's Legend would be in. It was! and so was Rideau—and a headline Two Poems by David Wevill![72] Ah David . . . Love. This was the first time something was published in absence. Hill green and abandoned to heat, every leaf out, dandelions so blase with May, some had already lost their heads. Blonde girl necking with a boy in glasses. Small dogs doing the usual. Vivid sense of everything unreal. What whit of luck, misfortune, has taken me out of the Hostel on the Hill and put me 15 years later[73] back on the grass opposite the dining room windows with another woman's husband? and he reading vaguely, looking for something to dredge out his stoniness.

69. Ted Hughes's "The Two Days of Man" is an unpublished script-libretto. Emory University holds a manuscript and corrected typescript. The British Library holds a notebook with autograph notes under this title as well.

70. A 213-foot hill, Primrose Hill is on the north side of Regent's Park; the hill offers a view of central London. The surrounding district is also known as Primrose Hill.

71. The *Listener* is an intellectual and cultural magazine, founded in London and published by the BBC from 1929 to 1991. Considered one of the most distinguished magazines in British journalism, it published literary work by Virginia Woolf and T. S. Eliot, among others.

72. DW's "A Legend" and "At Rideau Falls" were published in the *Listener* on May 23, 1963, 864.

73. AW married John Steele, her first husband, on May 17, 1947, and she listed her address as 6a Primrose Hill Road, NW5, at the office of the register (Koren and Negev, *Lover of Unreason*, 39). After her marriage to Steele, AW moved with him to a flat south of London, in Purley.

I suggested I leave, for a month, meaning for ever. Meaning May and him and David, leaving him for ever at the Airport in Barcelona waiting like a lunatic. It's Mrs. Plath's coming. At least that's what we decided it was. He preparing to meet[74] the Chief Plaintiff. Preparing to whiten, to corpsen with Guilt. The play is almost a petition. This is how it happened. I was vaguely longing, you see M'am, loving her all the time, but my sperm was playing havoc with my loins and my memories and then it slipped, because I'm dumb, and your beautiful doll earth queen fell and broke all by herself. Snapped in my hand. She did. My Beauty and yours. And now we're mourners.

I'm wicked and spiteful. What an evil running-away falseness this is.

Then we felt relieved. And kissed and ran and little. And it all fell away into the dry pavement,[75] no longer real and long ago. David. David. Where are you? why can't I love you like I used to? My dearest—David David, yellow boy, straight like cornstalk,[76] smelling of talcum and chocolate, locked with unripe seed. But I did love you more than anyone, ever. I did once, I'll never forget.

<AW's handwritten journal entries resume.—Eds.>

June 1st. 9:30 a.m. In Heptonstall. In Olwyn's bedroom where I slept alone last night.[77] Slept well, pleased to be alone. Went to visit him in his snow-flaked room next door with the whole valley ghosting at him first thing in the morning. He wears a vest at night, his day-vest, looked very fleshy and broad the flesh almost having expanded a little in the night, like a life-belt. I brought him coffee. He sneezes 1st thing in the morning. He asked for Kleenex. They probably slept in this room. It occurred to me, as I was looking at the sheep, that whereas before, it was I who'd "hit his imagination" in stealth, now we're in perfect reversal, it's Sylvia who's hit it again, and will remain there until he's middle-aged, when she'll be relieved by a very young girl. I'm crazy to stay with him. I must go.

74. "He ~~was~~ preparing to meet" appears in the original.

75. "the ~~sut of~~ dry pavement" appears in the original.

76. "straight ~~as~~ like cornstalk" appears in the original.

77. AW is with TH at The Beacon, the Hughes's family home, in Heptonstall, England.

12:00. I took an hour to bath and dress. If only I could dress well and carefully every day. I mean, if my function in life is mainly decorative[78] (but who's cast me?) then I may as well fulfill it with some brio. Ted's out picking up Frieda u Nick and shopping. He asked me to come. It would have meant dressing in a hurry. I need every inclination of vanity that I have, for today. I sense the day grim and bare. This house is a perfect mis-en-scene for all the Dolorosas[79] that Man invented. It heightens anything one's purile sensibilities happen to come across. Jealousy, abandon (God—to be ABANDONED HERE!) tenderness, cranky astrological tendencies, visionariness, the lot. The grass is bitterly green, three black with dandelions, black walls, black, little stunted men with parcels coming up the mountain. I sit near the window in this tiny child's, maid's, unwanted-guest room. Feeling fully unwanted, a quarter my size, stunted, not knowing what I should assert. Why do I need to assert anything? For God's sake, I'm fully grown, (I was fully possessed) why do I feel like a galaxy[80] of Theresa's left-over cups? Pits of chicken liver in glass . . . a boiled potato. Is this sulking? When he came near me I sulked. I sulk. I sulk. I sulk. The second bus has just gone by. He hasn't come yet.

1^{30} p.m. Still not home. I've tried to read Parade's End.[81] Can't concentrate. Is he punishing me for sulking?

I feel absolutely alien to him, to them all. I expect one always does. There's nothing as chilling as being in the bedroom of someone else's[82] family with all its secrets slammed close. In reality his loyalty to Sylvia means that he won't talk about her to me—surely by now he remembers nothing but the tenderest, the freshest, the most ever inaccessible again. (After I leave him he'll move from woman to woman. Perhaps he'll be lucky.) And he can't talk about that. Secret. I'm beginning to feel awful. It's too late to cash a cheque—I'd move out, buy cigarettes, take a train to London, pack, ring Pickford's[83] to cart the junk

78. "life is ~~largely~~ mainly decorative" appears in the original.

79. "all ~~kinds of~~ the Dolorosas" appears in the original. *Dolorosa* translates to "grieving" or "sorrowful" from Latin to English.

80. "like ~~Theresa's left-over~~ a galaxy" appears in the original.

81. AW cites a tetralogy of novels (*Some Do Not . . . ; No More Parades; A Man Could Stand Up—*; and *Last Post* [1924–28]) by British writer Ford Maddox Ford (1873–1939).

82. "in the bedroom of ~~another~~ someone else's" appears in the original.

83. Founded in 1646 in London, Pickfords is a moving and storage company.

away and take a train to Spain on Tuesday. I'm out of cigarettes . . . the third bus has just gone by.

11:15 p.m. He came finally, exhausted and in a foul temper. I went for a walk seething with the fantastic ineptitude of my position. He came after me. I glanced towards the house—saw him, and continued to walk. He walked towards me hard-faced and sweating. We didn't speak. the children were hungry and whiny. No welcomes. I made lunch—the dining room seething with sun—driven by enormous, Atlantic winds, and battering against the window. Everything became enlarged and uncontainable. As I was leaning over the table to give Frieda her food—we collided to—Kiss.[84] I then flared up with enormous love. It's lasted all day. He battered by every imaginable difficulty, exhausted, tinged[85] by insuperable after insuperable, and no time. He's belittled by all this. It presses and presses on him.

In the evening after F u N were returned to Hilda's brick nest, and Mr. Hughes and I had tea with television, he returned like thunder and very fresh with the winds. We went for a walk, in the most desolute valley. The Prototype Valley, soft, unenderable layers of green on green, green waters and ferns and black-green stones; and reins of bluebells, like songs, the whole valley saturated with the prime of love of generations of dead people, who descended, perhaps a dozen times in their lives into this green, unenderable cauldron, brimming with madness. I felt like Henry James governess, the one in The Turn of the Screw,[86] bewitched by this huge creative, who's touched off dreadful, magic things in me, I may never know what to do with.

In the late sun, the brick walls burn like evil furnaces[87]

JUNE 7TH (8TH?)

Heptonstall. Sunday.[88] 4th day of Big Summer. The Bedroom stews in the Great sun. The wind is sunny, gentle, the strange family, Vicky,[89] David[90] (naive-

84. "we collided to—Kiss ~~deeply~~" appears in the original.

85. It is unclear if this word is *tinged* or *ringed*.

86. Acclaimed American-British writer Henry James (1843–1916) wrote the Gothic novella *The Turn of the Screw* (1898).

87. This line written in the top margin of the page.

88. Likely this entry was written on Sunday, June 9, 1963.

89. Victoria Farrar Watling (1938–) is TH's cousin.

90. Probably AW is referring to David Watling, Victoria's husband.

travesty) stretching in the sun, idling not unhappily, all married, all irrevocable. Sheep hypnotized by individual grass blades, camouflaged to look exactly like mounds of rock of the district. Two good days with T. Today smouldering again. His time downstairs interrupted by Olwyn, creamy and harmlessly indolent tied with a dressing-gown (beware, beware dressing gowns!) wandering from room to room, waking. T. in mysterious repressing rage against her. Is it really concealed rage against me, or her old *Hate* against *Sylvia!* or both ours? Suddenly flaring of eagerness to not only wean himself completely, but cut himself off them. Establish his own Pater Familias establishment. He can't, won't commit himself to me entirely. S his wife. I'm his mistress, for ever and ever.

6$^{\underline{00}}$ Olwyn comes to say that T's gone to the Graveyard, to put flowers on Sylvia's Grave.[91] We shall have a properly gloomy journey back to London, with full honours. Olwyn and I made Tea for the whole lot, Papa Hughes[92] Vick u David like thirsty 'tomatoes,' the sun shining equally on the sinister ferns in the valley (Cragcastle) on the huge black Covent Rocks in the moor, merely trapped the tea drinkers and canned-salmon eaters. We were like sleepers in the body of a young whale, evading the privilege of summer and doing the duty-eating. Only I bleached outside them. I have no family. I refuse to sink my teeth into T. If I'm not claimed, I can't claim. Only David can claim me morally; there are no other claims, I think T's vascillation and regret at my living in his air, absolves me now from any feeling of having or wanting to take part in his revolving-spheres life. I am, quite obviously, quite outside his concern. All this has been a summer job. Reality is David, my own income. T is a long night of nightmares. Whatever the consequences for me, T. is unconcerned. He forces me to look out for myself.

JUNE 12$^{\underline{TH}}$.

The car journey to London began a new cycle. I explained, in what I hoped, was an objective, definitive voice[93] pretty well what I thought above. He sounded prepared for that, and at the same time, a little, gratifyingly bewildered. We spoke and accused each other for the full five hours the journey took. It was

91. SP is buried in the cemetery of St. Thomas the Apostle Church, Heptonstall.

92. William Henry Hughes (1894–1981) is TH's father.

93. "I explained, in what I hoped, ~~sounded~~ was an objective, definitive voice" appears in the original.

an exhilarating ride—the evening golden and green and stretching with new villages, and becoming brick, and T very brown and blue—intense. We've lived in peace for 5 days now—the longest (it seems) stretch since Sylvia died.

He explained last night again that his blackest, most demonic, most destructive moods come when he can't for one reason or another, write. On the other hand, I feel 'outside' in this mood, which continues into his mysterious writing periods and make me wretched. In "goodwill,"[94] I'm genuinely happy when he writes, I'm curious about it and concerned about its fate. When he's black—I resent it. We're both undergoing an anti-domestic mood. I wonder what the significance[95] is for T—and how he's arrived there? If it's in reaction to S. I'm pleased. If it's self-destructive, I'm apprehensive. I've noticed that whenever we're closest,[96] he complains, a little, about her—or at least mentions her openly and casually. Most apart, at his most close-toed, he fills the air[97] with her desirable and missed presence. This pretty well cancels his absolute assertion that his preoccupations do not necessarily always concern Sylvia. They must. We've decided to let the flat in Fitzroy Rd.[98] So. I've sold the carpet for £60 in Highbury—the book shelves for £22 and the cooker for £5. All the stuff will Go down to Court Green. He's raised Court Green's price to £4500 and will let the Compton[99] live there until the house is sold. Mrs. Plath[100] is expected any moment.

AUGUST 12TH. REMEMBER AUG. 10TH.

For the past six weeks in Heptonstall. A cage with six macaws wearing each other out with noises enough to occupy a whole street. Squalls. Orders. My own preserving indolence. There is absolutely no privacy whatsoever. I remember with pain the ½ hour of total privacy first thing in the morning when I just lived, with my skin all over open to the night's morning. David lightly asleep. I drink coffee, eat rolls with redcurrant jam, read, smoke.

94. "~~If~~ In "goodwill" appears in the original.
95. "I wonder what ~~this~~ the significance" appears in the original.
96. "whenever ~~he's~~ we're closest" appears in the original.
97. "he ~~per~~ fills the air" appears in the original.
98. There are three *X*s above the word *flat*.
99. Elizabeth Sigmund (1928–2017) and David Compton (1930–) lived at the time at Tythecott Mill, Tythecott, Buckland Brewer, Devon, England; they married in 1952 and divorced ca. 1967. For a time in 1963, the Comptons lived at Court Green. Elizabeth married William Sigmund in 1973. SP dedicated *The Bell Jar* (London: Heinemann, 1963) to Elizabeth and David Compton.
100. Aurelia Schober Plath (1906–94) is SP's mother.

T's practically bought the manor down the hill. "Bought" it enough to have fetched the Plath-Hughes belongings from Court Green. The house in Devon flimsy, weedy, like a stage house. But it felt exactly like the time DAW and I were there. Very secret, red, childishly furnished. Naively furnished. The whole look of it improvised, amateurish; the cobbled yard seemed larger than before, damp with hideous grass gorging on the smooth brown stones. Grass almost grew in the house. As we were leaving Court Green I saw a sight I had never seen before: a cock sewing one of the Comptons' hens.[101] T understandably charged with distress. I fetched Sylvia's clothes and drawers full of combs and ribbons and brushes and miscellaneous ½ discarded things from the Holy Study.* The enormous blue bed reverentially moved by the Comptons' from the God's bedroom and kept in the study. Soon it was empty. Without the elm desk[102] (made by T.)[103] without the red carpet, without the Baskin[104] etchings, without the marvelous photograph of the handsome T.—it turned relentlessly into just a room in North Devon. Through the window was the church,[105] the Elm,[106] the yew trees,[107] it was all over. It was the funeral all over again. DAW's and mine funeral. And Theirs. It was very sad.

*I noticed that David Compton used it for his study.

11 p.m.

The flat opposite. Strewn, animated, with legitimate domesticity. Blonde young wife, with straight shoulder-length yellow hair is leaning over her husband in white shirt. He's writing something. They're poor. There are no curtains.

101. "Comptons' ~~ducks~~ hens" appears in the original.

102. The elm plank desk is held by Smith College and was jointly made by SP's brother, Warren, and TH in September 1961. After SP's death, the desk was moved to the kitchen, where it was used for meals.

103. "(~~used~~ made by T.)" appears in the original.

104. American sculptor, illustrator, and wood engraver Leonard Baskin (1922–2000) collaborated with TH on artwork for TH's *Crow: From the Life and Songs of the Crow* (London: Faber and Faber, 1970), *Capriccio* (Searsmont, ME: The Gehenna Press, 1990), and *Howls & Whispers* (Rockport, ME: The Gehenna Press, 1999). Baskin met SP and TH at Smith College when SP taught English 11 in 1957–58.

105. AW refers to St. Peter's Church, North Tawton, Devon, England.

106. See SP's "Three Women," dated April 2, 1962; "Pheasant," dated April 7, 1962; and "Elm," dated April 19, 1962.

107. See SP's "The Moon and the Yew Tree," dated October 22, 1961; and "Little Fugue," dated April 2, 1962.

They have a Greyish electric light. There's her shopping basket, the kind they have here—it's like a flower-basket.—She wears a flowered skirt. He's concentrating hard. She has her arm over his shoulder—Quite relentless with its pressure. Two floors up there's their arty lodger—black wall, or very entire dark, bedecked with pictures. a figure spirals up the staircase—disappears. Reappears briefly. Vanishes. Basically, the household totally boring me.

Went to sleep—or tried to—at 9. Lonlelist sleep. Got up—the only thing I can do is listen to Bach. The only relief. Half my brain is attuned to the slow, exhausted braking outside—the other to the Great Cargo in the 3rd. I shall. I shall will myself to write. I shall will to read with more concentration,[108] less lasciviousness. less promiscuity. I'll start by willing myself back—to the earliest, darkest, most fearful bedroom in my life.

I've heard no birds all day long. Do I ever hear birds? Throughout the walk through Regents Park,[109] I heard wind, sails on the pond—but nothing as subtle as birds.[110] Perhaps because I walked throughout, with my head bowed. Birds in London, I hear with the difficulty I'd hear[111] bats in the country.

Observation: In fear, in apprehension, in expectancy, objects cling to that—objectless, and to the other objects they're connected to, with enormous rigidity. They seem absolutely immovable. They seem as though no force, ever could ever budge them again. In calm—they appear flimsy, fragile without life. During fear they hum with their positive death. They undergo their own rigor Mortis. A million times during their existence.

<On the inside front cover of the red exercise book appears the following.—Eds.>

Sarah (Merlin Rogers)
Sarah Hillsbae
60 Montpelier Walk SW7
KEN 3716

108. "to read ~~more~~ with more concentration" appears in the original.

109. One of London's eight royal parks, The Regent's Park encompasses 395 acres. The park contains formal gardens and tree-lined pathways. It is approximately two-fifths of a mile from 23 Fitzroy Road.

110. "as subtle ~~and~~ as birds" appears in the original.

111. "the difficulty ~~in~~ I'd hear" appears in the original.

<On page 1 of the journal appears the following.—Eds.>

Cher Raynfray—Leeds advertising

That was him, white shirt narrows waist
moving in the boat. He comes up the
gangway. The brown skin sweats. It sweats.

"SAYAH"—Burmese savant
KA BA—dance please
SA BAH—eat
LA BAH—Come here
Thakin—Lord—Sahib
Chezutunbadeh—Thank you.
Contretemp:
MASHEEBOO—Does not exist
MAKAMBOO—can't do
Yeé Noo-eh—not water
LAPAY—tea
HLA-ŔE—pretty
KW′E—dog
W′E—Pig
AH′A DE—"grace
AHA DH′E—graceful face-saving

YEH GEH—ice-water
THAN JIN—water festival
pice—penny

<The following notes appear between the May 19 and May 20, 1963, journal entries.—Eds.>

Robert Musil:[112] ". . . the only ones that never succeed (to conform to the beauty—standards of their time) are those faces born to strange triumphs, those in which the regal and exiled ideal beauty of another age is expressed without compromise. Such faces drift like corpses of earlier desires in the great insubstantiality of love's whirlwind."[113]

112. Austrian Robert Musil (1880–1942) is a philosopher.

113. The excerpt is from Robert Musil, *The Man Without Qualities*, vol. 1: *A Sort of Introduction and Pseudo Reality Prevails* (1930).The first American edition was translated from the German

GOOD AND EVIL

"good and evil are not constants at all, but "functional values," so that the goodness of works depends on the historical circumstances, and the goodness of human beings on the psycho-technical skill with which their qualities are exploited.[114]

Robert Musil—The Man Without Qualities.

"... they had their initials exquisitely[115] embroidered on their underclothing—and likewise, that is to say, not outwardly displayed, but, as it were, in the exquisite underlinen of their minds . . ."[116] (their personalities, bigotries).

<The following poems and notes appear between the May 27 and June 1, 1963, journal entries.—Eds.>

THERE ARE NO FLIES ON HIM . . .

With Germans the motive behind Fleiss
is to appear to have Fleiss!

Polish flag

many cherries[117]
of this blood[118]
become distinct in rebellion,
visual Persuade the bed into a red bed-bug. uncorrupt. . . .
The first frost counts beets, blind pools,[119]
Potato-fire over the horizon
And men half entangled in smoke
The days shrink, apples on the cupboard

---

and with a foreword by Eithne Wilkins and Ernst Kaiser (New York: Coward-McCann, 1953). The parenthetical phrase may be AW's.

114. Quotation is from Musil, *Man Without Qualities,* vol. 1.

115. "initials ~~significantly embroidered~~ exquisitely" appears in the original.

116. Quotation is from Musil, *Man Without Qualities,* vol. 1. AW slightly misquotes Musil's text and punctuation.

117. "cherries ~~which~~" appears in the original.

118. "~~out~~ of this blood" appears in the original.

119. "blind ~~tears~~ pools," appears in the original.

(liberty) Freedom froze, now she burns in the ovens
Cooks children's porridge, paints knuckles red.[120]

Düsseldorf

Ich esse—sie isst—she is
sies ist—she eats } the same

he eats therefore he is
young pregnant woman—woman at café in Bonn
respectably swelling belly[121]—pregnant,
protected by pearls.

<Drawing of a man wearing a bowtie and suit jacket with hands crossed over his stomach—Eds.>

In the snow of festival kerchiefs
Pilsudski's[122] heart, the horse's fifth hoof
beat at the barn, until the east star came

The flag bleeds without pattern[123]
And so came winter,[124]
and will find the step[125]
behind Warsaw's wolves.

(And so winter came)
(and was found a step)
(behind Warsaw's Wolves)

120. AW draws a line with an arrow pointing from the end of this page to two pages later, beginning "In the snow of festival kerchiefs."

121. "respectably ~~preg~~ swelling belly" appears in the original.

122. Possibly this is a reference to Polish statesman Józef Piłsudski (1867–1935).

123. "The flag ~~beats~~ bleeds without pattern" appears in the original.

124. "And so came winter, ~~with the~~" appears in the original.

125. "and will ~~be~~ find the step" appears in the original.

CHILDREN'S SONG

Who laughs here, has laughed?[126]
Here things have been laughed out.
The one who laughs here makes suspicious[127]
OR (He's suspect, who here laughs)[128]
Who weeps here, has wept?
There's no more weeping here.
The one who weeps here[129]
Weeps for a reason.

Who speaks here, speaks and keeps quiet?
The one who keeps quiet is betrayed.
The one who here speaks is discreet
about where his reasons lie.

Who plays here, in the sand?
Who plays must go to the wall.
She's gambled away his hand,
Burned it Away.[130]

Who plays here, who[131] plays in the sand?
The one who plays must go to the wall,
The one who's[132]
He has plays[133] gambled away his hand,[134]
burned it away.[135]

126. Handwritten above this line is "Who laughs, has laughed, here?" in DW's handwriting.

127. Above *suspicious* is the word *suspect* in DW's handwriting.

128. "(He's suspect, he who here laughs)" appears in the original. A line drawn leads to "That he laughs for a reason."—written by DW—which appears at the top of the page.

129. "The one who ~~here~~ weeps here" appears in the original.

130. This stanza is handwritten by DW.

131. This *who* is inserted by DW.

132. This line is added by DW.

133. The word *plays* is added by DW.

134. "gambled ~~his had away~~ away his hand," appears in the original.

135. "~~And~~ burned it away." appears in the original.

Who dies here & who[136] is dead?
The one who dies has been won over,
The one who dies, uncorrupted[137]
is dead for no reason.

in the room—

it is forbidden to “wash” to “press”
and “to kook”

Pension Pfistener
Heidelberg

many cherries of this blood
roll loose in rebellion
crush the bed into a red bed-bug

<The following texts appear at the end of the journal.—Eds.>

Pisciottas

e shot cut on irrelevant
shout—cuts to a newsreel shot—
very violent

cut from a shooting scene 2 details
of a Pocket eye view of funeral[138]

very bold variations in pace
great detail in one scene—and
cut suddenly to an oval view
of the whole situation,

136. “& who” is inserted by DW.

137. A line drawn points to the word *uncorrupt; uncorrupt* is added by DW.

138. “of a ~~dog’s~~ Pocket eye view of funeral” appears in the original.

Q's mother swoops on his corpse like
a black bird ,her ghoul hairs his,
suddenly his wounds are visible,
as though she'd pecked him.

violent speak of the Mafia men
photographed through the speaker's
backside. Black, huge back
against the white gravel pit.

DARK
WOMEN

    A
  L   C
B   K

Wo
 Me
  N

<Symbols and letters under a line—Eds.>

□△Z○
Z△○□
△□Ƶ○
○△Z□
□○△Ƶ

<The following notes are written on the inside of the back cover.—Eds.>

Note: man humming and driving—car; ears full of engine and road sounds,[139] sense of bodies rattling with the engine. Car stops—man looks, unselfconscious,[140] at corner of landscape—as though he's forgotten something—NOW—engine

139. "road ~~signs~~ sounds" appears in the original.
140. "unselfconscious~~ly~~" appears in the original.

sound stops, man continues humming—in short bursts. Sounds fantastically sad. Because marks distinct demarcation live in time—reality is suspended while driving, allows for play of memory; the minute it stops, it also stops the past, and jerks mercilessly into now. The times collide.

Note. Heptonstall moors. T. children and I, moody, walk up a path which curves and curves round the hill. We sit sheltering against the path wall. I sit up. The tallest. T. lies, rests on his elbow. Children preoccupied for a split second, with grass. The path curves up, with a way out for them on either side. I'm too tall. I only see the end of the bit of path we're on. Very sunny. The Green has a high content of yellow, and greens with the black frames of every bit of contour. The fields are lozenges.

<The three November 1966 journal entries are typed on three sheets of paper. —Eds.>

NOVEMBER 29 1966.

He's right. I'm idle. And I'm crossed by equal, hazy directions: on the one hand, to surface from the befuddled, lamenting pit on my own terms—pride intact, however patched, to confirm the rightness of my loss of the world, to burrow into the experimental tunnelling. Is there anyone there? who is there? rows of wax dolls in Edwardian laces, the candle light power of 39 years muzzing their baby cheeks into frog jowls. Margarine frogs in tatty lace and crepe de chine. What else? / the Dolls House.[141] In the Basement is Sarafand and mother's panic labours to keep us in Rindfleisch[142] and starched summer dresses. The lady ogres. The thin rat-cats. Frau Lischinsky's dog with the bright moving colony of lice crawling one on top of the other and out of the dog's ears. And she smells of faeces in the fine library, she opens her chamois necessaire and takes out a pair of tweezers her hands are grubby with gardening, washing up with cakes of soap, tenderly she pulls out the lice. The dog twitches. Avid revulsion. I cannot eat the chocolate she offers soon afterwards with the same hands. Cecilia goes for a ride on the obscure son's motorcycle. Was there a son. There was a motorcycle, therefore a son. Hot hot outside. There is a typewriter in the library.

141. AW may be alluding to the play *A Doll's House* (1879) by Norwegian dramatist and poet Henrik Ibsen (1828–1906).

142. German *Rindfleisch* means "beef" in English.

Lischintsy was a publisher in Frankfurt.[143] I play the typewriter like a piano. Then write my name. Walls with books. Pictures, Oriental rugs from Frankfurt. Their sweet, permissive Rhine German. Vati complains of the food. He is swinishly ungrateful. Frau Lischinsky hugs Mutti when she comes and when we depart. Why was she so loved? why did they all adore her? Mutti cancels us—out of arrogance? Their talk is of no interest. I am not interested in the Lishinksy's—only their possessions. They all sit in the end-less sand-coloured gardens—in deck chairs. The dull bouganvillia, and beyond it the road. Sometimes a car. An arab and a donkey carrying ballast in two huge baskets on either side. The garden wearies me. The son and Cecilia (little Cecilia, she's only 5) and the motorcycle have cut zig zag through the garden, the dust settling on the fine chocolate and turning the bouganvillia foliage two tones greyer. I sneak into the library. The bottom shelf is enormous with enormous books. First the cauldron monsters of Wilhelm KOCH[144] the boys, baker boys, butcher boys, chimney sweeps in voluptus orgies of soups and terrines huge napkins tied with enormous knots behind their skinny boy-necks. The table cloths reach the floor. Then fat maids in innocent enough debaucheries in feather beds. The boys' caps abandoned on the floor. Feathers and pillows everywhere. I am those boys, but not the serving girls. The traps which the cauldron sets them are the traps it sets for me Their punishment is so brutal. I weep. Frau Leschinsky says they're funny.

NOV. 29.66.

Out for a walk. T. gone just as I8d finished coming and powdering. Towards Burton Hall[145] in a blue velvet end of daylight. The church yews black charcoal soldiery monuments, one rider on top of the other. The top one, a slender one with a napoleonic hat, and one arm. Let North Tawton forever be like a town I drive through in twilight. I do not want to know the source of the country

143. Frankfurt is located in the center of the Rhine-Main Metropolitan Region in Germany and is an important global city. It has a long history in the profession of publishing. For example, it hosts the world's largest book fair, sponsored by the German Publishers and Booksellers Association; the fair was inaugurated in the seventeenth century and founded again in 1949.

144. This word is handwritten in this typed, loose entry. *Wilhelm Koch* may refer to the German writer (1845–91) of the same name.

145. Burton Hall is located in North Tawton, Devon, England; it is a large house that was brought from Norway to England by its owner in the 1870s.

lights, the marvels of the larders—let there be fantasies of bottled beans and cellars laddred with sausages. A squat man out to post a Sunday letter, in the miraculous country Sunday pillar-box. Face, cap, black coat in shadow. 'Good Evening.'

The miracle of the word, the reflection of an idea is in the pool in the middle of the maze of iron yews. The miracle comes out—trying one costume after another, and none are true, to stumble feeble and grotesque being a faulty flash bulb. Shura crying hideously. Frieda whimpering, amazed at the horrific results of a laxative. The end the end. Hair washing. Supper for 6, 7, bath, pity, love, story. Cup of milk.

The panels on the door are 1880 scenes of Heidelberg[146] with the crude stereotype early colour print colours of then—the effect nostalgic a little beyond bearing. There is a monk on the left side of the mirror, meditating on the platform just below Holderlin's[147] statue. A woman and child in Tracht.[148] Moon, sun sky, trees a cart drawn by horses through snows. Eternal winter twilight. Shura stops to point out, the man, mummy, Shura. Hoss hoss.

NOV. 30.66

Christ of the Ice Floes[149]—at last I bought a copy after the copious devoted, interested pleas. It is a ghost of a book. Where is the glossy abundance I remembered, the sense of solid, wrought, tough poems? where is the ice rapier, the framed, dense things—what a paltry, melancholy, disheveled book it is. I hardly dare read the admired Surgeon's tale,[150] just in case it too had withered in my absence. His eyes grow narrower in sorrow. He sits, troubled, grievous, disowning it in the cold. Soon he must leave the flat—where will he go? In my renewed embedding in T. I forget him more and more. He has diminished to thinning symbols of my treachery my selfishness. My withering selfishness. Invoke the endless, limitless thoughtfullness, the touching faith in all things falling somehow by sheer grace of time into their right place. His anguish. His terrible bereaved anguish. The thick veins on his elderly hands—sitting on the lowest part of his spinal cord, the hands helplessly falling on the arm rests of the

146. Heidelberg is a university and residential city in southwestern Germany.

147. Johann Christian Friedrich Hölderlin (1770–1843) is a German Romantic poet.

148. *Tracht* is German for traditional costume.

149. *A Christ of the Ice-Floes* (London: Macmillan, 1966) is DW's second poetry collection.

150. "The Surgeon's Tale" is a poem in *A Christ of the Ice-Floes.*

chair. His walking up and down the room—long pauses by the large windows to watch the tubs, the black cat with a bell. His flushed winter face, the coat collar up, carrying a large parcel. Sausages, peas, butter, bread, beer, cigarettes. The Evening Standard.[151] The breeze in the sitting room, while he turns to lock the door. I'm always moved by his arrival. All it takes are just these photographs for me to fall into self-loathing. How there was no hope. The fragile passing of white-printed on white, on grey, days and evenings, with the impatience for things to end, to begin again stewing in me. The nightmare duality, complete compleate duality of that life, cosy, private, smell-less, without bustle, without outside pressure. White into stained snow white, into pure grey, into browned grey into nothing, nothing. Murder.

NOV. 31ST

How the perfect, round, all-inclusive, transcendent words fall away from them like little suns. How clumsy, ugly, angled, halting my own are. My glaringfault in everything, I think everything, but most in writing, is to let the orphaned spangle drop into my lap and then opportunously let it blow out like a buble. Bust? then bust. This feels wrong, almost immoral. Still wallowing in S.'s notebooks. Once again a strong sensation of her repugnant live presence. ". . . work at femininity" in a list of resolutions and things to buy, including a bathrobe, slippers and nightgown. Were the elbows really sharp? the hands enormous and knuckled? or is this my imaginary shape-giving to the muscular brain, my envy of her splendid brilliance. How spoilt I am. I am spoilt to numbness—I must encourage a new daily name-giving, a counting of smells, of phenomena. My best world, my best past, lies before puberty. Buried. The rest is an accretion of sensation by reading, by what I have heard told and deemed desirable. In the past two years I have scraped the barnacles of my social education off, but gained nothing new for myself. Only a naked, talcumed self-love.

T.'s generousity and affection almost unsupportable. It reaches such luxuriance sometimes, that I buckle over, speechless. How is he? there, in the hut, he is. I expect the hut to smoke with the temperature of his presence in it. The bare apple-brances, the path brown and soggy with old brown leaves.[152] The

151. The *Evening Standard* is an English newspaper, founded in 1827.

152. "with ~~the~~ old brown leaves" appears in the original.

burnt out, evil looking dead nettle branches barking out against the walls. I have these fits of huge love and admiration for him—but it is still 2 parts that and one part memory of Ruthless. The Mouth. Mutti's probably silly remark, etched in, in warning. Stupid warning. There he is in his white shirt scything in the glossy Rousseau jungle.[153] In sweet sweat. There he is coming down the orchard in his plaid shirt carrying something. His superb legs and thighs—the beautiful Anatomical Man.[154] One of God's best creations. Is God squandering him on me? He carries so many perfections that I would in all truth not begrudge him an affair or two with other women—as long as he remains loyal to me. I would suffer bitterly—but this in all truth is the only due thanks I could give him for all his grace. He ventures everything. His lovely, long risks of grasp. Sometimes little yaps of greed, but all accounted for. He is one of God's best creatures. Ever. Ever.

<This journal spans August 1968 to March 1969 and is dated on the front cover "August 1968" by AW. Entries are handwritten in a black-and-white exercise book.—Eds.>

AUGUST 7TH 1968.

In Boppard[155]—evil, dangerous Boppard—to which I've returned shamelessly and guilty with my wretched passport, and Shura, and Ted and 3 pieces of luggage, all too many—and the damp warmth; the evening cool and a cold mist rising out of the river covering the million or so uniformly upstanding geraniums. The serious, unsmiling, unlovely people. I welcome being an outcast within them? I'm relieved that my connection with them is only historical. I'm about as German as I'm Israeli—in reality neither. For once I'm pleased to be unrooted here—my lust for Kläden[156] is almost completely gone.

153. Henri Rousseau (1844–1910) is a French Postimpressionist painter in the Primitive, or Naive, style. He is known for his paintings of jungles, and his work influenced avant-garde artists and writers, including Guillaume Apollinaire and Pablo Picasso.

154. AW probably is alluding to *The Vitruvian Man* (ca. 1487) by Leonardo da Vinci (1452–1519). The drawing was based on what was thought to be ideal body proportions for a man.

155. Boppard is a town in Germany.

156. Kläden was a municipality and village in Germany; it is now part of the German town Bismark.

Beethoven's[157] house in Bonn[158]—a crowd of Scandinavians lining up outside, withering little men in large lounge suits barring and allowing the way in and out—a lifeless choking little museum—his last piano immaculately Glassed in. His ear trumpets lying in lined cases like precious bellows—any magic they once possessed totally exorcised by the scholarship and commerce which discovered them.

AUG. 8TH

We woke with the room flooded in soft warm damp. Steamers and ferries sailed by almost continually. A huge breakfast of coffee and butter—flowers and rolls. Chocolate for Shura. And we sat there in front of the uniformly upright geraniums guarding the Rhine memorising the China-like landscape of vineyard terracing, the trees—unfamiliar, but rounded, bush-like, the foliage almost touching the river. The Rhine is muddy, as though still recovering from flood.

A waiter with large spectacles[159] came bearing the huge breakfast tray. He was young. I didn't tip him—I didn't think of it. The doors of the room are as tall as the ceiling, six panels, painted the colour of yoghurt. The curtains are unlined—flimsy.

On an impulse we went to Würzburg.[160] the journey took 6 hours in all.[161] It rained heavily almost throughout. We were there for 4. Ted hardly spoke through the journeys. I was sad, remembering the charge between us on that first journey to Spain. We posted cards to Amichai. Ted wrote on the pink stucco of the Valkenhaus,[162] "Yehuda Amichai lived here." A man classifying something in an inside room, in a ceiling decorated with birds and chinese plants, looked at the window with a flicker of suspicion—but he's used to tourists staring at the birds and the steel filing cupboards. On the day before yesterday, as I unpacked the suitcase filled with books and put them on top of the glass vitrine—'The Book of Hours"[163] fell, and bounced viciously off the tip of

157. Ludwig van Beethoven (1770–1827) is an acclaimed German musical composer and pianist.

158. The German city Bonn is where Beethoven was born. The Beethoven House serves as a museum, among other functions.

159. "A waiter ~~like~~ with large spectacles" appears in the original.

160. Würzburg is a city in Germany known for its architecture, art, and wines.

161. "6 hours ~~and~~ in all" appears in the original.

162. The eighteenth-century Falkenhaus is an iconic building located in downtown Würzburg.

163. *The Book of Hours* is a Christian devotional book, or prayerbook, that was popular in the Middle Ages. Also, the *Book of Hours* (1905) is a poetry collection by Rainer Maria Rilke (1875–1926). It is unclear which volume AW means.

my nose. It bled, and a small swelling came up.[164] It seemed such a savagery, from that adored book, where T. had written on the last page: 'All Hours." In the rain, on the cobbles leading to the closed dung-coloured Residenz,[165] I mentioned it for the 2nd time in 3 days. T burst out in impatience—there was nothing remarkable in that book hitting my nose. My eyes filled with tears. He remembers nothing. He uses the word sentimental frequently, whenever he refers to love between people. He condems himself. Us, whenever he says it. What he seems to say is that feeling, matters of the heart, matters of my heart, matters of his heart that were, are unworthy of life. Unimportant. Now I know how that woman in the bus in Hertford meant when she said to our (DAW u I) excruciated embarrassment—"Ah—young lovers." She was touched. That condition was forever out of her reach. And was hers once.

In this Hotel—I have taken, out of self defense to speak with a heavily accented German—I speak in deliberately with a scrabbled Grammar, hoping to be taken for a Roumanian or Pole, or even Italian. To be taken for a German, would imply the whole treacherous structure of a German woman with an Englishman. The enemy.

AUG 10TH

A reckless, enchanting day and ½ in Freiburg[166] after a weary 5 hours in a 1st class compartment on the amazing Lorelei Express.[167] Carpeted corridors, heavy interconnecting doors opening wide at the slightest pressure. We ate our cold meats and fruit guiltily in the cigar-scented compartment. Dry, manicured elderly men sit reading Die Frankfurter Allgemeine.[168] Then Freiburg opening gradually through a tunnel with an escalator, and a rail for prams. The prettily decorated Old town, memorials in murals and Roccoco arches of virgins, successful soap and candlemakers, gorgeous iron grilles hanging horizontally into the air, gilt and coloured, graped and beasted. The population much more easy going and leisurly. Bits and pieces of food so temptingly arranged, it be-

164. "a small ~~hillock~~ swelling came up" appears in the original.

165. AW probably means the Würzburger Residenz (Würzburg Residence), a palace renowned for its Baroque, Rococo, and Neocolassical architecture.

166. Freiburg is a German city that sits on the edge of the Black Forest.

167. AW and TH are likely aboard German Federal Railway (Deutsche Bundesbahn) express train passenger cars.

168. AW may mean the *Frankfurter Allgemeine Zeitung*, a newspaper founded in 1949.

comes impossible to resist yet another "Restervation." chocolate and marzipan shops are decked out as minor works of art. The serious assistants who serve as though their livelihood depended on the width of their smile. Their unctiousness grave. Victorian.

T. becoming more and more relaxed—his Good nature returning with magical abundance. He plays enchanting, serious games with Shura. Ravished by the meals. He is quite beguiling to travel with—he confirms rapidly the beginning of any boredom—and we move—on, to another path up the castle, with huge tree roots serving as stairs. A great rain storm begins, and we stand under an oak tree, looking down at a small, perfect orchard, lovely rosy pears and ripening apples hanging from the glossy wet boughs. The rain doesn't stop—we walk through it, down to the arches of the town-gates, and stand, shivering with 2 fat nuns.

His sense of direction is almost flawless—time u again he knew just the way back to the hunter's shop where we bought him 2 green huntsmens' shirts. Me a white blouse, and Shura 2 little wooden birds. She responds to him with complete but slightly impertinent adoration.

With an absurdly misguided romanticism we took a train to Titisee[169] today. The train climbed up through huge oak and black conifer forests promising trout in green-blue rivers—a faint, pale English girl with a flat, sick face and perfect, long pink nails collapsed on the outside seat.

Titisee is in fact a garish, silly, overpriced, boring little resort with the spirit of Victorian Bournemouth.[170] grave, middle aged "walkers" with sticks and raincoats march along the lakeside inhaling the hard to come by mountain air. All the hotels have a uniform, neat cuteness which cancels out any marvel this place may once have promised. Streams of cars pass by regularly. But the forests in the distance continue to promise a mythical black damp; wolves, deer.

SCHLIRCHSEE[171] 11.8.68

In 48 hours in the rotten, Greedy heart of the Black forest, we saw 1 black tail, 2 black birds and a Goldfinch. Bird sounds are almost nonexistent. Clean white raincoats wrap to mid-calf, tart German women—heavy, robin-chested

169. Titisee is a lake in the Black Forest and is a popular tourist attraction. Titisee-Neustadt is a municipality in southern Germany.

170. Bournemouth is a resort town on the southern coast of England.

171. Schliersee is a small town in Bavaria.

middle-aged men sit on freshly painted benches on the edge of the lake—wearing shorts, sandals and silly little socks. But they're ready to be friendly. Honey bees swarm every where. Yesterday very bleak, with T's chemistry gone amok, an ugly impatient mood setting in. Later, in the feather bed in the Pension Post (11 D.M.[172] pro person inklusiv Frühstück)[173] his lavish glühwein[174] mood returned. We sat in the Rotbräu, watching a company of 3 standard-ugly-German hags, and 4 men cowed by the Women's exuberance, giggling richly over bottle after bottle of champagne. The serene young waiters working away doggedly sober, amused only by the Baroque bills. Their arithmetic rapid and correct, orders splitting the stainless steel kitchen, a rumble of anger surrounds the cashier's frontage.

This morning T. rowed us round the black lake, hikers peeping round orderly wastebaskets in the forest. Shura's walking stick and the plastic whistle attached to it, her brave participation. It's raining again—we sit at the railway station, outside, on benches still sun-warmed.

AUG. 28TH.

God—you are my might horse.
Loved you are.

<The next three journal entries are handwritten on a single sheet of paper removed from a spiral-bound notebook.—Eds.>

SEP. 6TH 1968

It is only inevitably that the life I have lead should end like this. That I should be sup planted (sub-planted!) by others. I was endowed with too many minor qualities, but with neither the will nor huge intelligence to bring them a life of their own.

That Cilly should only ever see me again at my end—which no doubt she had always predicted for me, like this. And Vati—who expected nothing, and too weak.

172. *D.M.* stands for deutsche marks.
173. AW lists that breakfast is included ("inklusiv Frühstück").
174. Glühwein is mulled wine or claret.

JAN. 16/69

morning rushhour—state funeral of the day.

As if all life was a preparation for the grotesque shapes of middle age.—this final shape, is the only product of such a long process.

UNDATED ENTRY

1. One thing never dies—the doom of a dead man.
2. The grave straightens the hunchback.

<These final two entries are in the journal labeled "August 1968."—Eds.>

HAWORTH, YORKSHIRE

March 20th 1969

I pretend to be alive and ask the lard-white landlady if she knew of a house for sale. Yes. And an ensuing conversation—before 3 men come in and I retreat into the corner seat, neither daring to read nor write. In the late afternoon I went down the almost precipe-high street, to the surgery, the only new building in the whole town. Managed to get 35 soneryl.[175] Felt criminal. Snow hardening and deep—an iron town. The pub, real Inn, warm and comfortable in that new-old, false wood-wormed way. In the dining room (steak u salad u chip £1.4.0) plummy velvet curtains. My Shura. Feel totally bankrupt. Can't write Wellington.[176] No point. It's 9 p.m.—will go to bed. Trying to read Herbert.[177] I admire—but no reaction. The marvelous black church—and black cemetry, and black trees—and the Brontes[178] as dead and false as the plastic pine-apple which is the lampbase, in the light. I am sinking—further and further inwards. Ted on television[179]—

175. Soneryl is a barbiturate used to treat insomnia.

176. In personal correspondence to the editors on November 20, 2019, Martin Baker writes, "I believe that this is a reference to my children's book, *Wellington the Tin Soldier* . . . Assia suggested she and Ted write the story."

177. Probably AW is referring to Polish poet Zbigniew Herbert (1924–98).

178. AW is alluding to English writers Charlotte Brontë (1816–55), Emily Brontë (1818–48), and Anne Brontë (1820–49).

179. According to Jonathan Bate, TH read eleven poems, including "Hawk Roosting," "An Otter," "The Thought-Fox," "Six Young Men," "View of a Pig," "Wind," and "Wodwo," at Holly Royde College, Manchester, England (*Ted Hughes*, p. 273).

I pacing in the hall outside—he didn't want me there. Owen[180] adamant on refusing me into the monitor van—got very drunk and weepy at the meal afterwards. Ted drunk—stroking my shoulder. The terrible talk in the "lounge" of the Elm Hotel. "It's Sylvia—it's because of her"—I can't answer that. No more than if it were a court-sentence. It says die—die, soon. But execute yourself and your little self, efficiently. But I can't believe it—anymore than I could believe hearing of my own death. How tall cats' front legs seem, when they sit up.

What I want is some base reason—the truth—as though that would be some comfort. A pity about Wellington. A pity about the 3 children. "They're just in average despair"—he says. About F u N. Poor little Shoe isn't even mentioned. "I can't bear any more show of temperament from anyone"—curious how he's becomes more and more extravagant. How angry and mottled he was as he got off the train in Manchester.[181] Sunless. And I in high spirits. He feels as though he has already buried me—that feels hideously accurate.[182] That which allowed him pervious graces was desire—and I know it's dead in him.

MARCH 21ST

Woke after a long sleep to a white window, with no demarcation between sky and snow on the opposite roof-top. Tried the museum[183] again—too early. Fell asleep to Beethoven's 130th[184]—the coicidence—when the bed-light went off because of a fault—I couldn't bear the dark with the quartet playing. It was sinister. It's thawing, slowly. Bricks of ice are heaped in the car park, twigs of oak lie spread over the yard. People have a huddled look. They're huddled over account books, fires, car wheels. The short walk between the street and the parsonage is immaculately rural and Victorian. The house looms, genuine, terrorising, closed, as the tomb it is;—round the corner the American-built plate glass extension and a sentimental "yearning" bronze of the 3 sisters destroys the very presence of anything that may have taken place here. Nothing to be seen of the moors—covered with snow—all wood, every gate, stump, roof, has shrunk to the most absolute of black. I woke in optimism—it's receding in caution.

180. Probably Owen is New Zealand–born writer and radio broadcaster Owen Leeming (1930–).

181. Manchester is a city in northwestern England; it is second in population only to London.

182. "that ~~seems~~ feels hideously accurate." appears in the original.

183. AW means the Brontë Parsonage Museum.

184. Beethoven String Quartet No. 13 in B-flat Major, Op. 130, aired on "Beethoven and Tonality," BBC Radio 3, March 19, 1969 at 10:00 p.m.

A programme on Dorothy Wordsworth[185] last night on the radio—"The Exquisite sister"[186]—readings from a pedestrian journal—she ended mad and old. The tenderness with which these terrible relationships are evoked, once the players are dead. Their lives are so compost for the sentimental bouquets of "compilers" of the future.

Ted is to pick me up this morning. He went to visit his mother in hospital yesterday—spent the night at the Beacon. 10$^{\underline{30}}$, he said[187]

185. Dorothy Wordsworth (1771–1855) is a posthumously published British Romantic writer and sister to famed poet William Wordsworth (1770–1850). At the end of her life, Dorothy Wordsworth faced mental health challenges and addictions to opium and laudanum. Her brother was her primary caretaker.

186. "The Exquisite Sister: A Glance at Dorothy Wordsworth" aired on BBC Radio 4 on March 19, 1969, at 9:40 p.m.

187. The journal ends here; blank pages follow.

Valentine's Day card from Assia Wevill to Ted Hughes, February 14, 1967. Courtesy of the Stuart A. Rose Manuscript, Archives, and Rare Book Library, Emory University. © Estate of Assia Wevill.

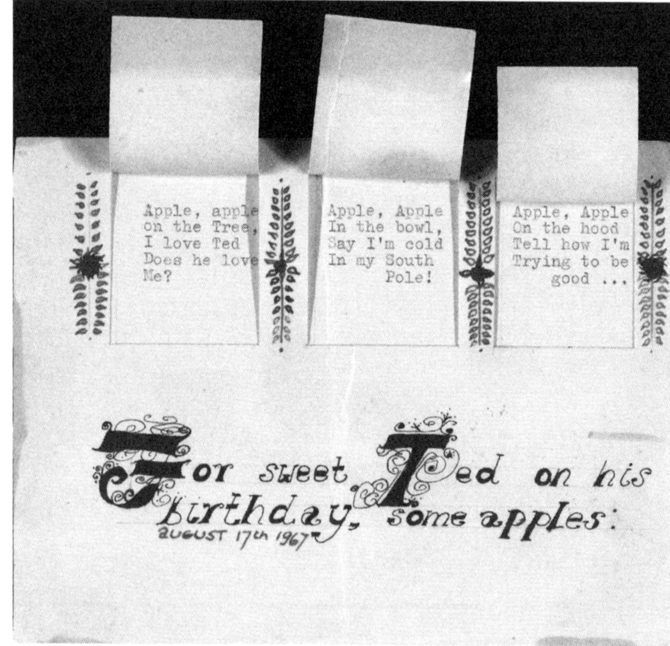

Birthday card from Assia Wevill to Ted Hughes, August 17, 1967. Image below shows the flaps open. Courtesy of the Stuart A. Rose Manuscript, Archives, and Rare Book Library, Emory University. © Estate of Assia Wevill.

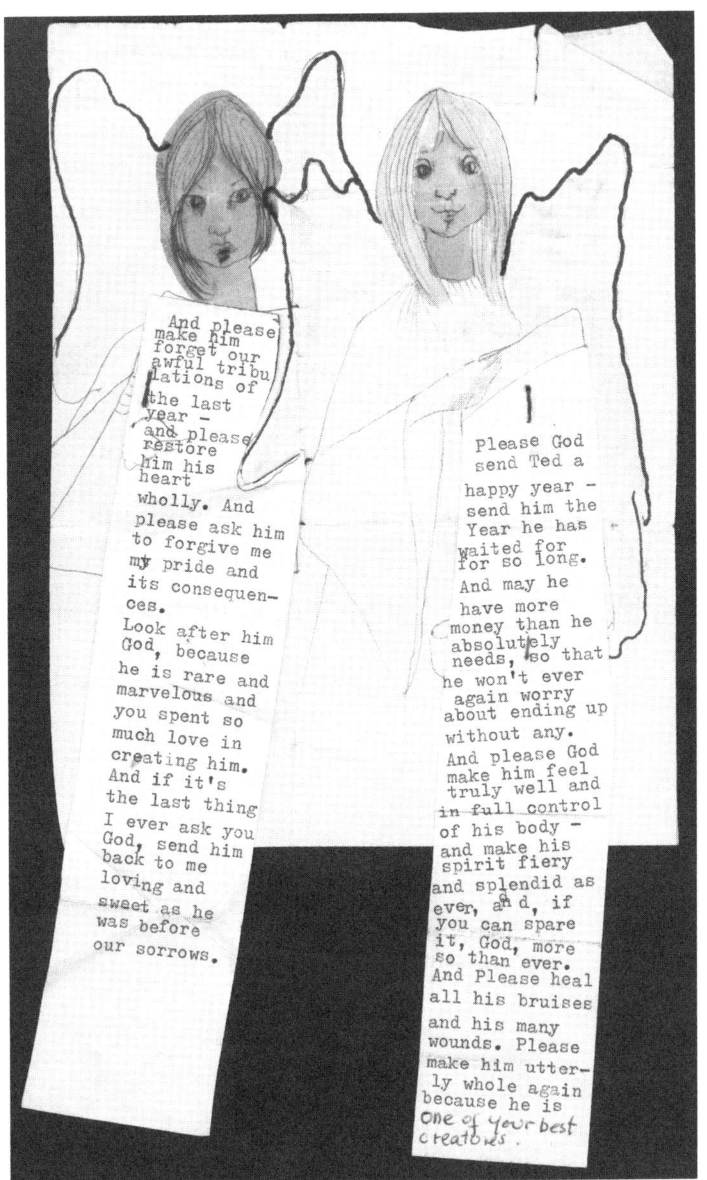
And please
make him
forget our
awful tribu
lations of
the last
year -
and please
restore
him his
heart
wholly. And
please ask him
to forgive me
my pride and
its consequen-
ces.
Look after him
God, because
he is rare and
marvelous and
you spent so
much love in
creating him.
And if it's
the last thing
I ever ask you
God, send him
back to me
loving and
sweet as he
was before
our sorrows.

Please God
send Ted a
happy year -
send him the
Year he has
waited for
for so long.
And may he
have more
money than he
absolutely
needs, so that
he won't ever
again worry
about ending up
without any.
And please God
make him feel
truly well and
in full control
of his body -
and make his
spirit fiery
and splendid as
ever, and, if
you can spare
it, God, more
so than ever.
And Please heal
all his bruises
and his many
wounds. Please
make him utter-
ly whole again
because he is
one of your best
creatures.

Card from Assia Wevill to Ted Hughes, April 4, 1968. Courtesy of the Stuart A. Rose Manuscript, Archives, and Rare Book Library, Emory University.

which allowed him [illegible] pervious
graces was desire – and I know
it's dead in him.

[March 21st]

Woke after a long sleep to a white window, with no demarcation between sky and snow on the opposite roof-top. Tried the museum again – too early. Fell asleep to Beethoven's 130th – the coincidence – when the bed-light went off because of a fault – I couldn't bear the dark with the quartet playing. It was sinister. It's thawing, slowly. Bricks of ice are heaped in the car park, twigs of oak lie spread over the yard. People have a huddled look. They're huddled over account books, tires, car wheels. The short walk between the street and the parsonage is immaculately rural and Victorian. The house looms, genuine, terrorising, closed, as the tomb it is; – round the corner the American-built plate glass extension and a sentimental "yearning" bronze of the 3 sisters destroys the very presence of anything that may have taken place here. Nothing to be seen of the moors – covered with snow – all wood, every gate, stump, roof, has shrunk to the most absolute of black. I woke in optimism – it's receding in caution.

A programme on Dorothy Wordsworth last night on the radio – "The Exquisite Sister" – readings from a pedestrian journal – she ended mad and old. The tenderness with which these terrible relationships are evoked, once the players are dead. Their lives are so compost for the sentimental bouquets of "compilers" of the future.

Ted is to pick me up this morning.
He went to visit his mother in hospital yesterday – spent the night at the Beacon.
10^{30}, he said

Assia Wevill's last journal entry, March 21, 1969. Courtesy of the Stuart A. Rose Manuscript, Archives, and Rare Book Library, Emory University.

Once there was a large, flat stone.

It was a pebble really. Someone, a long, long time ago picked it up on a beach and left it on mantlepiece. It was so ordinary that no one bothered to look at it carefully.

Then the mantlepiece had new owners - and taking the pebble down the stairs, they thought it would keep the milk-bottles from turning over outside. And so, for years, the stone stopped milk-bottles from turning over.

Slowly, it grew moss. At first a fine, pale green moss which looked like grassy icicles when you looked closely, and then, more slowly it grew a blackish-green honeycomb of woolly moss.

As the years passed, a little wall of earth formed between the mossy stone and the cobbles near it, and the earth sprouted thin grasses which never grew very high.

One spring, amongst the grasses grew a strange, thick seedling. The seedling became a stalk, and the stalk grew taller and taller and thicker and thicker. But each of its leaves was different: it had oak leaves, and strawberry leaves and poppy leaves and lily leaves.

But only God knew about this plant. And only God saw it.

As the summer went on, the stalk flowered - it sprouted a lily, whichsprouted a poppy, which sprouted a strawberry flower. When summer ended, this 3-flower flower dropped off, and when November came an oak kernel sat tight on the hollow wavering stalk, moving back and forth with the wind.

One day, when the milkman rang the bell, waiting to be paid, he noticed the oak kernel, and because he didn't have much else to do, he pulled it out. But as he pulled, he heard a song which he hadn't heard since he was a very young man, and it seemed to come from the stalk. He tugged once more, and the stalk came away, roots and all. But, at the end of the roots there dangled half a bright red heart.

The other half of the heart lay hugging the mossy stone, red and ragged - and he looked again, and saw that the icy white milk bottles were splattered with tiny drops of steaming blood.

Then he went back to his van, and thought about it all morning.

"Once there was a large, flat stone" poem, ca. February 14. Courtesy of the British Library. © Estate of Assia Wevill.

AMICHAI

IN MY WORST DREAMS

In my worst dreams
You, with ~~pure~~ bright eyes
Are always standing near walls
Whose foundation stone
Is a heart.

Of all the things I do,
Parting is the inevitable one.

In my dreams I always hear a voice -
It is not my voice -
And not yours,
Neither is it the daughter of your voice.

Eyes creased, my eyes are
Like the eyes of exhausted beasts
Lusting for days
~~Interchangeable for~~ nights.
That have passed with the

additional stanza

They have taken a love-mask off me
Just as they take a death-mask.
They took it without my noticing
As I lay beside you.

It is my true face.

Until my death I must remember
The heavy scent of fig trees,
Heavy, like my father's eyes.
The fig, the Jew's tree.

Typescript with markings by Assia Wevill of "In My Worst Dreams," translation of a poem by Yehuda Amichai, n.d. Courtesy of the Stuart A. Rose Manuscript, Archives, and Rare Book Library, Emory University. © Estate of Assia Wevill.

Assia Wevill and John Steele, May 1, 1943. Courtesy of the Stuart A. Rose Manuscript, Archives, and Rare Book Library, Emory University.

Assia Wevill at the beach in Bat Yam, Israel, August 1945. Courtesy of the Stuart A. Rose Manuscript, Archives, and Rare Book Library, Emory University.

Assia Wevill and Richard "Dick" Lipsey with Keith and Pam Gems on a ski holiday, 1952–53. Courtesy of Yehuda Koren and Eilat Negev.

Studio photograph of Assia Wevill, 1954. Courtesy of the Stuart A. Rose Manuscript, Archives, and Rare Book Library, Emory University.

Assia Wevill in a tea dress, August 1956. The others in the photo are unidentified. Courtesy of the Stuart A. Rose Manuscript, Archives, and Rare Book Library, Emory University.

Assia Wevill working at a desk, 1957. The man to the right is unidentified. Courtesy of the Stuart A. Rose Manuscript, Archives, and Rare Book Library, Emory University.

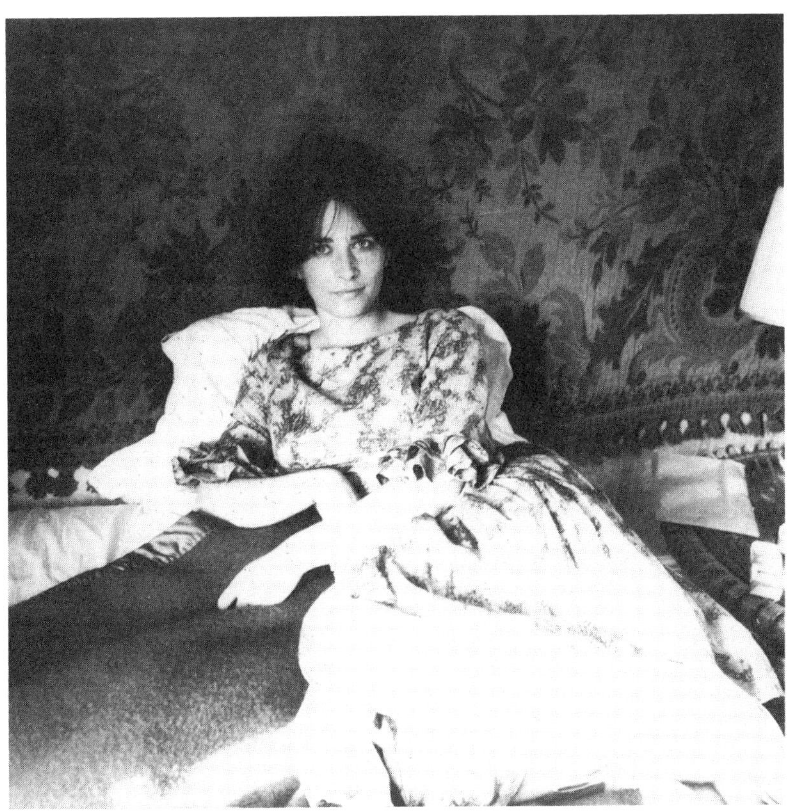

Assia Wevill in Burma, ca. 1959–60. Courtesy of the Stuart A. Rose Manuscript, Archives, and Rare Book Library, Emory University. © David Wevill.

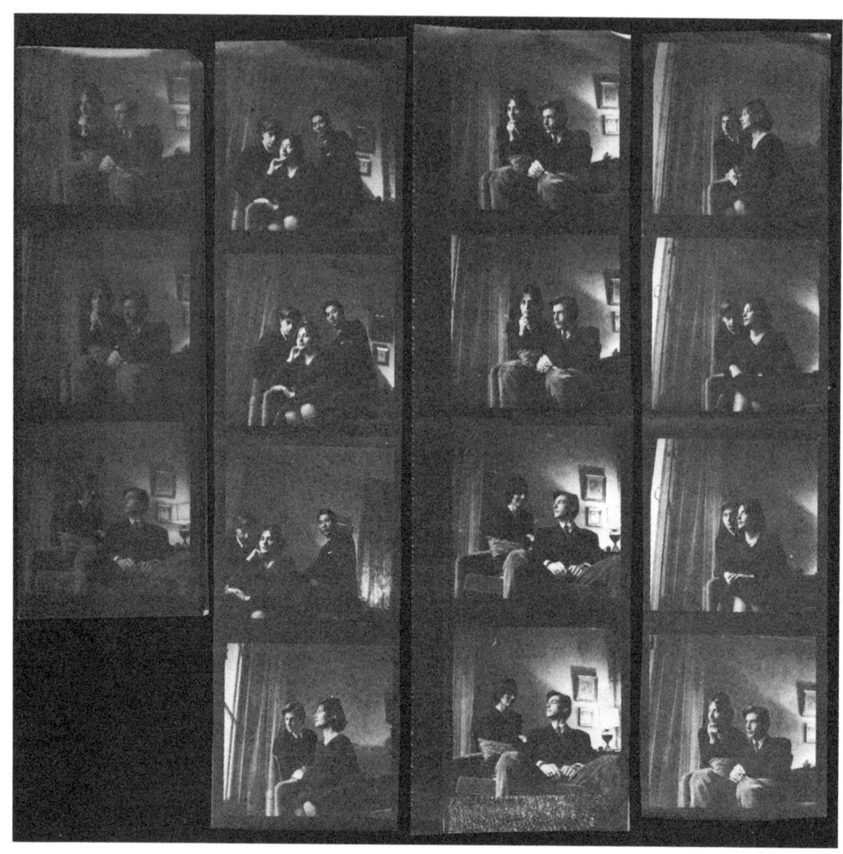

Assia Wevill and David Wevill featured in contact sheets, ca. early 1960s. Courtesy of the Stuart A. Rose Manuscript, Archives, and Rare Book Library, Emory University.

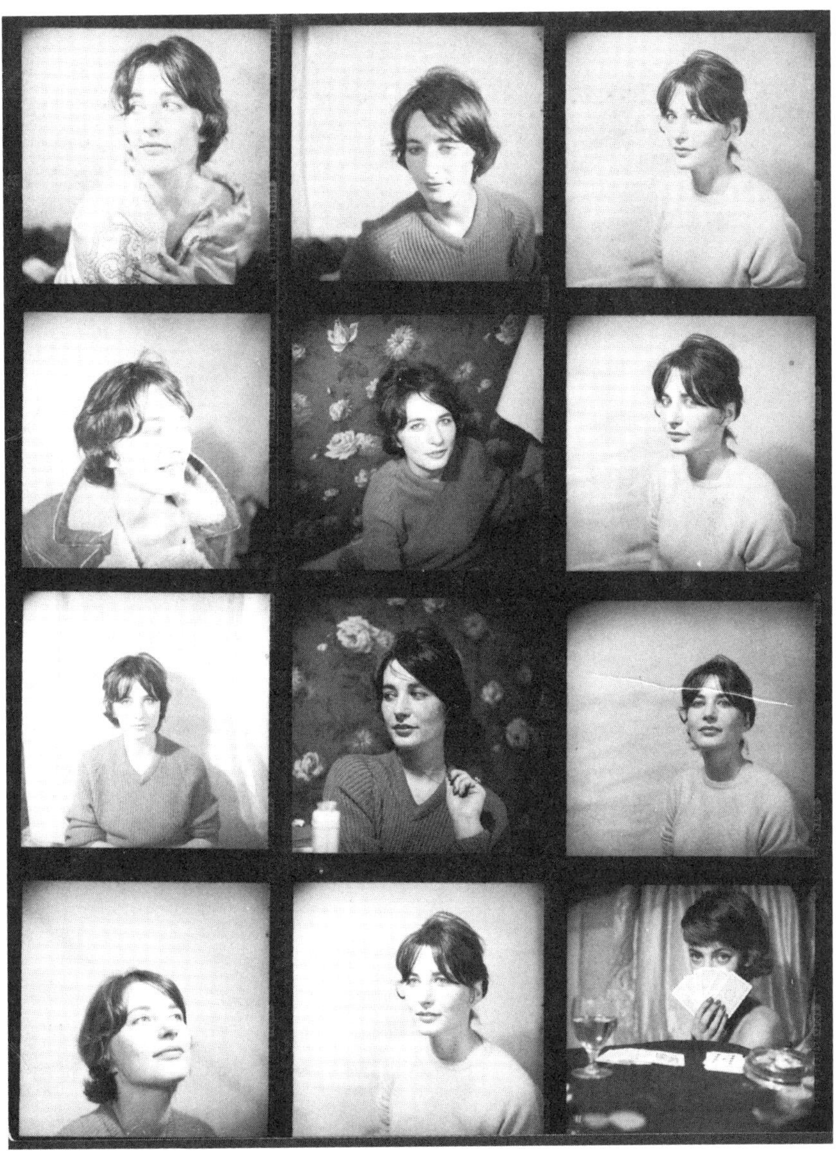

Assia Wevill featured in contact sheets, n.d. Courtesy of the Stuart A. Rose Manuscript, Archives, and Rare Book Library, Emory University.

Assia Wevill's father, Vati, from Assia Wevill's personal collection of photographs, n.d. Courtesy of the Stuart A. Rose Manuscript, Archives, and Rare Book Library, Emory University.

From left: Celia Chaikin holding her daughter Tamara Chaikin; Assia and Celia's mother, Mutti; and Assia Wevill, ca. 1961. Courtesy of the Stuart A. Rose Manuscript, Archives, and Rare Book Library, Emory University.

Assia Wevill and Celia Chaikin in Montreal, 1961. Courtesy of the Stuart A. Rose Manuscript, Archives, and Rare Book Library, Emory University.

Assia Wevill and Shura Wevill in London, 1966. Courtesy of the Stuart A. Rose Manuscript, Archives, and Rare Book Library, Emory University.

Ted Hughes, Assia Wevill, and Shura Wevill, ca. 1966. Courtesy of the Stuart A. Rose Manuscript, Archives, and Rare Book Library, Emory University.

Shura Wevill, 1968.

Assia Wevill and Shura Wevill, 1968. © Martin Baker.

III. POEMS

ORIGINAL POEMS

MAGNIFICAT[1]

For the shy sun, for the dull hour
I give praise.
Not the raging forests of summer or
The maniacal autumn moon, the flight
Of bugs or slug-fat gardens, or sight
Of seed growing, do I praise—

But thin sunlight, and the waiting.

And I do praise the force that falls
With loosened stones and plunging force
Of clear ghost-rivers in dried beds.
And besides this watchful course
Of hours and currents, watersheds
Of welcome, do I praise the eye
That finds me welcome
needing no reply.

Assia Lipsey

WINTER-END, HERTFORDSHIRE[2]

At this time's end
Lulled by the end alone
I look through all the windows
Of this time's passing

1. Typescript is held by Emory University.
2. Typescript is held by Emory University.

To look again and no more
At the triple death of
Thomas Head and no identity
Like his child and bitter wife
Stalled in their moss eroded cattle grave
In a pauper's winter.

Unhollied, unmarked, spring less
Thomas, tamer of yew partridge
Master of none but the brewer's weeds
Procurer of rat tails and winter lover
of Mrs. Head's, has eaten his fifty
Year old death and had no time,
No sun, no annotation.

To see again no more
The black northern pond,
Its autumn spent
Its eye burning with crippled cedar wings
And four black feet deep with
Summer's rotting rooks,
Like Thomas Head's and my time's
Unlamented, springless, passed.

A. Lipsey

WHY MR. L. IS NOT A SWINE[3]

Why Mr. L. is not a swine
And why anyone suggesting that
He might be
Is a homosexual American Scene Setting
Anti Vietnam, Thomas-loving liberal-cultural Fendango Gimmick master of the moment.

3. Typescript is held by Emory University.

To begin with,
Mr. L. is a Cornishman.
He therefore automatically ennobles
Three qualities, which,
In any man not from Cornwall
Would be dismissed as offences.
The first Virtue-Offence is
Plainess of manner. The manner is
The hand of the thought, its hat,
Crown, seat. It shakes, devoures,
Slurps up, rips into all the crevices
Of Natural Secrets. This the hand scatters
into the upward worshipping eyes of
Very old and very young fellow Cornishmen.
Mr. L. Is their creation. Their myth.
Their gorgeous Fart.

Mr. L. correctly and courageously
Asserts his masculinity. He is no
Woman's slave. Or flunkey, or Giggolo.
He is Everyman's Robin Hood. He takes
From those who are blessed to bestow on
Those who are deprived of blessing. Any
Blessing. Above all, the blessing of
St. Thomas, of which he has almost succeeded
In making a new South West Religion. Incorporating
The Lord Buddha, The Lord Jesus, The Lord Jehovah,
Count Allah, The Duke of Pluto, Graf Tolstoy,
The Count of County Clare, The Prelate of Boston,
St. Sybilla of Wellesley and Johann Sebastian Bach.
Its Goddesses bleached blondes, its priestesses
Sturdy Celtic peasant women with chill-blained
Thighs. Or young negresses tatooed with signs
of the Zodiac in surprising places.

MAYBE IT'S A GOOD THING[4]

Maybe it's a good thing
that we're now.
And not, say, in Coblenz
even a hundred years ago.
You'd be the black Englishman
making faces in the windows
of the Hotel Bristol—
and I, the apphrensively
employed Emma,
not much good with Mehlspeisen,
but reliably friendly
on wine festivals.
I'd be stoned
(By the mothers of Boppard)
bitten
(by wolves)
spat at
(by frogs)
frozen by sleet and
pregnant with twins.
Oh.

ONCE THERE WAS A LARGE, FLAT STONE.

Once there was a large, flat stone.[5]

It was a pebble really. Someone, a long, long
time ago picked it up on a beach and left it
on mantelpiece. It was so ordinary that no
one bothered to look at it carefully.

---

4. Typescript is held by the British Library. "Oh." is written in pencil by AW as the last line, and "by Assia" is written in red ink at the bottom in an unknown hand.

5. Typescript is held by the British Library. AW has drawn a necklace with an insect-like pendant and handwritten "FOR TEDDY A VALENTINE."

Then the mantelpiece had new owners—and
taking the pebble down the stairs, they thought
it would keep the milk-bottles from turning
over outside. And so, for years, the stone
stopped milk-bottles from turning over.

Slowly, it grew moss. At first a fine, pale
green moss which looked like grassy icicles
when you looked closely, and then, more slowly
it grew a blackish-green honeycomb of wooly moss.

As the years passed, a little wall of earth formed
between the mossy stone and the cobbles near it,
and the earth sprouted thin grasses which never
grew very high.

One spring, amongst the grasses grew a strange,
thick seedling. The seedling became a stalk, and
the stalk grew taller and taller and thicker and
thicker. But each of its leaves was different:
it had oak leaves, and strawberry leaves and poppy
leaves and lily leaves.

But only God knew about this plant. And only God saw it.

As the summer went on, the stalk flowered—it sprouted
a lily, which sprouted a poppy, which sprouted a
strawberry flower. When summer ended, this 3-flower
flower dropped off, and when November came an oak
kernel sat tight on the hollow wavering stalk, moving
back and forth with the wind.

One day, when the milkman rang the bell, waiting to
be paid, he noticed the oak kernel, and because he
didn't have much else to do, he pulled it out. But
as he pulled, he heard a song which he hadn't heard

since he was a very young man, and it seemed to
come from the stalk. He tugged once more, and the
stalk came away, roots and all. But, at this end of
the roots there dangled half a bright red heart.

The other half of the heart lay hugging the mossy
stone, red and ragged—and he looked again, and
saw that the icy white milk bottles were splattered
with tiny drops of steaming blood.

Then he went back to his van, and thought about it all morning.

TRANSLATIONS[6]

Editors' note: Assia Wevill met the Israeli poet Yehuda Amichai through Ted Hughes. Her translations of Amichai's poetry were published under her maiden name, Assia Gutmann. Two editions appeared in book form: *Selected Poems* (London: Cape Goliard, 1968) and *Poems* (New York: Harper & Row, 1969). Both editions are out of print; the text in this section is printed from the 1969 edition. Several poems appeared in periodicals in advance of the books. Though it was not possible to trace them all, the translations were printed, among possible others, in *Afrasian, Encounter,* the *New Yorker,* and possibly the *Scotsman.* Please see the appropriate footnotes in the Letters section for citations.

KING SAUL AND I

1

They gave him a finger, but he took the whole hand.
They gave me the whole hand; I didn't even take the little finger.
While my heart
Was weight-lifting its first feelings
He rehearsed the tearing of oxen.

6. The poems in this section are Assia Gutmann Wevill's English translations of Hebrew poems by Yehuda Amichai.

My pulsebeats were like
Drips from a tap,
His pulsebeats
Pounded like hammers on a new building.

He was my big brother,
I got his used clothes.

2
His head, like a compass, will always bring him
To the sure north of his future.

His heart is set, like an alarm clock,
For the hour of his reign.
When everyone's asleep, he will cry out
Until all the quarries are hoarse.
Nobody will stop him!

Only the asses bare their yellow teeth
At the end.

3
Dead prophets turned time wheels
When he went out searching for asses
Which I, now, have found.
But I don't know how to handle them.
They kick me.

I was raised with the straw,
I fell with heavy seeds.

But he breathed the winds of his histories.
He was anointed with the royal oil
As with wrestlers' grease.
He battled with olive trees,
Forcing them to kneel.

Roots bulged on the earth's forehead
With the strain.
The prophets escaped from the arena;
Only God remained, counting:
Seven . . . eight . . . nine . . . ten . . .
The people, from his shoulders downward, rejoiced.
Not a man stood up.
He had won.

4
I am tired,
My bed is my kingdom.

My sleep is just,
My dream is my verdict.

I hung my clothes on a chair
For tomorrow.

He hung his kingdom
In a frame of golden wrath
On the sky's wall.

My arms are short, like string too short
To tie a parcel.

His arms are like the chains in a harbor
For cargo to be carried across time.

He is a dead king.
I am a tired man.

IBN GABIROL

Sometimes pus
Sometimes a poem.

Something always bursts out.
And always pain.

My father was a tree in a forest of fathers
Covered in green cotton wool.

Oh, widows of the flesh, orphans of the blood,
I must escape.

Eyes sharp as tin openers
Opened heavy secrets.

But through the wound on my chest
God peers into the world.

I am the door
To his apartment.

THE PLACE WHERE I HAVE NOT BEEN

The place where I have not been
I never shall be.
The place where I have been
Is as though I have never been there. People stray
Far from the places where they were born
And far from the words which were spoken
As if by their mouths
And still wide of the promise
Which they were promised.

And they eat standing and die sitting
And lying down they remember.
And what I shall never in the world return to
And look at, I am to love forever.
Only a stranger will return to my place. But I will set down
All these things once more, as Moses did,

After he smashed the first tablets.

OUT OF THREE OR FOUR IN A ROOM

Out of three or four in a room
One is always standing at the window.
Forced to see the injustice among the thorns,
The fires on the hill.

And people who left whole
Are brought home in the evening, like small change.

Out of three or four in a room
One is always standing at the window.
Hair dark above his thoughts.
Behind him, the words.
And in front of him the words, wandering, without luggage.
Hearts without provision, prophecies without water
And big stones put there
And staying closed, like letters
With no addresses, and no one to receive them.

IF WITH A BITTER MOUTH

If with a bitter mouth you will speak
Sweet words, the world will
Neither sweeten nor become bitterer.

And it is written in the book that we shall not fear.
And it is also written, that we also shall change,
Like the words,
In future and in past,
In the plural or in isolation.

And soon in the coming nights
We shall appear, like strolling players,
Each in the other's dream.

And into these dreams
There shall also come strangers
We did not know together.

IN MY TIME, IN YOUR PLACE

We were together in my time, in your place.
You gave the place and I the time.
Quietly your body waited for the seasons to change.
Fashions passed over it, to shorten, to lengthen,
With flowers or in white silk, clinging.

We swapped human values for those of beasts,
Calm and tigerlike and forever.
And for all that, ready to burn any moment
With the dry grass of the end of summer.

I divided the days with you, nights.
We exchanged a look with rain,
I was your Lent and your Mardi gras
In one body. We were not like dreamers,
Even in our dreams.

And in the unquiet, nestled the quiet,
In my time, in your place.

The many dreams I now dream of you
Prophesy your end with me—

As the multiplying crowds of seagulls
Come where the sea ends.

IN MY WORST DREAMS

In my worst dreams
You, with bright eyes,
Are always standing near walls
Whose foundation stone
Is a heart.

Of all the things I do,
Parting is the inevitable one.

In my dreams I always hear a voice—
It is not my voice
And not yours,
Neither is it the daughter of your voice.

Eyes creased, my eyes are
Like the eyes of exhausted beasts
Lusting for days
That have passed with the nights.

They have taken a love mask off me
Just as they take a death mask.
They took it without my noticing
As I lay beside you.

It is my true face.

FAREWELL, YOU

Farewell, you; your Face, already the Face of memory,
Wandering, rising from the world of the dead, and flying, flying.
Face of beasts, Face of water, Face of going
And a forest of whispers,
Face of the womb, Face of child.

No longer ours the hours of touch,
No longer ours to say: Now. Now.
Yours was the name or winds, once the wife
Of directions, purpose, mirror, and autumn.

Whatever we failed to understand, we sang together.
Generations and the dark, Face of alternation.
No longer mine, unsolved,
Locked nipples, buckles, mouths, screws.

Farewell then, you, the never sleeping,
All was fulfilled by our word; that all is of sand.
From now on
Dream through your own dreams, the world and all.

Go in peace, go, bundles and cases of death.
Threads, feathers, the household mash, pawn of hair,
Whatever will not be, no hand writes,
Whatever was not of the body will leave no memory.

A PITY. WE WERE SUCH A GOOD INVENTION

They amputated
Your thighs off my hips.
As far as I'm concerned
They are all surgeons. All of them.

They dismantled us
Each from the other.
As far as I'm concerned
They are all engineers. All of them.

A pity. We were such a good
And loving invention.
An airplane made from a man and wife.
Wings and everything.
We hovered a little above the earth.

We even flew a little.

IT WAS SUMMER, OR THE END OF SUMMER

It was summer, or the end of summer,
And I heard then your footsteps, as you went from east to west
For the last time. And in the world
Handkerchiefs were lost, and books, and people.

It was summer, or the end of summer,
There were hours in the afternoon,
You were;
And you wore your shroud
For the first time.
And you never noticed
Because it was embroidered with flowers.

TWO SONGS ON CAESAREA BEACH

I
The sea preserves in salt.
Jerusalem preserves in dryness.
And where shall we go?

Now, in the exacting twilight,
To choose.
Not what we shall do
Or how we shall live
But to choose the life
Whose dreams
Will hurt least
In all the nights to come.

II
"Come again next summer"
Or words like that
Hold my life,
Take away my days,
Like a line of soldiers
Passing over a bridge
Marked for exploding.
"Come again next summer."

Who hasn't heard these words?

But who comes again?

LIKE OUR BODIES' IMPRINT

Like our bodies' imprint,
Not a sign will remain that we were in this place.
The world closes behind us,
The sand straightens itself.

Dates are already in view
In which you no longer exist,
Already a wind blows clouds
Which will not rain on us both.

And your name is already on the passenger lists of ships
And in the registers of hotels
Whose names alone
Deaden the heart.

The three languages I know,
All the colors in which I see and dream:

None will help me.

GOD HAS PITY ON KINDERGARTEN CHILDREN

God has pity on children in kindergartens,
He pities school children—less.
But adults he pities not at all.

He abandons them,
And sometimes they have to crawl on all fours
In the roasting sand
To reach the dressing station,
And they are streaming with blood.

But perhaps
He will have pity on those who love truly
And take care of them
And shade them,
Like a tree over the sleeper on the public bench.

Perhaps even we will spend on them
Our last pennies of kindness
Inherited from mother,

So that their own happiness will protect us
Now and on other days.

TWO QUATRAINS

1

Once I escaped, but I do not remember why or from which God,
I shall therefore travel through my life, like Jonah in his dark fish,
We've settled it between us, I and the fish, we're both in the world's bowels,
I shall not come out, he will not digest me.

2

The last rains came on a warm night, in the morning my disaster blossomed.
The race is over. Who is first, who second?
After our death we could play: I shall be you, you—me,
In the dead moon, in the returning ancient time, in my window's tree.

EYE EXAMINATION

Go back a bit. Close your left eye.
Still?
Go back a bit further. The wall has moved on.
What do you see?
What do you recognize in the dimness?
I remember a lovely song which went . . .
Now? What do you see now?
Still?—All the time.
Don't leave me. Please. Please.
You're not leaving.
I'm not.
Close one eye. Speak in a loud voice.
I can't hear—I'm already far away.
What do you recognize? What do you see?

Close one sad eye.
Yes.
Close the other sad eye. Yes.
I can see now.
And nothing else.

IN THE MIDDLE OF THIS CENTURY

In the middle of this century we turned to each other
With half faces and full eyes
Like an ancient Egyptian picture
And for a short while.

I stroked your hair
In the opposite direction to your journey.
We called to each other,
Like calling out the names of towns
Where nobody stops
Along the route.

Lovely is the world rising early to evil,
Lovely is the world falling asleep to sin and pity,
In the mingling of ourselves, you and I,
Lovely is the world.

The earth drinks men and their loves
Like wine,
To forget.
It can't.
And like the contours of the Judean hills,
We shall never find peace.

In the middle of this century we turned to each other,
I saw your body, throwing shade, waiting for me,
The leather straps for a long journey
Already tightening across my chest.
I spoke in praise of your mortal hips,
You spoke in praise of my passing face.

I stroked your hair in the direction of your journey,
I touched your flesh, prophet of your end,
I touched your hand, which has never slept,
I touched your mouth, which may yet sing.

Dust from the desert covered the table
At which we did not eat.
But with my finger I wrote on it
The letters of your name.

POEM IN AN ORANGE GROVE

I am abandoned by God. "You're abandoned by God,"
Said my father.
God forgot me—
So did he, later.

The scent of orange groves in blossom
Was in me for a while. You. Hands sticky
With juice and love. You cried a great cry
And threw two of your last thighs into battle.
And then silence.
You, whose handsome head learned history,
Know that only what's past is silent.
Even battles,
Even the scent of orange groves.
Blossoms and fruit were on one and the same tree,
Above us, in that double season.

Even then we spoke with that foreign
And strange accent of those who will die.

I WAS THE MOON

My child is very sad.

Whatever I teach him—
Geography of love,
Strange languages which can't be heard
Because of the distance—
My child rocks his little bed towards me in the night.

What am I?
More than forgetting.
The very language of forgotten.
And until he understands what I did
I am as good as dead.

What are you doing with our quiet child?
You cover him with a blanket
Like heaven, layers of clouds—
I could be the moon.

What are you doing with your sad fingers?
You dress them with gloves
And go out.

I was the moon.

AS FOR THE WORLD

As for the world,
I am always like one of Socrates' disciples,
Walking by his side,
Hearing his opinions and histories;
It remains for me to say:
Yes. Yes, it is like that.
You are right again,
Indeed your words are true.

As for my life,
I am always like Venice:
Whatever is mere streets in others
Within me is a dark streaming love.

As for the cry, as for the silence,
I am always a shofar:
All year long hoarding its one blast
For the Terrible Days.

As for action,
I am always like Cain:
Nomad
In the face of the act, which I will not do,
Or, having done,
Will make it irredeemable.

As for the palm of your hand,
As for the signals of my heart
And the plans of my flesh,
As for the writing on the wall,

I am always ignorant;
I can neither read nor write
And my head is like the
Heads of those senseless weeds,

Knowing only the rustle and drift
Of the wind
When a fate passes through me
To some other place.

SHE KNOWS

I know that she knows.
They think she doesn't, but know otherwise.
She knows.

My heart tears with this game
And in the night its blood hears the cry
Like the cry of paper tearing
Across the forty-two years of my life.

Under a broad vine,
In the yard of a house
In the Valley of Hinnom,
An old woman once told me:

"Because he was burned inside,
His head turned white as snow."
I forget what she was talking about
Or whom—
My life is forty-two years of torn paper.

TOURIST

She showed me her swaying hair
In the four winds of her coming.
I showed her some of my folding ways of life
And the trick, and the lock.
She asked after my street and my house
And I laughed loudly.
She showed me this long night
And the interior of her thirty years.
I showed her the place where I once laid tefillin.

I brought her chapters and verses
And sand from Eilat
And the handing of the Torah
And the manna of my death
And all the miracles that have not yet healed in me.

She showed me the stages of joy
And my childhood's double.
I revealed to her that King David is not buried in his tomb
And that I don't live in my life.
While I was reflecting and she was eating,
The city map lay open on the table—
Her hand on Qatamon,
My hand on hers—
The cup covered the Old City,
Ash dropped on the King David Hotel,
And an ancient weeping
Allowed us to lie together.

GOD'S FATE

God's fate
Is now
The fate of trees rocks sun and moon,
The ones they stopped worshipping
When they began to believe in God.

But he's forced to remain with us
As are the trees, as are the rocks
Sun moon and stars.

MY MOTHER ONCE TOLD ME

My mother once told me
Not to sleep with flowers in the room.
Since then I have not slept with flowers.
I sleep alone, without them.

There were many flowers.
But I've never had enough time.
And persons I love are already pushing themselves
Away from my life, like boats
Away from the shore.

My mother said
Not to sleep with flowers.
You won't sleep.
You won't sleep, mother of my childhood.

The bannister I clung to
When they dragged me off to school
Is long since burned.
But my hands, clinging,
Remain
Clinging.

MY PARENTS' MIGRATION

And my parents' migration has not yet calmed in me.
My blood goes on shaking at its walls,
As the bowl after it is set down.
And my parents' migration has not yet calmed in me.
Winds continually over stones.
Earth forgets the footsteps of those who walk.
An awful fate. Stumps of talk after midnight.
An achievement, a retreat. Night reminds
And day forgets.
My eyes, which have looked a long time into a vast desert,
Are a little calmed. One woman. The rules of a game
Nobody had ever completely explained. The laws of pain and weight.

Even now my heart
Makes only a bare living
With its daily love.
My parents in their migration.
On the crossroads where I am forever orphaned,
Too young to die, too old to play.
The weariness of the miner
The emptiness of the quarry
In one body.
Archaeology of the future,
Museums of what is still to happen.
And my parents' migration has not yet calmed in me.
And from bitter peoples I learned bitter languages
For my silence among the houses
Which are always
Like ships.

Already my veins, my tendons
Are a tangle of ropes I will never undo.
Finally, my own death
And an end to my parents' migration.

TO SUMMON WITNESSES

When did I last weep?
The time has come to summon witnesses.
Of those who last saw me weep
Some are dead.

I wash my eyes with a lot of water
So as to see the world once more
Through the wet and the hurt.

I must find witnesses.

Lately, I have felt for the first time
Needle stabs in my heart.
I am not frightened,
I am almost proud, like a boy
Who discovers the first hairs in his armpits
And between his legs.

THE END OF ELUL*

I'm tired of summer.
The smoke rising from the convent of the silent nuns
Is all I have to say.
This year winter will come late
When we're ready for its coming,
And we won't be.

I'm tired. And curse the three Great Religions,
Which won't let me sleep at night
What with bells and howls of muezzins and loud shofars and noisy atonements.
Oh, God, close your houses, let the world rest.
Why hast thou *not* forsaken me?
This year the year hesitates.

The summer drags on.
If it weren't for the tears that I have kept back all these years,
I'd have dried up like thorns.

Great battles are conducted within me in dreadful quiet,
With only the sighs of thousands of sweating, naked wrestlers.
There is no iron, and no stone, only flesh, like snakes;
And afterwards, they'll fall away one from the other with surfeit and weakness,
And there will be clouds, and there will be rain
When we're ready for it, and we won't be.

* *Elul* is the last month of summer.

QUICK AND BITTER

The end was quick and bitter.
Slow and sweet was the time between us,
Slow and sweet were the nights
When my hands did not touch one another in despair
But with the love of your body
Which came between them.

And when I entered into you
It seemed then that great happiness
Could be measured with the precision
Of sharp pain. Quick and bitter.

Slow and sweet were the nights.
Now is as bitter and grinding as sand—
"We shall be sensible" and similar curses.

And as we stray further from love
We multiply the words,
Words and sentences long and orderly.
Had we remained together
We could have become a silence.

LUXURY

My uncle is buried at Sheik Bad'r.
The other one is scattered in the Carpathian mountains.

My father is buried at Sanhedria,
My grandmother on the Mount of Olives.
And all their forefathers
Are buried in the ruined Jewish cemeteries in the villages of Lower Franconia,
Near rivers and forests which are not Jerusalem.

My father's father kept heavy-eyed
Jewish cows in their sheds below the kitchen—

And rose at four in the morning.
I inherited his early rising,
My mouth bitter with nightmares
I attend to my bad dreams.

Grandfather, Grandfather,
Chief Rabbi of my life,
As you sold unleavened bread on the Passover Eve,
Sell my pains—
So they stay in me, even ache—but not mine,
Not my property.

So many tombstones are scattered behind me—
Names, engraved like the names of long-abandoned railway stations.

How shall I cover all these distances,
How can I keep them connected?
I can't afford such an intricate network.
It's a luxury.

TWO SONGS OF PEACE

I

My son smells of peace when I lean over him.
It isn't just the soap.
Everybody was once the child with the smell of peace.
(And in the whole country there isn't a single windmill which turns.)

O torn country, like torn clothes
Which can't be mended,
And hard, lonely forefathers in Hebron's grave
In childless silence.

My son smells of peace.
His mother's womb
Promised him that
Which God can't promise us.

II

My love was not in the war.
She learns love and history
Off my body, which was in two, or three.
And at night.
When my body makes battles into peace
She is bewildered.
Her perplexity is her love. And her learning.
Her wars and her peace, her dream.

And I am now in the middle of my life.
The time when one begins to collect
Facts, and many details,
And exact maps
Of a country we shall never occupy
And of an enemy and lover
Whose borders we shall never cross.

MY CHILD

When I last saw my child
He ate only porridge.
Now he's sad.

He eats bread and meat with a fork and knife
And with manners, which already prepare him
to die politely, and quietly.

He thinks that I'm a sailor,
But knows I have no ship.
And that we have no sea.
Only vast distances, and winds.

My father's movements in prayer
And my own in love
Lie already folded in his small body.

To be grown-up is
To bake the bread of longing,
To sit the whole night long
With a reddening face
Opposite the open oven.

My child sees everything.

And that magic spell "See you,"
which he's learned to say,
Is only valid among the dead.

SONG OF RESIGNATION

1
I resign!

My son has my father's eyes,
My mother's hands,
And my own mouth.
There is no further need of me. Many thanks.
The refrigerator is beginning to hum towards a long journey.
An unknown dog sobs over the loss of a stranger.

2
I resign!

I paid my dues to so many funds.
I am fully insured.
Let the world care for me now;
I am knotted and tied with it and all of them.
Every change in my life will cost them cash.
Every movement of mine will hurt them,
My death will dispossess them.
My voice passes with clouds
My hand, stretched out, has turned into paper. Yet another contract.
I see the world through the yellow roses
Someone has forgotten
On the table near my window.

3
Bankruptcy!
I declare the whole world to be a womb.
And as of this moment
I appoint myself,
Order myself
At its mercy.
Let it adopt me. Let it care for me.

I declare the President of the United States to be my father,
The Chairman of the Soviet Union to have my power of attorney,
The British Cabinet to be my family,
And Mao Tse-tung to be my grandmother.

I resign!

I declare the heavens to be God:
They all together go ahead and do those things
That I never believed they would.

TO MY MOTHER

1
Like an old windmill,
Two hands always raised
To howl at the sky
And two lowered
To make sandwiches.

Her eyes are clean and glitter
Like the Passover eve.

2
At night she will put
All the letters
And the photographs
Side by side.

So she can measure
The length of God's finger.

3
I want to walk in the deep
Wadis between her sobs,
I want to stand in the terrible heat
Of her silence.

I want to lean on the
Rough trunks
Of her pain.

4
She laid me
As Hagar laid Ishmael
Under one of the bushes.

So that she won't have to be at my death
In the war,
Under one of the bushes
In one of the wars.

MAYOR

It's sad
To be the Mayor of Jerusalem.
It is terrible.
How can any man be the mayor of a city like that?

What can he do with her?
He will build, and build, and build.

And at night
The stones of the hills round about
Will crawl down
Towards the stone houses,
Like wolves coming
To howl at the dogs
Who have become men's slaves.

MY FATHER FOUGHT THEIR WAR FOR FOUR YEARS

My father fought their war for four years
And he didn't hate his enemies or love them.
But I know that even there
He formed me daily out of his little calms,
So rare; he gathered them out of the bombs
And the smoke,
And he put them in his frayed knapsack
With the last bits of his mother's hardening cake.

And with his eyes he gathered nameless dead;
He gathered many dead on my behalf,
So that I will know them in his look and love them.

And not die, like them, in horror . . .

And he filled his eyes with them in vain:

I go out to all my wars.

THE UNITED NATIONS' COMMAND IN JERUSALEM

The mediators, the peace makers, the compromisers, the pacifiers
Live in the white house
And receive their nourishment from far away,
Through twisting channels, through dark veins, like a foetus.

And their secretaries are lipsticked and laughing,
And their immune chauffeurs wait below, like horses in a stable,
And the trees whose shadow shades them have their roots in disputed territory,
And the delusions are children who go out into the fields to find cyclamen
And do not come back.

And the thoughts circle above, uneasily, like scout planes,
And they take photographs, and return, and develop the film
In dark, sad rooms.

And I know that they have very heavy chandeliers,
And the boy that I was sits on them and swings
In and out, in and out, and out, and does not come back.

Later on, the night will bring
Rusty and crooked conclusions out of our ancient lives,
And above all the houses the music
Will gather all the scattered things,
Like a hand gathering crumbs off the table
After the meal while the talk continues
And the children are already asleep.

And hopes come to me like daring sailors,
Like discoverers of continents
To an island,
And they rest for a day or two,
And then they sail away.

YOU ALSO WERE SO TIRED

You also were so tired of being an advertisement for
The world, for the angels to admire. It's lovely here.
Take a rest from smiling. And without complaint,
Let the sea wind pleat your mouth.

You won't mind, like flying paper
Your eyes also fly; fruit also dropped off the sycamore.
How does one say "to love" in the language of water?
What are we in the language of earth?

Here is the road and the going on it, what does it mean?
Whatsoever hill, the Last Wind. Which prophet . . . ?
And at night, out of my sleep you speak.
And how shall I answer, and what shall I bring?

TWO BEDOUIN SONGS

I
He Lives in a House in the City

Buttons fall away, one by one,
Not in battles, not in rape—
From time to time they jump off in little explosions.
A dry sob of trousers and shirts.

Across the wall a yellow woman
Teaches children to play the guitar and a harmonica.
I provide her
With the dry air, the air longing for harmonicas.

Against my will
The barber cuts off a black straggling hair growing in my nose,
Extinguishing the rage,
Castrating the fury
In my nose.

And in the nights
Moonlight pierces through the crack in the letter box,
Lights it,
White
Like a letter.

II
He Loves

No house would have us.

I stretched myself above you, like a tent,
I spread myself beneath you,
A straw mattress.

Your red dress opened up heavenwards,
Like a goblet—
You sat on me upright
To keep your thighs off the hard ground.

"Madman," you said in your strange language.

His dog died in his chains.
His friends remote—
His son dreams the saying of Kaddish.

INDIAN SUMMER IN PRINCETON

Indian summer is a Jewish summer.
Your eyes are so heavy they almost fall out—
Held back, they are, by the sadness of your face.
They do not fall out because of dryness,
And the forgetting of the fruit,
But because of the weight of the remembering.
The ground beneath us moves further away—
This falling away will go on,
And go on.

It was Sunday, their Sabbath,
Time to sit down and ask ourselves
Whom we really love.
In the house lives someone whose name is not the same as the name on the gate—
A woman told me that she does not love her life
And which of the trees are sick, just as people are sick.

But in my dreams I look at bright, blinding Jerusalem—
And that's why Jerusalem's black now,
Like an underexposed photograph.

THE HEART IS A CORRUPT DIRECTOR[7]

The last days of summer
Are the last days of two, together.

The heart is a corrupt director.

Departing departs from departing.
And in the nights it is written:
Despair which despaired of us
Became hope.

I think that even Newton discovered
Whatever he discovered
In the lull between
One pain and another.

What bearing could this have
On the headiness of our lives?
What bearing on the soft talk
Which surrounds them?
What manner of things have to fall
From which tree, for us to learn?

It is terrible to battle against love
With sleeping pills. What have we come to!

NATIONAL THOUGHTS

You: trapped in the homeland of the Chosen People.
On your head a cossack's fur hat,
Child of their pogroms.
"After these words." Always.
Or, for instance, your face: slanting eyes,

7. In archived drafts at Emory University, AW placed an asterisk after the title and included the note "Theatrical Director."

Pogrom Year eyes. Your cheekbones, high,
Hetman's cheekbones, Hetman the rabble king.
Hassid dancing, dutiful, you, naked on a rock in the early evening by the
  canopies of water at Ein Geddi
With eyes closed and your body open like hair.

After these words, "Always."
Every day I know the miracle of
Jesus walking upon the waters,
I walk through my life without drowning.

To speak, now, in this tired language
Torn from its sleep in the Bible—
Blinded, it lurches from mouth to mouth—
The language which described God and the Miracles,
Says:
Motor car, bomb, God.

The squared letters wanted to stay closed,
Every letter a locked house,
To stay and to sleep in it forever.

IF I FORGET THEE, JERUSALEM

If I forget thee, Jerusalem,
Then let my right be forgotten.
Let my right be forgotten, and my left remember.
Let my left remember, and your right close
And your mouth open near the gate.

I shall remember Jerusalem
And forget the forest—my love will remember,
Will open her hair, will close my window,
Will forget my right,
Will forget my left.

If the west wind does not come
I'll never forgive the walls,
Or the sea, or myself.
Should my right forget,
My left shall forgive,
I shall forget all water,
I shall forget my mother.

If I forget thee, Jerusalem,
Let my blood be forgotten.
I shall touch your forehead,
Forget my own,
My voice change
For the second and last time
To the most terrible of voices—
Or silence.

RAIN ON A BATTLEFIELD

It rains on my friends' faces,
On my live friends' faces,
Those who cover their heads with a blanket.
And it rains on my dead friends' faces,
Those who are covered by nothing.

THE FIRST BATTLES

The first battles raised
Terrible love flowers
With near-killing kisses
Like shells.
The boy soldiers
Are driven in our city's handsome buses:
Number 12, number 8, and number 5 go to the front.

HIGH-HEELED SHOES

The earth answered several times:
Come in!
When you crossed the road in your tapping
High-heeled shoes,
It said, Come in!
But you couldn't hear.

THEY CALL ME

Taxis below
And angels above
Are impatient.
At one and the same time
They call me
With a terrible voice.

I'm coming, I am
Coming,
I'm coming down,
I'm coming up!

IT'S A LONG TIME SINCE ANYBODY'S ASKED

It's a long time since anybody's asked
Who lived in these houses, and who last spoke; who
Forgot his overcoat in these houses,
And who stayed. (Why didn't he run away?)

A dead tree stands among the blossoming trees. A dead tree.
It's an old mistake, never understood,
And at the edge of the country; the beginning
Of somebody else's time. A little silence.
And the ravings of the body and hell.

And the end of the end which moves in whispers.
The wind passed through this place
And a serious dog watched humans laugh.

IV. MISCELLANEOUS TEXTS

NOTE, CIRCA EARLY MARCH 1965[1]

We, the undersigned patients in the Maternity Ward in your hospital, protest at the unbelievable and disgraceful squalor of the lavatories in this ward.[2] The clean condition of these lavatories we feel, are the responsibility of the hospital's Guardians—since the patients' hygienic sensibilities cannot be relied upon. What is clearly needed is a fully trained, full time cleaner who is responsible for maintaining standards[3] of hygiene appropriate to lavatories in a maternity ward as famous and as otherwise excellent as yours.[4]

NOTE[5]

Aye, but it hath a sting,
To come to reason; yet the name
Of madness is an awful thing.—
Could I but die in one swift flame
Unthinking, unknowing!

1. The note is handwritten on slate gray–blue paper in blue ink and is held by Emory University.

2. After this sentence, "~~Since this hospital has had so much bad publicity recently, we shall not hesitate to write to the press and describe the conditions in which we~~" appears in the original.

3. "for maintaining ~~appropriate~~ standards" appears in the original.

4. On the verso side is this list:

   Swab results?
   delactation pills?
   bath?
   feed?
   midwife?
   Tranquilisers
   anti-hystamin

5. Note is handwritten on light-pink paper and is held by Emory University.

Phaedre,
Hyppolytus
Euripides.[6]

THE WILL OF ASSIA ESTHER WEVILL[7]

The Will of Assia Estre Wevill of Flat 14, 51 Marlborough Place, N.W. 8. Dated April 27th 1967.[8]

In the event of my death, I wish all my furniture and furnishings to be sold by auction and the proceeds to go towards my estate which I leave wholey to my only daughter, Alexandra Tatiana Elise Wevill. In the event of my daughter not surviving, I wish the proceeds as well as the rest of my savings at a Deposit Account[9] at Lloyd's Bank, Berkley Sq., W.1. to go to my sister, Cecilia Chaikin at 4395 Walkley Ave, N.D.G. 28, Montreal, P.Q., Canada. I also wish my sister to be the beneficiary of any royalties accruing to my estate on the publication of a translation of Yehuda Amichai's poems by Cape Golliard (Jonathan Cape Ltd.) Penguin Books and Harper Row in New York.[10]

To my dear friends Mr. & Mrs. Michael Mendelson of 21 Kidderpore Gdns., .3., I wish to to leave any 10 objects or books they may care to have.

My sister Cecilia Chaikin to have any manuscripts of Ted Hughes in my possession and inscribed books by him, as well as all manuscripts and inscribed books by David Wevill. She is also to have sole charge of my journal, to do with as she pleases.

To my dear friend, Martin Graham,[11] barrister, of Garden Court, Temple, I wish to leave any ten objects he may care to have, in gratitude for a long and thoughtful friendship.

6. Euripides (ca. 480 or 484–ca. 406 BCE) wrote the Greek tragic play *Hippolytus* (performed in 428 BCE), in which Phaedra is a character.

7. This unsigned will is a typescript held by Emory University.

8. As AW's biographers note, this document was likely drafted in 1968, not 1967. The year given is a typographical error, as is Assia's middle name ("Estre" instead of "Ester" or "Esther").

9. "at ~~the~~ a Deposit Account" appears in the original.

10. "Harper Row ~~Ltd~~ in New York." appears in the original.

11. "Martin ~~Grham~~ Graham" appears in the original. According to Koren and Negev, Martin Graham was a lawyer and friend with whom AW went skiing when she was married to RL (71).

To my recent friend, Fay Weldon,[12] of 3 Chalcot Crescent N.W.1., I wish to leave any piece or pieces of china she may care to have.

To my old friend, Janice Porter, of Cleveland Square, W.2., any pieces of jewelry she may care to have. To her husband, Peter Porter, any records or books he may care to possess.

The two oil paintings in gilt frames plus a 19th Century water colour of an archway, also in a gilt frame to go to my sister, Cecilia Chaikin.

All silver pieces as well as the plated silver samovar and any pieces which belonged to my mother and father, to be in possession of my sister, Cecilia Chaikin. Whom I hereby name as executor.[13]

I wish my cadaver to be buried in any rural cemetry in England, the vicar of its parish not objecting to its burial. I wish a tombstone to be erected within six months of my death inscribed with my name and dates of birth and death, and the epitaph: "Here lies a lover of unreason and an exile." The parish church to be given £50 for the permission to be buried there.

To Nicholas Farrar Hughes, since he is too young for possessions, I will all my most tender love. To Frieda Rebecca Hughes, I will also my love and all the lace, ribbons and silks she can find, as well as a fine gold chain. To Ted Hughes, their father, I leave my no doubt welcome absence and my bitter contempt.

To David Wevill I leave any photograph albums he may care to have. All other photographs to be given to my sister.

To my father, I leave my regret, and love.

To Myra Coopman of 36 Hanover Mansions, N.W.1., I leave the Bulgarian rug with birds on it. Also some mystification.

My sister to have the three oriental rugs in the sitting room.

To Christopher Wilkins,[14] my colleague at Ogilvy & Mather, Brettenham Ho[15]

12. Fay Weldon (1931–) is an award-winning British writer.

13. "hereby name as executor." is handwritten.

14. Christopher Wilkins is a former colleague of AW at Ogilvy & Mather with whom she shared an office.

15. AW means *House*, as Ogilvy & Mather had offices at Brettenham House, Lancaster Place, London, WC2E 7EZ.

POEMS BY YEHUDA AMICHAI BY ASSIA GUTMANN

BBC typescript, Emory[16]

Poems by Yehuda Amichai by Assia Gutman
PRE-RECORDED: Friday, June 28th: 2.0–3.30
TAPE NO: TLN 26/ TT 305D DURATION:
TRANSMISSION: PRODUCER: George MacBeth
THIRD

Yehuda Amichai was born in Wurzburg in 1923, and left Germany in 1937, near the height of the German-Jewish migration to Palestine. There, during the 1950s, he became the best known of the generation who made the effort to free Hebrew poetry from its heavy traditions, making it colloquial and supple enough to deal with the complexities of modern life in Israel.

His mixed background is typical of his whole generation; but in Amichai's poems it becomes something more than a shared circumstance: it deepens his sense of the placeless, nation-less, and equivocal mixture of people contained within Israel's struggle to make itself into a rooted nation. On the plane on nationality, even of identity, it remains a dilemma. Here is My Father Fought Their War for Four Years:

My father fought their war for four years
And he didn't hate his enemies or love them.
But I know, that even there
He formed me daily out of his little calms
So rare; he gathered them out of the bombs
And the smoke,
And he put them in this frayed knapsack
With the last bite of his mother's hardening cake.

And with his eyes he gathered nameless dead,
He gathered many dead on my behalf,

16. Broadcast on BBC Radio 3, December 12, 1968. Assia Wevill wrote the introduction and text; poems were read by Ted Hughes.

So that I will know them in his look and love them.
And not die, like them, in horror . . .
And he filled his eyes with them in vain:
I go out to all my wars.

His personal dilemmas open quite naturally, within the poems, to express the historical dilemmas of being a Jew. Through this next poem, for instance, which is based on a common enough circumstance, which it never really leaves, comes something much wider and older—a lament for the weariness of Jewish wandering. My Parents' Migration.

And my parents' migration has not yet calmed in me.
My blood goes on shaking at its walls,
As the bowl after it is set down.
And my parents' migration has not yet calmed in me.
Winds continually over stones.
Earth forgets the footsteps of those who walk.
An awful fate. Stumps of talk after midnight.
An achievement, a retreat. Night reminds
And day forgets.
My eyes which have looked a long time into a vast desert,
Are a little calmed. One woman. The rules of a game
Nobody had ever completely explained. The laws of pain and weight.

Even now my heart
Makes only a bare living
With its daily love.
My parents in their migration.
On the cross roads where I am forever orphaned,
Too young to die, too old to play.
The weariness of the miner
The emptiness of the quarry
In one body.
Archaeology of the future
Museums of what is still to happen.

And my parents' migration is not yet calmed in me,
And from bitter peoples I learned bitter languages
For my silence among the houses
Which are always
Like ships.
Already in my veins, my tendons
Are a tangle of ropes I will never undo
Finally, my own
Death
And an end to my parents' migration.

Amichai's poems are open, innocent, good-humoured, often funny, always sad, always fundamentally elegiac—lamenting something lost or foredoomed, a separation. Their most striking quality is the wealth of invention, the ingenuity and freshness of the imagery used everywhere. The poems are freely and even loosely shaped—following out their forms through trains of imagery and a subtle music of cadences and phrasing. And the imagery is never just descriptive or atmospheric. It is organic, a form of argument—blended with the musical core of the poem so that the two become one. It is also deeply integral to Amichai's main conflict: the relationship between Israel of the Old Testament and the modern state—between the heroic intensities of the Prophets and the secular intensities of the New State—between Jehova's terrifying pragmatic imperatives and a modern Israeli's struggle to lead his own life, which in Amichai's case is essentially a love-life, an unheroic opting for the daily round. The wit and imagination with which he brings this debate off can be seen quite well in this next poem, King Saul and I.

1.
They gave him a finger, but he took the whole hand
They gave me the whole hand: I didn't even take the little finger.
While my heart
Weightlifted its first feelings
He rehearsed the tearing of oxen.

My pulse-beats were like
Drips from a tap

His pulse-beats
Pounded like hammers on a new building.

He was my big brother.
I got his used clothes.

2.
His head, like a compass, will always bring him
To the sure north of this future.

His heart is set, like an alarm clock
For the hour of his reign.
When everyone's asleep, he will cry out
Until all the quarries are hoarse.
Nobody will stop him!

Only the asses bare their yellow teeth
At the end.

3.
Dead prophets turned time-wheels
When he went out searching for asses
Which I, now, have found.
But I don't know how to handle them.
They kick me.

I was raised with the straw,
I fell with heavy seeds.

But he breathed the winds of his histories.
He was anointed with the royal oil
As with wrestler's grease.
He battled with olive-trees
Forcing them to kneel.
Roots bulged on the earth's forehead
With the strain.

The prophets escaped from the arena;
Only God remained, counting:
Seven . . . eight . . . nine . . . ten . . .
The people, from his shoulders downwards, rejoiced.
He had won.

4.
I am tired,
My bed is my kingdom.
My sleep is just
My dream is my verdict.

I hung my clothes on a chair
For tomorrow.
He hung his kingdom
In a frame of golden wrath
On the sky's wall.

My arms are short, like string too short
To tie a parcel.

His arms are like the chains in a harbour
For cargo to be carried across time.

He is a dead king.
I am a tired man.

The debate recurs, in a slightly different manner, in the following poem, As for the World.

As for the world,
I am always like one of Socrates' disciples,
Walking by his side,
Hearing his opinions and histories
It remains for me to say:
Yes. Yes it is like that.

You are right again,
Indeed your words are true.

As for my life,
I am always like Venice:
Whatever is mere streets in others
Within me is a dark streaming love.

As for the cry, as for the silence,
I am always a <u>shofar:</u>
All year long hoarding its one blast
For the Terrible Days.

As for the action
I am always like Cain:
Nomad
In the face of the act, which I will not do,
Or, having done,
Will make it irredeemable.

As for the palm of your hand,
As for the signals of my heart,
And the plans of my flesh,
As for the writing on the wall,
I am always ignorant,
I can neither read nor write
and my head is like the
Heads of those senseless weeds

Knowing only the rustle and drift
Of the wind
When a fate passes through me
To some other place.

One could say that Amichai, like Jewish history, is obsessed with Jehova, but the relationship is far from simple. Mainly, this poet is concerned to protect human beings from this overwhelming inheritance of theirs. There is never any doubt that he is in God's house, but Amichai acts towards him like a licensed court jester, defending love and pity. Here is God Has Pity on Kindergarten Children.

God has pity on children in Kindergartens,
He pities school-children—less.
But adults he pities not at all.

He abandons them,
And sometimes they have to crawl on all fours
In the roasting sand
To reach the dressing station,
And they are streaming with blood.

But perhaps
He will have pity on those who love truly
And take care of them
And shade them
Like a tree over the sleeper in the public bench.

Perhaps even we will spend on them
Our last pennies of kindness
Inherited from mother,

So that their own happiness will protect us
Now and on other days.

Amichai is mainly a love-poet. Writing about love, he is able to bring all his concerns to bear most powerfully. Love appears as the most valuable element in life—but vulnerable, and doomed. Homeless, nationless, striving to live in the niches and shadows of a world as terrible and abstract and unconcerned as Jehovah: In the Middle of This Century.

In the middle of this century we turned to each other
With half faces and full eyes

Like an ancient Egyptian picture
And for a short while.

I stroked your hair
In the opposite direction to your journey,
We called to each other,
Like calling out the names of towns
Where nobody stops
Along the route.

Lovely is the world rising early to evil,
Lovely is the world falling asleep to sin and pity,
In the mingling of ourselves, you and I,
Lovely is the world.

The earth drinks men and their loves
Like wine,
To forget.
It can't.
And like the contours of the Judean hills,
We shall never find peace.

In the middle of this century we turned to each other,
I saw your body, throwing shade, waiting for me,
The leather straps for a long journey
Already tightening across my chest.
I spoke in praise of your mortal hips,
You spoke in praise of my passing face,

I stroked your hair in the direction of your journey,
I touched your flesh, prophet of your end,
I touched your hand which has never slept,
I touched your mouth which may yet sing.

Dust from the desert covered the table
At which we did not eat.

But with my finger I wrote on it
The letters of your name.

In the following love poem, the same themes emerge more clearly. Like Our Bodies' Imprint.

Like our bodies' imprint
Not a sign will remain that we were in this place
The world closes behind us,
The sand straightens itself.

Dates are already in view
In which you no longer exist,
Already a wind blows clouds
Which will not rain on us both.

And your name is already in the passenger lists of ships
And in the registers of hotels,
Whose names alone
Deaden the heart.

The three languages I know,
All the colours in which I see and dream:

None will help me.

Under these elegies there is something close to a foreboding all too fulfilled: despair would be the word, if Amichai hadn't come to terms with it. Here is It Was Summer, Or The End of Summer.

It was summer, or the end of summer
And I heard then your footsteps, as you went from east to west
For the last time. And in the world
Handkerchiefs were lost, and books, and people.

It was summer or the end of summer
There were hours in the afternoon,

You were;
And you wore your shroud
For the first time.
And you never noticed
Because it was embroidered with flowers.

It's not an easy sadness: we feel it has been earned, if we are never quite sure when. Love is merely where it shows itself most inevitably, where he can feel it most keenly. Here is A Pity. We Were Such a Good Invention.

They amputated
Your thighs off my hips.
As far as I'm concerned
They are all surgeons. All of them.

They dismantled us
Each from the other.
As far as I'm concerned
They are all engineers. All of them.

A pity. We were such a good
And loving invention.
An aeroplane made from a man and wife.
Wings and everything.
We hovered a little above the earth.

We even flew a little.

Perhaps this sadness goes right back into his childhood—as his good humour and warmth seem to. More than in most poets, one can feel his purest self still alive, still at the surface, as in To My Mother.

Like an old windmill
Two hands always raised
To howl at the sky
And two lowered
To make sandwiches.

Her eyes are clean and glitter
Like the Passover eve.

At night she will put
All the letters
And the photographs
Side by side,

So she can measure
The length of God's finger.

I want to walk in the deep
Wadis between her sobs
I want to stand in the terrible heat
Of her silence.

I want to lean on the
Rough trunks
Of her pain.

She laid me,
As Hagar laid Ishmael
Under one of the bushes.

So that she won't have to be at my death
In the war,
Under one of the bushes
In one of the wars.

This unspoilt self is always there, even in his most occasional pieces like Mayor.

It's sad
To be the Mayor of Jerusalem.
It is terrible.
How can any man be the mayor of a city like that?

What can he do with her?
He will build, and build, and build.

And at night
The stones of the hills round about
Will crawl down
Towards the stone houses,
Like wolves coming
To howl at the dogs
Who have become mens' slaves.

Even in his near-satirical pieces, it isn't the anger of an intellectual adult that we feel, but something much more refreshing. Here, to end with, is The United Nations.

The mediators, the peace-makers, the compromisers, the pacifiers,
Live in the white house
And receive their nourishment from far away,
Through twisting channels, through dark veins, like a foetus.

And their secretaries are lipsticked and laughing,
And their immune chauffeurs wait below, like horses in a stable
And the trees whose shadow shades them, have their roots in disputed
    territory,
And the delusions are children who go out into the fields to find cyclamen
And do not come back.

And the thoughts circle above, uneasily, like scout-planes,
And they take photographs, and return, and develop the film
In dark, sad rooms.

And I know that they have very heavy chandeliers,
And the boy that I was sits on them and swings
In and out, in and out, and out, and does not come back.

Later on, the night will bring
Rusty and crooked conclusions out of our ancient lives

And above all the houses, the music
Will gather all the scattered things
Like a hand gathering crumbs off the table
After the meal, while the talk continues
And the children are already asleep.

And hopes come to me like daring sailors
Like discoverers of continents
To an island
And they rest for a day or two,
And then they sail away.

MAM
17.6.68.

INDEX

Abbreviations used: AW (Assia Wevill); DW (David Wevill); SP (Sylvia Plath); TH (Ted Hughes).